Robert A. Geffner, PhD, ABPN
Marti Loring, PhD, LCSW
Corinna Young, MS
Editors

WITHDRAWN

Bullying Behavior: Current Issues, Research, and Interventions

Bullying Behavior: Current Issues, Research, and Interventions has been co-published simultaneously as *Journal of Emotional Abuse*, Volume 2, Numbers 2/3 2001

*Pre-publication
REVIEWS,
COMMENTARIES,
EVALUATIONS . . .*

"**D**ESERVES TO BE READ BY EVERYONE WHO WANTS TO REDUCE YOUTH VIOLENCE. . . . Bullying has rightfully become a major consideration in our efforts to reduce the incidence and prevalence of school violence and other forms of aggression in young people. This book makes a significant contribution to the literature. Not only does it expand our understanding of various theoretical perspectives and dynamics; it also takes a close look at interventions that can address the problem of bullying."

Joseph T. McCann, PsyD, JD
Editor
Journal of Threat Assessment

Bullying Behavior: Current Issues, Research, and Interventions

Bullying Behavior: Current Issues, Research, and Interventions has been co-published simultaneously as *Journal of Emotional Abuse* Volume 2, Numbers 2/3 2001.

The *Journal of Emotional Abuse* Monographic ''Separates''

Below is a list of " separates," which in serials librarianship means a special issue simultaneously published as a special journal issue or double-issue *and* as a "separate" hardbound monograph. (This is a format which we also call a "DocuSerial.")

"Separates" are published because specialized libraries or professionals may wish to purchase a specific thematic issue by itself in a format which can be separately cataloged and shelved, as opposed to purchasing the journal on an on-going basis. Faculty members may also more easily consider a "separate" for classroom adoption.

"Separates" are carefully classified separately with the major book jobbers so that the journal tie-in can be noted on new book order slips to avoid duplicate purchasing.

You may wish to visit Haworth's Website at . . .

http://www.HaworthPress.com

. . . to search our online catalog for complete tables of contents of these separates and related publications.

You may also call 1-800-HAWORTH (outside US/Canada: 607-722-5857), or Fax 1-800-895-0582 (outside US/Canada: 607-771-0012), or e-mail at:

getinfo@haworthpressinc.com

Bullying Behavior: Current Issues, Research, and Interventions, *edited by Robert A. Geffner, PhD, ABPN, Marti Loring, PhD, LCSW, and Corinna Young, MS (Vol. 2, No. 2/3 2001). "Shows how to stop schoolyard terror before it escalates to tragedy with timely intervention strategies and up-to-date reports on the dynamics of bullying."*

Bullying Behavior: Current Issues, Research, and Interventions

Robert A. Geffner, PhD, ABPN
Marti Loring, PhD, LCSW
Corinna Young, MS
Editors

Bullying Behavior: Current Issues, Research, and Interventions has been co-published simultaneously as *Journal of Emotional Abuse* Volume 2, Numbers 2/3 2001

HMTP

The Haworth Maltreatment & Trauma Press
An Imprint of
The Haworth Press, Inc.
New York • London • Oxford

KH

Published by

The Haworth Maltreatment & Trauma Press, 10 Alice Street, Binghamton, NY 13904-1580 USA

The Haworth Maltreatment & Trauma Press is an imprint of The Haworth Press, Inc., 10 Alice Street, Binghamton, NY 13904-1580 USA.

Bullying Behavior: Current Issues, Research, and Interventions has been co-published simultaneously as *Journal of Emotional Abuse*, Volume 2, Numbers 2/3 2001.

The development, preparation, and publication of this work has been undertaken with great care. However, the publisher, employees, editors, and agents of The Haworth Press and all imprints of The Haworth Press, Inc., including The Haworth Medical Press® and The Pharmaceutical Products Press®, are not responsible for any errors contained herein or for consequences that may ensue from use of materials or information contained in this work. Opinions expressed by the author(s) are not necessarily those of The Haworth Press, Inc.

Cover design by Thomas J. Mayshock Jr.

Library of Congress Cataloging-in-Publication Data

Bullying behavior: current issues, research, and interventions / Robert A. Geffner, Marti Loring, and Corinna Young editors.
     p. cm.
    "Bullying behavior : current issues, research, and interventions has been co-published simultaneously as 'Journal of emotional abuse,' vol. 2, nos. 2/3 2001."
    Includes bibliographical references and index.
    ISBN 0-7890-1435-1 (alk. paper)–ISBN 0-7890-1436-X (pbk: alk. paper)
    1. Bullying. 2. Bullying–Prevention. 3. School violence. I. Geffner, Robert. II. Loring, Marti Tamm. III. Young, Corinna. IV. Journal of emotional abuse.
BF637.B85 B857 2002
371.5′8–DC21   2002017190

Indexing, Abstracting & Website/Internet Coverage

This section provides you with a list of major indexing & abstracting services. That is to say, each service began covering this periodical during the year noted in the right column. Most Websites which are listed below have indicated that they will either post, disseminate, compile, archive, cite or alert their own Website users with research-based content from this work. (This list is as current as the copyright date of this publication.)

(continued)

Special Bibliographic Notes related to special journal issues
(separates) and indexing/abstracting:

- indexing/abstracting services in this list will also cover material in any "separate" that is co-published simultaneously with Haworth's special thematic journal issue or DocuSerial. Indexing/abstracting usually covers material at the article/chapter level.
- monographic co-editions are intended for either non-subscribers or libraries which intend to purchase a second copy for their circulating collections.
- monographic co-editions are reported to all jobbers/wholesalers/approval plans. The source journal is listed as the "series" to assist the prevention of duplicate purchasing in the same manner utilized for books-in-series.
- to facilitate user/access services all indexing/abstracting services are encouraged to utilize the co-indexing entry note indicated at the bottom of the first page of each article/chapter/contribution.
- this is intended to assist a library user of any reference tool (whether print, electronic, online, or CD-ROM) to locate the monographic version if the library has purchased this version but not a subscription to the source journal.
- individual articles/chapters in any Haworth publication are also available through the Haworth Document Delivery Service (HDDS).

Bullying Behavior: Current Issues, Research, and Interventions

CONTENTS

ABOUT THE EDITORS

Robert A. Geffner, PhD, ABPN, is Founder and President of the Family Violence & Sexual Assault Institute now in San Diego, California. Dr. Geffner is a former Professor of Psychology at the University of Texas at Tyler, and currently is Clinical Research Professor of Psychology at the California School of Professional Psychology, Alliant International University in San Diego. A licensed psychologist and licensed marriage and family therapist, he was the Clinical Director of a large, private practice mental health clinic for over 15 years. He has a diplomate in clinical neuropsychology.

He is a founding member and former President of the Board of the East Texas Crisis Center and Shelter for Battered Women & Their Children. Dr. Geffner is a member of the American Psychological Association, the American Professional Society on Abuse of Children, the International Society for Traumatic Stress Studies, the National Academy of Neuropsychologists, and several other related organizations. He has been an adjunct faculty member of the National Judicial College for 10 years. In addition to editing several international journals, he is Editor-in-Chief of The Haworth Maltreatment & Trauma Press. He has also served as a consultant to several national and state agencies and has served on numerous national and state committees concerning child abuse, program evaluation, family violence, and forensic psychology issues.

Marti Loring, PhD, LCSW, is a clinical social worker and sociologist. She is Director of the Center for Mental Health and Human Development and The Emotional Abuse Institute in Atlanta, Georgia. Dr. Loring has authored two books, *Emotional Abuse* and *Stories from the Heart: Case Studies of Emotional Abuse*, as well as numerous articles in the area of emotional abuse, trauma, and bizarre post-incident behavior.

Dr. Loring's forensic work includes expert witness testimony for abused and traumatized individuals across the country. She is co-editor of the *Journal of Emotional Abuse*.

Corinna Young, MS, is Assistant Editor of the *Journal of Emotional Abuse* and the *Journal of Child Sexual Abuse* and on the staff of the Family Violence & Sexual Assault Institute. She is currently completing her doctorate in health psychology at the California School of Professional Psychology at Alliant International University in San Diego. Ms. Young works with chronic pain patients at the SHARP Pain Rehabilitation Center in San Diego and does outcomes research with both medical patients and psychiatric patients with various institutions in the local area. She has published in both psychiatric and medical journals and co-authored a biopsychosocial treatment manual for chronic pain.

Bullying Behavior: Current Issues, Research, and Interventions

Bullying Behavior: Current Issues, Research, and Interventions has been co-published simultaneously as *Journal of Emotional Abuse* Volume 2, Numbers 2/3 2001.

Preface

This special volume focuses on a topic that has become more relevant recently with increased media attention on various violent crimes perpetrated by adolescents in schools throughout the United States. These incidents have sparked renewed interest and research concerning bullying behavior in schools, and a focus on understanding more about the dynamics so that effective intervention and prevention can be implemented. We are pleased that the contributors to this volume agreed to report on their latest perspectives, research, and interventions. This volume contains state-of-the-art information that should be useful for researchers, practitioners, and others who work with children and youth. We hope this will stimulate more research and funding for a problem that has been recognized for decades, but has not yet received sufficient attention. This volume is an important step to begin rectifying this situation.

Robert A. Geffner
Marti Loring
Corinna Young

[Haworth co-indexing entry note]: "Preface." Geffner, Robert A. Co-published simultaneously in *Journal of Emotional Abuse* (The Haworth Maltreatment & Trauma Press, an imprint of The Haworth Press, Inc.) Vol. 2, No. 2/3, 2001, p. xvii; and: *Bullying Behavior: Current Issues, Research, and Interventions* (ed: Robert A. Geffner, Marti Loring, and Corinna Young) The Haworth Maltreatment & Trauma Press, an imprint of The Haworth Press, Inc., 2001, p. xiii. Single or multiple copies of this article are available for a fee from The Haworth Document Delivery Service [1-800-HAWORTH, 9:00 a.m. - 5:00 p.m. (EST). E-mail address: getinfo@haworthpressinc.com].

xiii

Introduction–
What a Difference a Discipline Makes:
Bullying Research and Future Directions

Nan Stein

The array of articles in this special issue on bullying present new directions in research on bullying in the United States. This introduction discusses the challenges that remain for researchers on bullying and also briefly focuses on the contributions of the articles in this volume.

With these articles and others previously published, we finally have access to a series of research studies conducted in the United States, and we no longer have to rely largely on studies from other countries (predominately Norway, Sweden, Britain, Spain, Netherlands, Australia, Canada, and Japan). As ground breaking and inspiring as those studies from other countries have been, their findings always posed lurking dangers and limitations for us in the U.S. for several obvious reasons. First of all, many of those countries have populations that are much more homogenous than ours in the U.S. (northern Europe, in particular), and any attempt to extrapolate their conclusions to our context was problematic. Secondly, all of those countries have much less overt, public violence than the United States, so the meaning (and forms) of bullying varied greatly. These differences meant that we always had to approach the findings from other countries cautiously, because many of those countries do not provide us with a viable comparison sample or context.

Nan Stein, EdD, is Senior Research Scientist, Center for Research on Women at Wellesley College, where she directs several research projects on bullying, sexual harassment, and gender violence in K-12 schools.

[Haworth co-indexing entry note]: "What a Difference a Discipline Makes: Bullying Research and Future Directions." Stein, Nan. Co-published simultaneously in *Journal of Emotional Abuse* (The Haworth Maltreatment & Trauma Press, an imprint of The Haworth Press, Inc.) Vol. 2, No. 2/3, 2001, pp. 1-5; and: *Bullying Behavior: Current Issues, Research, and Interventions* (ed: Robert A. Geffner, Marti Loring, and Corinna Young) The Haworth Maltreatment & Trauma Press, an imprint of The Haworth Press, Inc., 2001, pp. 1-5. Single or multiple copies of this article are available for a fee from The Haworth Document Delivery Service [1-800-HAWORTH, 9:00 a.m. - 5:00 p.m. (EST). E-mail address: getinfo@haworthpressinc.com].

Thankfully, several of the articles in the present volume discuss research projects with large samples, and in some cases are part of longitudinal studies (see articles by Jeffrey, Miller & Linn, and Espelage & Holt), while other articles with smaller samples employ methodology that informs and deepens our understanding of children's experiences with bullying, whether as target/victim, harasser/perpetrator, or witness/bystander (Espelage & Asidao; Swearer & Song; Gottheil & Dubow in this issue).

Moreover, the strategies that have been developed in other countries (for example, all the European countries, Britain, Australia, Canada, and Japan) to reduce and prevent bullying generally rely on the existence of a nationalized curriculum for elementary and secondary schools, thus permitting a coordinated, nationwide effort. This is lacking from the U.S. context. In the U.S., not only is curriculum often not coordinated state-by-state, but even building-by-building (some would argue, classroom-by-classroom) within the same school district (see articles by Sanchez, Robertson, Lewis, and Rosenbluth in this issue for a discussion of a three-year coordinated effort of curriculum intervention on bullying with fifth graders, and another article by Howard, Horne and Jolliff involves the evaluation of a much smaller study of the effectiveness of an intervention program that several of the authors had developed; in addition, a final article by Swearer and Doll argues for an ecological framework within which to approach interventions to reduce bullying).

However original and uniquely American the research has become, it is of concern that the definition of bullying that seems to be in vogue, and utilized by many of the authors in this volume, is very elastic. Under the prevailing definition of bullying, almost anything has the potential to be called bullying, from raising one's eyebrow, giving "the evil eye," making faces (all very culturally constructed activities), to verbal expressions of preference towards particular people over others. I fear that there may be a tyranny of sameness that is implicitly being proposed in this pursuit to eradicate bullying behaviors. Yet, on the other hand, sometimes very egregious behaviors are named as bullying, when in fact they may constitute criminal hazing or sexual/gender harassment.

What appears to be lacking from many of the research studies on bullying is an acknowledgment that bullying is not against the law in the U.S. Unlike hazing or sexual or gender-based harassment which are illegal behaviors in an educational context, some researchers (and educators) may be predisposed to name these illegal behaviors as "bullying." This may be due to a lack of recognition that what has happened is in fact against the law, or conceivably because they prefer to "soft-pedal" what is going on by avoiding the legal consequences, and thus they apply the milder term of bullying. Regardless of the motives, we are left with confusion over terms, which may lead to the elasticity mentioned above, and ultimately contribute to a climate of permission for illegal conduct. This liberal use of the term bullying may also be part of a general trend to label children, particularly in a culture that tends to psycho-pathologize behaviors.

Furthermore, among researchers, this expansionist trend to call all sorts of behaviors as "bullying" may in fact be due to a lack of familiarity with other disciplines, in particular educational research, sociology, anthropology, and feminist legal scholarship. A wealth of studies and articles from researchers who have employed widely different methodologies have long argued for a gendered critique of children's behaviors, and in some cases, have named these behaviors as sexual harassment. Included among these scholars are Thorne (1989, 1993), Eder (1995, 1997), Fineran (1996), Fineran and Bennett (1995, 1998), Lever (1976), Lee and colleagues (1996), Shakeshaft and colleagues (1995, 1997, 2000), and Stein (1981, 1992, 1993a & b, 1995, 1999). Among the articles published in this volume, two seem familiar with some of this scholarship (Espelage & Holt, and Sanchez et al.). While other articles in this volume acknowledge the existence of sexual harassment in schools as documented through survey research and recent legal developments in the U.S. Supreme Court (see Pellegrini's article in this issue), I look forward to future contributions from the discipline of psychology that will build upon researchers from other fields who have long studied the arena of gender violence and sexual harassment in schools.

Finally, there appears to be an unfortunate failure of bullying researchers to consider the policing of masculinity and the imposition of compulsive heterosexuality. Not to factor in or even name these potent elements is to deny a central and operating feature of boy culture which is strongly driven by tireless efforts to define oneself as "not gay." Researchers such as Kimmel (1987, 2000), Connell (1995), Messner (1990), and Pleck (1981), to list just a few, have written about this phenomenon and its consequences for several decades.

In conclusion, it is important to reemphasize, "What a difference a discipline makes." Our research will be all the stronger when we draw upon various disciplines and reach across those disciplines to shape and inform further research. Hopefully, too, this will not simply be an academic exercise of expanding our citations and references, but also will be one that will benefit children, their teachers and their families. This issue takes a great first step while also showing us how much further we have to go.

REFERENCES

Bennett, L., & Fineran, S. (1998). Sexual and severe physical violence of high school students: Power beliefs, gender and relationship. *Journal of Orthopsychiatry 64*(4), 645-652.

Connell, R.W. (1995). *Masculinities*. Berkeley, CA: University of California Press.

Eder, D. (1997). Sexual aggression within the school culture. In B.J. Bank & P.M. Hall (Ed.), *Gender, equity, and schooling: Policy and practice* (pp. 93-112). New York: Garland.

Eder, D., with Evans, C.C., & Parker, S. (1995). *School talk: Gender and adolescent culture.* New Brunswick, NJ: Rutgers University Press.

Fineran, S. (1996). *Gender issues of peer sexual harassment among teenagers.* Unpublished doctoral dissertation, University of Illinois at Chicago.

Fineran, S., & Bennett, L. (1995, July). *Gender and power issues of peer sexual harassment among teenagers.* Paper presented at Fourth International Family Violence Research Conference, University of New Hampshire, Durham, NH.

Fineran, S., & Bennett, L. (1998). Teenage peer sexual harassment: Implications for social work practice in education. *Social Work, 43,* 1, 55-64.

Kimmel, M.S. (1987). *Changing men: New directions in research on men and masculinity.* Newbury Park, CA: Sage Publications.

Kimmel, M.S., with Aronson, A. (2000). *The Gendered society reader.* New York: Oxford University Press.

Lee, V.E., Croninger, R.G., Linn, E., & Chen, X. (1996, Summer). The culture of sexual harassment in secondary schools. *American Educational Research Journal, 33* (2), 383-417.

Lever, J. (1976). Sex differences in the games children play. *Social Problems 23,* 478-487.

Messner, M.A. (1990). Boyhood, organized sports and the construction of masculinities. *Journal of Contemporary Ethnography, 18*(4), 416-444.

Pleck, J. (1981). *The myth of masculinity.* Cambridge: MA: M.I.T. Press.

Shakeshaft, C. (1997, March). *Peer harassment and the culture of schooling: What administrators need to know.* Paper presented at American Educational Research Association conference, Chicago, IL.

Shakeshaft, C., Barber, E., Hergenrother, M.A., Johnson, Y., Mandel, L., & Sawyer, J. (1995). Peer harassment in schools. In J.L. Curcio & P.F. First (Eds.), *Journal for a just and caring education* (pp. 30-44). Thousand Oaks, CA: Corwin Press.

Shakeshaft, C., & Mandel, L. (2000). Heterosexism in middle schools. In N. Lesko (Ed.), *Masculinities at school* (pp. 75-103). Thousand Oaks, CA: Sage Publications.

Stein, N. (1981). *Sexual harassment of high school students: Preliminary research results.* Boston, MA: Massachusetts Department of Education, unpublished manuscript.

Stein, N. (1992). *Secrets in public: Sexual harassment in public (and private) schools.* (working paper #256). Wellesley, MA: Wellesley College Center for Research on Women.

Stein, N. (1993a). No laughing matter: Sexual harassment in K-12 schools. In E. Buchwald, P. R. Fletcher, & M. Roth (Eds.), *Transforming a rape culture* (311-331). Minneapolis, MN: Milkweed Editions.

Stein, N. (1993b). It happens here, too: Sexual harassment and child sexual abuse in elementary and secondary schools. In S.K. Biklen & D. Pollard (Eds.), *Gender and*

Education: 92nd yearbook of the National Society for the Study of education (pp. 191-203). Chicago, IL: University of Chicago Press.

Stein, N. (1995, summer). Sexual harassment in K-12 schools: The public performance of gendered violence. *Harvard Educational Review, Special issue: Violence and youth, 65*,(2),145-162.

Stein, N. (1999). *Classrooms and courtrooms: Facing sexual harassment in k-12 schools.* New York: Teachers College Press.

Thorne, B. (1989). Girls and boys together . . . but mostly apart: Gender arrangements in elementary school. In M.S. Kimmel & M. A. Messner, *Men's lives* (pp. 61-73). Needham Heights, MA: Allyn & Bacon.

Thorne, B. (1993). *Gender Play: Girls and Boys in School.* New Brunswick, NJ: Rutgers University Press.

Bullying in Schools:
An Ecological Framework

Susan M. Swearer
Beth Doll

SUMMARY. In this paper, we will argue that careful examination of research on bullying and victimization establishes that these are ecological phenomenon that emerge from social, physical, institutional and community contexts as well as the individual characteristics of youth who are bullied and victimized. Consequently, we will use an ecological framework to review prominent definitions and explanations of the problem of bullying and to make suggestions for linking intervention to research findings. It is hoped that this paper will fur-

Susan M. Swearer, PhD, is Assistant Professor, School Psychology, Department of Educational Psychology, University of Nebraska–Lincoln. Beth Doll, PhD, is Associate Professor, School Psychology, Department of Educational Psychology, University of Nebraska–Lincoln.

Address correspondence to: Susan Swearer, Department of Educational Psychology, The University of Nebraska-Lincoln, 130B Bancroft Hall, Lincoln, NE 68588-0345 (E-mail: sswearer@unlserve.unl.edu).

[Haworth co-indexing entry note]: "Bullying in Schools: An Ecological Framework." Swearer, Susan M., and Beth Doll. Co-published simultaneously in *Journal of Emotional Abuse* (The Haworth Maltreatment & Trauma Press, an imprint of The Haworth Press, Inc.) Vol. 2, No. 2/3, 2001, pp. 7-23; and: *Bullying Behavior: Current Issues, Research, and Interventions* (ed: Robert A. Geffner, Marti Loring, and Corinna Young) The Haworth Maltreatment & Trauma Press, an imprint of The Haworth Press, Inc., 2001, pp. 7-23. Single or multiple copies of this article are available for a fee from The Haworth Document Delivery Service [1-800-HAWORTH, 9:00 a.m. - 5:00 p.m. (EST). E-mail address: getinfo@haworthpressinc.com].

ther bridge the gap between the empirical knowledge about bullying and resultant prevention and intervention efforts. *[Article copies available for a fee from The Haworth Document Delivery Service: 1-800-HAWORTH. E-mail address: <getinfo@haworthpressinc.com> Website: <http://www.HaworthPress.com> © 2001 by The Haworth Press, Inc. All rights reserved.]*

KEYWORDS. Bullying, intervention, ecological framework

Bullying may be the most prevalent type of school violence (Batsche, 1997). Worldwide incidence rates for bullying in school-aged youth range from 10% of secondary students to 27% of middle school students who report being bullied often (Whitney & Smith, 1993). Studies in the United States have yielded slightly higher rates of bullying, ranging from a low of 10% for "extreme victims" of bullying (Perry, Kusel, & Perry, 1988) to a high of 75% of school-aged children who reported being bullied at least one time during their school years (Hoover, Oliver, & Hazler, 1992). In a review of the literature on bullying, Batsche and Knoff (1994) concluded that 15% to 20% of all students will encounter bullying during their school careers. These statistics suggest that bullying is a prevalent problem that directly affects one-fourth of school-aged youth.

National and international evidence suggests that present day bullying occurs more frequently and with greater lethality then it did in the 1970s and 1980s (Olweus & Alsaker, 1991). Moreover, emerging research suggests that there is a positive relationship between bullying and more serious forms of violence (Baldry & Farrington, 2000). Consequently, bullying in schools has become the focus of increased public attention as part of the larger media examination of prominent incidents of school crime and violence. In response to public scrutiny, the federal government has established multiple projects to foster school safety within the U. S. Departments of Education, Justice, and Health and Human Services (U. S. Departments of Education and Justice, 1998; 1999). Ninety percent of the nation's public schools have established zero-tolerance policies that mandate predetermined consequences or punishments for specific criminal or violent offenses (National Center for Education Statistics, 1997). Seventy-eight percent of public schools adopted some type of formal school violence prevention program by the 1996-97 academic year (U.S. Departments of Education and Justice, 1998). There are now more than 300 available violence-prevention programs targeted towards schools (Howard, Flora, & Griffin, 1999).

Indeed, the public's urgent interest in the prevention of intimidation and violence closely resembles an educational fad–interest in the topic is sudden, violence prevention programs are seen as panaceas, and the proliferation of violence prevention programs marketed to schools has occurred in the absence of methodologically rigorous research proving that the programs are effective.

This is reflected by the fact that fewer than a quarter of the 300 published violence prevention programs report outcome data showing that they reduce or prevent violence (Howard et al., 1999). The danger of such fads is that they create an atmosphere of false hope and unrealistically high expectations for rapid change, and they fade quickly when it becomes apparent they cannot guarantee safe schools (Sternberg, 1997). To confront faddism, it is critically important that school policies and practices that confront bullying be predicated on research and empirically supported interventions.

In this paper, we will argue that careful examination of the research on bullying and victimization establishes that these are ecological phenomenon that emerge from social, physical, institutional and community contexts as well as the individual characteristics of the bully and the victim. Consequently, we will propose an ecological framework for understanding bullying and victimization. The application of such a framework to the research that exists will highlight six important implications for school policies and practices that address bullying behaviors in school.

These six assertions are based on previous research on the dynamics underlying bullying and victimization. We will list our assertions here, and then we will discuss them in detail throughout the paper. First, we assert that bullying must be defined as a constellation of behavioral interactions. Second, we assert that internalizing disorders contribute to bullying and victimization but are too often overlooked. Third, families must be active partners in anti-bullying interventions. Fourth, anti-bullying interventions must interrupt and neutralize the peer support for bullying behavior. Fifth, anti-bullying interventions must alter the responses toward bullying of teachers and other supervising adults. Finally, our sixth assertion is that anti-bullying interventions require changes within the upper reaches of administration to have a lasting impact. The reaction of school personnel and adult family members toward bullying behaviors is critical in developing a healthy school (and home) environment. These six assertions are directly linked to intervention and this link will be outlined in the remainder of this paper.

ECOLOGICAL THEORY AND BULLYING

Our empirical discussion of bullying borrows heavily from the ecological systems perspective of Bronfenbrenner (1977, 1979), Dishion and Patterson (1997) and their contemporaries. Ecological theory presumes that simultaneous with development in language, cognition, social competence and physical integrity, children also accommodate to their immediate social and physical environment. This environment, in turn, is mediated by more remote forces in the larger community and society. These act as ecological systems (Capra, 1996), and competence or problems that are evidenced in the child are reflecting properties of this integrated system and not just their individual characteristics. Complex interactions between children and their environments work to develop or inhibit prosocial and antisocial behaviors in each child (Lerner, Hess & Nitz, 1991; Sameroff, 1975). Thus, problems do not "reside" within the children or within the context but instead are the result of ongoing transactions between the two (Pianta & Walsh, 1996).

When the ecological perspective is applied to bullying, a bullying interaction occurs not only because of individual characteristics of the child who is bullying, but also because of actions of peers, actions of teachers and other adult caretakers at school, physical characteristics of the school grounds, family factors, cultural characteristics, and even community factors. Bronfenbrenner (1977) describes this ecosystem with his classic diagram resembling a target, with the child at the center and concentric circles representing contexts from those closest to the child (family) to those furthest away (community). In our discussion of the ecological phenomenon of bullying, we are most directly interested in the reciprocal interplay between the individual and the contexts of family, peers, teachers and other supervising adults in the school, school policies, and the physical setting of schools.

The ecological model of bullying does not overlook contributions to bullying of individual characteristics of children but views these as they interact with the child's social context. Within this perspective, children who bully are predisposed to do so because they are prone to be impulsive, unempathetic, domineering (Olweus, 1997b), inflexible and easily discouraged (Scholte, 1992), aggressive and advocates of aggressive means towards solving conflicts (Olweus, 1997a). Still, these characteristics of the children are mediated by families when they encourage bullying by modeling bullying behaviors, tolerating it when it occurs, and contributing to the child's emotional sense of ill-being and unhappiness (Olweus, 1993b, 1997b; Smith & Myron-Wilson, 1998). Peer contributions to bullying incidents reflect more direct social learning influences, in which peers' immediate and cumulative respect for the bullying behavior reinforces the child who bullies, as does the peers' immediate and cumulative devaluing of the victim (Pellegrini, Bartini, & Brooks, 1999). Teachers and other adults who supervise children in school can inadvertently enable bullying when they create pockets of unsupervised times and spaces where bullying can easily occur and by being unresponsive to the reports of victims and onlookers to incidents of bullying (Craig, Pepler, & Atlas, 2000; Olweus, 1993a). Ultimately, decisions made within the upper levels of school administration contribute to bullying by providing insufficient levels of adult supervision, physical settings that facilitate bullying behaviors, and policies that discourage prompt and effective responses when bullying occurs (Olweus,

1993b). When this ecosystem of the child, family, peers and school exist within a community characterized by high levels of violence (Jonson-Reid, 1998), bullying becomes an event that rises out of a complex interaction of conditions at several levels within the child's ecological context.

THE SIX ASSERTIONS

Bullying Must Be Defined as a Constellation of Behavioral Interactions

Researchers have struggled to reconcile varying definitions of bullying and victimization. Much of the previous research has defined bullying in person-centered terms, in which some children are "bullies" and others are "victims." For example, in several bullying prevention programs, some students are referred to as the "bully" and others as the "victim" and children are taught ways to respond differentially to each (Garrity, Jens, Porter, Sager, & Short-Camilli, 1994; Newman, Horne, & Bartolomucci, 2000). Still, person-centered definitions of bullying cannot account for Olweus' (1993b) evidence that one out of six bullies were themselves victims in other situations and one out of four victims had also acted as bullies. Thus, person-centered definitions of bullying appear to create a false dichotomy between bullies and victims that does not account for the large numbers of children who move fluidly between these two groups (Smith, 1991).

Other researchers have defined bullying as a set of discrete behaviors. For example, bullying behaviors have been classified as physical, verbal, and non-verbal behaviors (Rigby, 1996). Still, definitions that describe bullying as a set of observable behaviors cannot account for the different meanings that social behaviors often assume depending on whether these occur between friends or non-friends (Brown, 1989). When interacting with their friends, children tolerate a wide range of name-calling, physical jostling, and verbal insults that they will not tolerate from children outside their circle of friends (McConnell & Odom, 1986). Similarly, there is evidence to suggest that children enjoy vigorous mock fights with their friends and that these pretend conflicts contribute to their social competence, especially in young children (Humphreys & Smith, 1984; Pellegrini, 1993). Behavioral observers are not always able to discriminate between these pretend conflicts and authentically coercive behaviors (Walker & Severson, 1992). Moreover, not all bullying behavior is observable. Olweus (1994) has pointed out that bullying may take the form of direct attacks on the victim, which can be observed, or social isolation and intentional exclusion from a group, which may be too subtle to be observed.

Olweus' (1993a) seminal definition of bullying describes a behavioral interaction rather than merely a person or a behavior: "A person is being bullied when he or she is exposed, repeatedly and over time, to negative actions on the part of one or more other persons" (p. 9). Slee (1995) supplements this definition by delineating specific aspects of the interaction that must be present for it to be classified as "bullying": (1) an imbalance of physical and/or psychological power exists between the bully and the victim; (2) the bully's negative action towards the victim must be repeated; (3) the bully must deliberately intend to hurt the victim; and (4) the bully's negative action towards the victim must be largely unprovoked (i.e., the victim does not intentionally provoke the bully). Within this definition, a violent attack may not be considered bullying if it is directed by a relatively powerless person towards a relatively powerful one, violent behaviors that are intentionally provoked would not be classified as an instance of bullying, and violent behaviors that inadvertently harm another person would not be considered bullying. By defining bullying within the interaction, Olweus' definition acknowledges the constellation of critical features of the socio-ecological system that contributes to the occurrence of an incident of bullying behavior.

Internalizing Disorders Contribute to Bullying and Victimization but Are Too-Often Overlooked

When bullying is vested within the child who bullies, then attempts at intervention will focus on strategies to stop the problem child's behavior either by punishing it (i.e., office referrals, withdrawal of recess), teaching the child alternative behaviors and rewarding those (i.e., social skills training, positive peer reporting), or restricting the child so that he or she is unable to bully (i.e., in-school suspension, expulsion). Once bullying is viewed as a constellation of behaviors emerging out of a complex social interaction, then some attempts at intervention can be redirected towards understanding why a particular child is vulnerable to contextual influences favoring bullying. In fact, this is beginning to occur within the bullying literature as research has begun to examine the contributions of internalizing factors across bully subtypes. Research conducted with bullies, victims, and bully-victims (youth who are both bullied and victimized) suggests that bullies are more depressed than controls (Kaltiala-Heino, Rimpela, Marttunen, Rimpela, & Rantanen, 1999; Swearer, Song, Cary, Eagle, & Mickelson, 2000); bully-victims are both more depressed and more anxious than controls (Swearer, Song et al., 2000); and victims are more anxious than bullies and controls (Craig, 1998; Swearer, Song et al., 2000). These data indicate that comorbidity of internalizing factors are present across bully and victim subtypes and need to be considered when developing effective intervention programs. To this end, individual cognitive-behavioral therapy and an established system of appropriate referral sources should be an integral part of a bullying prevention program.

Families Must Be Active Partners in Anti-Bullying Interventions

Family members are not typically present on the school grounds when bullying occurs, and so most family contributions to bullying are indirect and long-term. Moreover, Olweus' (1993a) survey suggested that parents of children who are bullied or who bully others are often not aware of the problem and do not discuss it with the children. Still, three of Olweus' (1993a, 1997b) four risk factors leading to bullying fall firmly within the family circle of Bronfenbrenner's (1977) ecological framework. First, Olweus argues that a lack of parental warmth and involvement increases the risk that a child may become hostile and aggressive towards others. Second, children are also more likely to be aggressive towards others when parents permit them to be inappropriately aggressive towards other children, their siblings, or even adults. Third, children are more likely to be aggressive when their parents have used physical punishment and emotional outbursts in disciplining them. Olweus' arguments gain further support from the research of Farrington (1993) who has similarly linked the bullying behavior of children to the aggressive actions of their parents and from the research of Loeber and Dishion (1984) who suggest that "bullies at school are often victims at home" (Batsche, 1997; p. 172). Moreover, evidence suggests that bullying behavior may be transmitted across generations, as both Farrington (1993) and Eron and Huesmann (1990) have reported that male bullying during the teenage years predicted bullying by his child a decade or two years later.

More recent research has began to identify similar links between parenting practices and victimization (Baldry & Farrington, 2000). For example, being a victim of parental violence is related to children's social withdrawal and running away (Gray, 1998). Children who are victimized tend to have overly supportive and authoritarian parents (Baldry & Farrington, 1998). Thus, family patterns of interaction can predispose victims to accede in the face of threat and withdraw in ineffective ways from bullying overtures.

It is no surprise, then, that family participation played an important role in the Olweus and Limber (1999), "Bullying Prevention Program," the only anti-bullying program to meet the criteria for a proven program in the *Blueprints for Violence Prevention*, edited by Delbert S. Elliot (1999) at the University of Colorado at Boulder. Family components of anti-bullying interventions that are essential to interrupt the bullying interaction include (1) increasing family awareness of the bully-victim problem; (2) actively involving parents and the family in confronting bullying; (3) developing clear family rules against bullying; and (4) providing support and protection for youth who are victimized.

Anti-Bullying Interventions Must Interrupt and Neutralize the Peer Support for Bullying Behavior

The peer influences that support bullying behavior are powerful and must be dismantled if effective intervention is to occur. We have identified two types of peer influence that must underlie effective attempts at intervention: The influence of onlookers on the bullying incident, and the influence of victims on bullying.

Onlooking peers can directly encourage or inhibit incidents of bullying because they are almost always present when bullying occurs (O'Connell, Pepler, & Craig, 1999; Pepler, Craig, & O'Connell 1999). Peer onlookers can reinforce the bully's feelings of dominance and power as a result of bullying. Indeed, there is evidence that students who bullied gained social status relative to their victims (Oliver, Hoover & Hazler, 1994). In some special instances of bullying, a one-on-one bullying situation gradually evolves into group-perpetrated bullying, as several students join in to jointly bully a victim. Olweus (1993b) has explained how, in these instances, bullying is perpetuated by the students' mutual endorsement and encouragement of each other's aggressive acts, and their weakened sense of responsibility for a shared act of bullying. Moreover, when such bullying continues over time, the students as a group come to view the victim as diminished and even deserving of the bullying. In other instances, peer onlookers observe the bullying without actively taking part and are called "passive bullies" by Olweus (1991). Passive bullies can encourage incidents of bullying by perpetuating the reputational bias against victims outside of the bullying situation (Merton, 1996).

Further evidence of the power of the peer group is found in the research on group interventions for antisocial youth which has shown that, in many cases, the group serves to perpetuate and encourage continued offenses by aggressive youth even while intervention is occurring (Dishion, McCord, & Poulin, 1999). Generalizing this finding to bullying intervention suggests that group interventions for bullying are unlikely to be effective when these are comprised of children who bully and the onlooker peers who may be their silent partners in the bullying incident. Despite the best intentions of the facilitators, such groups are likely to become another stage upon which bullying behavior is celebrated and admired. Instead, peer interventions must serve to interrupt the cycle of support and encouragement that peers provide for bullying by removing the peer audience, altering the peer contingencies for bullying that they observe, or challenging the peer attitudes that value power and dominance at the expense of tolerance and caring.

One contextual way to interrupt the peer support for bullying is to alter the physical setting of the school playground so that there are more games and more attractive things to do than to stand around observing bullying. Another approach is to include students who are not involved in bullying in the intervention. In this way, all students can be trained to help intervene in bully incidents by establishing a zero-tolerance toward bullying and by following a no-bullying school policy.

Victims' relationships with bullies and with their other peers represent a unique feature of the peer context to bullying. Victims are often younger and physically weaker than the children who bully them (Olweus, 1993b). In fact, rates of bullying tend to drop temporarily at the point where a cohort of children move from elementary to middle, or middle to high school, presumably because being the youngest grade within a school limits the bullies' access to weaker victims (Olweus, 1993b). These interactions mimic the coercive cycle that Patterson (1982) has identified. When victims attempt to resist or confront the bullying behavior, they are met with heightened aggression such that the victims learn, over time, that quickly succumbing to the bully results in the least amount of pain and humiliation. In this way, the victim's quick accession reinforces the bullying behavior and increases the likelihood of its reoccurrence. Moreover, when such bullying continues over time, peers come to view the victim as diminished and even deserving of the bullying. In this way, victim reputations tend to be perpetuated by peers even after a victim has altered their behavior or acquired new skills, and may only be overcome when the victim moves into a new school with an unfamiliar peer group.

While several interventions incorporate strategies for victims to protect themselves from bullying behavior, others stress the importance of not holding the victims responsible for stopping the intimidation. Schools need to foster an environment of peer support for bullying behavior (Craig et al., 2000; Olweus, 1997b). Still, some of the best advice for victims has emerged from the youth themselves. In one second-grade classroom where we worked, a small troupe of boys was terrorizing several of the children in the class as well as first grade children in the class next door. As part of a larger classroom intervention to diminish bullying, a group of eight of their victims met to talk about times when they had been bullied and times when they had themselves been a bully. By the end of the discussion, they had decided that bullying occurred primarily when they were alone and outside the sight of adults who were supervising, that it happened because the bully was having fun or getting even for something mean that they had done to the bully, and that there were things that they could do to stop bullying. Their list of seven 'bully tricks' provides a striking exam-

.ple of ways to use the ecological context to interrupt the peer context that supports bullying (see Table 1: Seven Bully Tricks).

Bullying Interventions Must Alter the Responses Toward Bullying of Teachers and Other Supervising Adults

Teachers rarely observe bullying directly since children who bully usually avoid doing so when they can be seen by adult supervisors. Still, Olweus' (1978) Bergan study suggested that teachers' estimates of bullying closely corresponded to those of the children in a school. Thus, while not altogether unaware of the problem, teachers do relatively little to stop bullying from happening. This is the case despite the research showing that much of the bullying occurs in hallways and classrooms, where teachers are immediately available to observe it or intervene (Swearer, Cary, Song, & Eagle, 2000). Children who have been bullied report that teachers ignore their requests for help more than half the time. At the same time, Olweus (1993b) suggests that rates of bullying drop significantly when all adults in a building are trained to use consistently and immediately respond to bullying with non-hostile and non-physical consequences.

The ecological perspective on bullying makes it clear that the cycle of coercion is perpetuated by the reactions to its occurrence by supervising adults. Consequently, attempts to interrupt that cycle will be counterproductive unless they include strategies that increase the visibility of bullying to adult supervisors and that enhance supervisors skills in recognizing and responding appropriately to bullying incidents that come to their attention. In most schools, enhanced supervision will require attitude changes on the part of teachers and other staff, so that they come to recognize second-hand reports of bullying as incidents that require prompt and effective responses on their part. In almost

TABLE 1. Seven Second Grade "Bullying Tricks" for Victims

1. Camouflage yourself by trying to fit into the background.

2. Be with a group of other kids.

3. Stay near grown-ups.

4. Stay busy playing.

5. Don't give other kids an excuse for payback.

6. Swings are a good place to play because bullies can't get to you.

7. Leave and join a group of other kids if it starts to be a problem.

every case, an effective response to bullying will require an increased understanding of bullying, its antecedents, and its varying forms, if adults are to recognize it effectively and know what to do.

The "Bullying Prevention Program" (Olweus & Limber, 1999) serves as an example of the kind of intervention that prepares a school's adults to confront bullying. The schoolwide program prepares adults to be simultaneously warm, interested and involved with children and firm in their limits on unacceptable behavior. It teaches them to use non-hostile, non-physical sanctions with good consistency when bullying did occur. Finally, it shows them how to maximize their monitoring and surveillance of children's activities in and out of school.

Anti-Bullying Interventions Require Changes Within the Upper Reaches of Administration to Have a Lasting Impact

Almost all of the bullying reported to Olweus (1993b) occurred at school, with the majority of that occurring on the playground, in the classroom or the halls of the building. Consequently, it is no surprise that bullying decreases significantly in the face of school-wide practices that increase adult-child ratios during out-of-classroom times and that mandate immediate responses towards bullying can significantly decrease its occurrence (Olweus, 1993a). Still, Olweus' work and the experience in U. S. schools (Walker, Colvin, & Ramsey, 1995) show that school authorities are slower to recognize when problems with bullying exist and slow to engage themselves in seeking solutions to the problem.

The school building and its surrounding grounds provide the physical context for most bullying incidents and school practices that alter that environment can impact the occurrence of bullying. Children report that most bullying occurs in hidden alcoves or blind corners around the building that most teachers cannot readily observe. In other cases, common playground equipment can serve to shelter bullying incidents from adult eyes, including concrete pipes or enclosed climbing structures. Less obvious, bullying is also encouraged by playground designs that provide children with too few games to play, such that fighting and intimidation become attractive alternatives for things to do (Doll, 1993). Moreover, Blatchford (1988) has shown that aggression becomes more likely to occur towards the end of an hour long lunchtime recess, suggesting that policies related to the length and timing of recess periods can unintentionally foster bullying. School policies often determine whether school play areas are adequately equipped with age-appropriate play equipment and sufficient supervision. Table 2 describes two schools encountered in our work, one whose playground policies inadvertently encouraged bullying and another whose policies acted as bullying deterrents.

In many schools, enhanced adult supervision will require policy changes and even changed budgetary priorities, so as to increase the ratio of supervisors to students at key points during the school day. Other school policies are necessary to restrict children to areas on the school grounds that are highly visible and easily supervised by adults. Because many schools use a combination of certified and uncertified staff for supervision duties, school practices to discourage bullying must providing effective training for those adults to recognize intimidation when it occurs, interrupt it and respond appropriately. Schools also have the option using mental health professionals to teach children how to recognize and respond to bullying.

Substantial reductions in bullying and victimization have been reported (over 50%) as a result of the altered policies and practices of the Bullying Prevention Program (Olweus & Limber, 1999). This was the only bullying intervention showing empirical support sufficient to meet the criteria of the Center for the Study and Prevention of Violence at the University of Colorado at Boulder. Key policies and practices of the program include: (1) creating a school environment characterized by warmth, positive interest, and involvement from adults and firm limits to unacceptable behavior; (2) in cases of vio-

TABLE 2. Two Examples of Building Recess Practices That Affected Bullying

School One was a suburban elementary school that, in the face of budget cuts, combined the early elementary (K, 1, 2) and late elementary (3, 4, 5) recess periods and supervised them with a single playground aide. The combined recess period met on the younger children's playground, which was richly supplied with swings and sand boxes but had relatively few games for the older children to play. There were no balls available for a tetherball pole, and the four-square court had been painted on a small hill, making the game impossible to play. As a result, the older children tended to play soccer on a large open field without marked goal posts or sidelines. Also, additions to the school had created numerous small cubby holes between or behind walls and doorways, so there was no place that an aide could stand and see all corners of the playground. The combination of not enough to do and too many hidden spots contributed to an inordinate amount of physical and verbal bullying during the recess period.

School Two was an inner city school with a much smaller playground, surrounded by a high chain-link fence perimeter. In this school, the physical education teachers were responsible for co-supervising the lunch recess as part of their teaching load. They used the lunch period as an extension of the skills that they taught during regular class gym periods, and so the activities available for the children were rich and varied. In addition to swings, sandboxes and climbing equipment, the children could play basketball, tetherball, jump rope in all its varied forms, four square, soccer on a far end field, and other various activities that had been introduced as part of their physical education curriculum. A limited number of children also had the option of spending the lunch recess in the library working on the computers. Moreover, due partly to its size, this playground had relatively few hidden corners within the fenced yard, and an aide was available to assist the physical education teacher with the supervision duties. The combination of diverse activities, higher levels of supervision, and good visibility on the playground contributed to this school having a much lower rate of bullying and intimidation during recess period.

lations of limits and rules, non-hostile, non-physical sanctions should be applied consistently; (3) a certain degree of monitoring and surveillance of the student's activities in and out of school; and (4) adults at both home and school are supposed to act as authorities. Additional goals include: (1) increasing awareness of the bully-victim problem; (2) active involvement from adults; (3) developing clear rules against bullying; and (4) teachers provide support and protection for the victims. Demonstration of a "dosage-response" outcome established that larger reductions in bullying occurred when more components of the program were implemented (Olweus & Limber, 1999).

CONCLUSIONS FROM AN ECOLOGICAL FRAMEWORK

The preceding discussion suggests that bullying is best conceptualized as an interaction between the individual and his or her peer group, school, family, and community. Internal factors in the individual interact with the social environment, which then serves to reinforce bullying and/or victimization behaviors. Additionally, the complexity of bullying and victimization suggests that these behaviors are both overt and covert. These behaviors may occur in a variety of contexts and typically are not marked by the discreteness that their labels imply. In order to develop truly effective intervention programs, it is imperative that we understand the complex ecological environment in which bullying and victimization takes place.

While our schools, homes and communities may never be completely bully-free environments, we can do much to help youth break out of the bullying and victimization cycle and perpetuate a healthy cycle of functioning. Given that bullying is best conceptualized as a constellation of behavioral interactions, interventions need to address the complexity of these behaviors. Effective interventions must address internalizing disorders that contribute to bullying and victimization. Additionally, effective interventions include partnering with families in anti-bullying interventions and interrupting and neutralizing peer support for bullying behavior. Schools that adopt anti-bullying interventions must directly include teachers, other supervising adults, and the administration in order to impact bullying and victimization. When we adopt empirically supported anti-bullying intervention programs, we can transcend faddism and develop a healthy school (and home) environment. An understanding of an ecological framework of bullying and victimization is the first step.

REFERENCES

Baldry, A. C., & Farrington, D. P. (2000). Bullies and delinquents: Personal characteristics and parental styles. *Journal of Community and Applied Social Psychology, 10*, 17-31.

Batsche, G. M. (1997). Bullying. In G. C. Bear, K. M. Minke and A. Thomas (Eds.), *Children's needs II: Development, problems and alternatives* (pp. 171-179). Bethesda, MD: National Association of School Psychologists.

Batsche, G. M. & Knoff, H. M. (1994). Bullies and their victims: Understanding a pervasive problem in the schools. *School Psychology Review, 23*, 165-174.

Blatchford, P. (1988). *Playtime in the primary school.* Windsor, Englend: NFER-Nelson.

Bronfenbrenner, U. (1977). Toward an experimental ecology of human development. *American Psychologist, 32*, 513-531.

Bronfenbrenner, U. (1979). *The Ecology of Human Development: Experiments by Nature and Design.* Cambridge, MA: Harvard University Press.

Brown, B. B. (1989). The role of peer groups in adolescents' adjustment to secondary school. In T. J. Berndt & G. W. Ladd (Eds.), *Peer relationships in child development* (pp. 188-215). New York: John Wiley & Sons.

Capra, F. (1996). *The Web of Life.* New York: Doubleday.

Craig, W. (1998). The relationship among bullying, victimization, depression, anxiety, and aggression in elementary school children. *Personality and Individual Differences, 24* (1), 123-130.

Craig, W. M., Pepler, D. & Atlas, R. (2000). Observations of bullying in the playground and in the classroom. *School Psychology International, 21*, 22-36.

Dishion, T. J., McCord, J., & Poulin, F. (1999). When interventions harm: Peer groups and problem behavior. *American Psychologist, 54*, 755-764.

Dishion, T. J., & Patterson, G. R. (1997). The timing and severity of antisocial behavior: Three hypotheses within an ecological framework. In David M. Stoff, James Breiling, & Jack D. Maser (Eds.), *Handbook of antisocial behavior* (pp. 205-217). New York, NY: John Wiley & Sons.

Doll, B. (1993). Evaluating parental concerns about children's friendships. *Journal of School Psychology, 31*, 431-447.

Elliott, D. S. (Ed.), (1999). *Blueprints for Violence Prevention.* Boulder, CO: Regents of the University of Colorado.

Eron, L. D., & Huesmann, L. R. (1990). The stability of aggressive behavior–even onto the third generation. In M. Lewis & S. M. Miller (Eds.), *Handbook of developmental psychopathology* (pp. 147-156). New York: Plenum.

Farrington, D. P. (1993). Understanding and preventing bullying. In M. Tonry (Ed.), *Crime and Justice* (pp. 381-458). Chicago: Chicago University Press.

Garrity, C., Jens, K., Porter, W., Sager, N., & Short-Camilli, C. (1994). *Bully-proofing your school.* Longmont, CO: Sopris West.

Gray, E. (1988). The link between child abuse and juvenile delinquency: What we know and recommendations for policy and research. In G.T. Hotaling, D. Finkelhor, J. T. Kirkpatrick, & M. A. Straus (Eds.), *Family abuse and its consequences: New directions in research* (pp. 109-123). NY: Sage Publications.

Hoover, J. H., Oliver, R., & Hazler, R. J. (1992). Bullying: Perceptions of adolescent victims in the Midwestern U.S.A. *School Psychology International, 13*, 5-16.

Howard, K. A., Flora, J., & Griffin, M. (1999). Violence-prevention programs in schools: State of the science and implications for future research. *Applied & Preventive Psychology, 8*, 197-215.

Humphreys, A. & Smith, P. K. (1984). Rough and tumble in preschool and playground. In P. K. Smith (Ed.), *Play in animals and humans* (pp. 241-270). London: Basil Blackwell.

Jonson-Reid, M. (1998). Youth violence and exposure to violence in childhood: An ecological review. *Aggression and Violent Behavior 3* (2), 159-179.

Kaltiala-Heino, R., Rimpela, M., Marttunen, M., Rimpela, A., & Rantanen, P. (1999). Bullying, depression, and suicidal ideation in Finnish adolescents: School survey. *British Medical Journal, 319*, 348-351.

Lerner, M. R., Hess, L. E., & Nitz, K. (1991). A developmental perspective on psychopathology. In M. Hersen & C. G. Last (Eds.), *Handbook of child and adult psychopathology: A longitudinal perspective* (pp. 9-32). Elmsford, NY: Pergamon Press.

Loeber, R., & Dishion, T. J. (1984). Boys who fight at home and school: Family conditions influencing cross-setting consistency. *Journal of Consulting and Clinical Psychology, 52*, 759-768.

McConnell, S. R., & Odom, S. L. (1986). Sociometrics: Peer-referenced measures and the assessment of social competence. In P. S. Strain, M. J. Guralnic, & H. M. Walker (Eds.), *Children's Social behavior: Development, assessment and modification* (pp. 215-285). New York: Academic Press.

Merton, D. E. (1996). Visibility and vulnerability: Responses to rejection by nonaggressive junior high school boys. *Journal of Early Adolescence, 16*, 5-26.

National Center for Education Statistics. (1997). *National Assessment of Educational Progress.* Washington, DC.

Newman, D. A., Horne, A. M., & Bartolomucci, C. L., (2000). *Bully-busters: A teacher's manual for helping bullies, victims, and bystanders.* Champaign, IL: Research Press.

O'Connell, P., Pepler, D., & Craig, W. (1999). Peer involvement in bullying: Insights and challenges for intervention. *Journal of Adolescence, 22*, 437-452.

Oliver, R., Hoover, J. H., & Hazler, R. (1994). The perceived roles of bullying in small-town midwestern schools. *Journal of Counseling & Development, 72*, 416-420.

Olweus, D. (1978). *Aggression in the schools: Bullies and whipping boys.* Washington, D.C.: Hemisphere Press (Wiley).

Olweus, D. (1991). Bully/victim problems among schoolchildren: Basic facts and effects of a school-based intervention program. In D. Pepler & K. H. Rubin (Eds.), *The development and treatment of childhood aggression* (pp. 411-448). Hillsdale, NJ: Lawrence Erlbaum Associates.

Olweus, D. (1993a). Bullies on the playground: The role of victimization. In C. H. Hart (Ed.), *Children on playgrounds: Research perspectives and applications* (pp. 85-128). Albany: State University of New York Press.

Olweus, D. (1993b). *Bullying at school.* Cambridge: Blackwell.

Olweus, D. (1994). Annotation: Bullying at school: Basic facts and effects of a school-based intervention program. *Journal of Child Psychology and Psychiatry, 35,* 1171-1190.

Olweus, D. (1997a). Tackling peer victimization with a school-based intervention program. In D. P. Fry & K. Bjorkqvist (Eds.), *Cultural Variation in Conflict Resolution: Alternatives to Violence* (pp. 215-231). Mahwah, NJ: Lawrence Erlbaum Associates.

Olweus, D. (1997b). Bully/Victim problems in school: Knowledge base and an effective intervention program. *The Irish Journal of Psychology, 18* (2), 170-190.

Olweus, D., & Alsaker, F. D. (1991). Assessing change in a cohort-longitudinal study with hierarchical data. In D. Magnusson, L. R. Bergman, G. Rudinger, & B. Rorestad (Eds.), *Problems and Methods in Longitudinal Research: Stability and Change.* Cambridge: Cambridge University Press.

Olweus, D. & Limber, S. (1999). *Blueprints for Violence Prevention: Bullying Prevention Program.* Boulder, CO: Institute of Behavioral Science, Regents of the University of Colorado.

Patterson, G. R. (1982) *Coercive family process.* Eugene, OR: Castalia.

Pellegrini, A. D. (1993). Elementary-school children's rough-and-tumble play and social competence. *Developmental Psychology, 24,* 802-806.

Pellegrini, A. D., Bartini, M., & Brooks, F. (1999). School bullies, victims, and aggressive victims: Factors relating to group affiliation and victimization in early adolescence. *Journal of Educational Psychology, 91,* 216-224.

Pepler, D., Craig, W. M., & O'Connell, P. (1999). Understanding bullying from a dynamic systems perspective. In A. Slater and D. Muir (Eds.), *The Blackwell Reader in Developmental Psychology* (pp.440-451). Blackwell Publishers.

Perry, D., Kusel, S., & Perry, L. (1988). Victims of peer aggression. *Developmental Psychology, 24,* 807-814.

Pianta, R C., & Walsh, D. J. (1996). *High-risk children in schools: Constructing sustaining relationships.* New York: Routledge.

Rigby, K. (1996). *Bullying in schools and what to do about it.* Melbourne, Australia: ACER.

Sameroff, A. J. (1975). Transactional models in early social relations. *Human Development, 18,* 65-79.

Scholte, E. M. (1992). Prevention and treatment of juvenile problem behavior: A proposal for a socio-ecological approach. *Journal of Abnormal Child Psychology, 20* (3), 247-262.

Slee, P. T. (1995). Peer victimization and its relationship to depression among Australian primary school students. *Personality and Individual Differences, 18*(1), 57-62.

Smith, P. K. (1991). The silent nightmare: Bullying and victimization in school peer groups. *The Psychologist: Bulletin of the British Psychological Society, 4,* 243-248.

Smith, P. K., & Myron-Wilson, R. (1998). Parenting and school bullying. *Clinical Child Psychology and Psychiatry, 3,* 405-417.

Sternberg, R. (1997, July). Fads in psychology: What we can do. *APA Monitor*, p. 19. Washington D. C.: American Psychological Association.

Swearer, S. M., Cary, P. T., Song, S. Y., & Eagle, J. W. (August, 2000). Self-monitoring as a means of assessing bullying and victimization. Poster presented at the American Psychological Association National Conference; Washington, DC.

Swearer, S. M., Song, S. Y., Cary, P. T., Mickelson, W. M. (2000, this volume). Psychosocial correlates in bullying and victimization: The relationship between depression, anxiety, and bully/victim status. *Journal of Emotional Abuse*.

U.S. Departments of Education and Justice. (1998). *1998 Annual Report on School Safety*. Washington, DC: U. S. Department of Education, Education Publications Center.

U.S. Departments of Education and Justice. (1999). *1999 Annual Report on School Safety*. Washington, DC: U. S. Department of Education, Education Publications Center.

Walker, H. M., Colvin, G., & Ramsey, E. (1995). Antisocial behavior in school: Strategies and best practices. Pacific Grove, CA: Brooks/Cole Publishing Company.

Walker, H. M., & Severson, H. (1992). *Systematic screening for behavior disorders*. Longmont, CO: Sopris Press.

Whitney, I. & Smith, P. K. (1993). A survey of the nature and extent of bullying in junior/middle and secondary schools. *Educational Research, 35*(1), 3-25.

Tripartite Beliefs Models of Bully and Victim Behavior

Neil F. Gottheil

Eric F. Dubow

SUMMARY. Tripartite beliefs models are proposed as potential explanations for the stability of bully and victim behavior. These models include normative beliefs about acceptability of weakness, and provoked and unprovoked aggression; self-efficacy beliefs about the ability to use aggression and inhibit aggressive impulses; and outcome-expectancy beliefs regarding the use of aggression.

Children from grades 5 and 6 (N = 120) completed measures representing each of the belief categories, as well as three indices of bully and victim behavior. The relation of each belief category with the behavioral measures of bully and victim behavior were examined.

Strong support was found for the tripartite beliefs model of bully behavior, lending support to the notion that beliefs about aggression and bullying that are supportive, justifying, accepting, and encouraging of bullying, might be related to its actual expression. No support was found for the tripartite beliefs model of victim behavior. Perhaps, unlike bullies, victims are passive recipients of the aggression they receive, and hence, their social

Neil F. Gottheil, PhD, is Clinical Psychologist, Children's Hospital of Eastern Ontario and an associate in a private practice. Eric F. Dubow, PhD, is Professor, Department of Psychology, Bowling Green State University.

Address correspondence to: Neil F. Gottheil, PhD, 2249 Carling Avenue, Suite 314, Ottawa, Ontario, Canada, K2B 7E9 (E-mail: Ngottheil@home.com).

[Haworth co-indexing entry note]: "Tripartite Beliefs Models of Bully and Victim Behavior." Gottheil, Neil F., and Eric F. Dubow. Co-published simultaneously in *Journal of Emotional Abuse* (The Haworth Maltreatment & Trauma Press, an imprint of The Haworth Press, Inc.) Vol. 2, No. 2/3, 2001, pp. 25-47; and: *Bullying Behavior: Current Issues, Research, and Interventions* (ed: Robert A. Geffner, Marti Loring, and Corinna Young) The Haworth Maltreatment & Trauma Press, an imprint of The Haworth Press, Inc., 2001, pp. 25-47. Single or multiple copies of this article are available for a fee from The Haworth Document Delivery Service [1-800-HAWORTH, 9:00 a.m. - 5:00 p.m. (EST). E-mail address: getinfo@haworthpressinc.com].

role might be imposed upon them regardless of their beliefs. Implications for prevention/intervention are discussed. *[Article copies available for a fee from The Haworth Document Delivery Service: 1-800-HAWORTH. E-mail address: <getinfo@haworthpressinc.com> Website: <http://www.HaworthPress.com> © 2001 by The Haworth Press, Inc. All rights reserved.]*

KEYWORDS. Bullying, peer victimization, aggression, beliefs, self-efficacy, outcome-expectancy, normative, prevention, intervention

Social conflict can be a productive forum through which individuals learn and develop resolution skills that in turn promote smoother future relationships. Conflict resolution is a necessary component of productive social experiences and fosters the development of skills such as empathy, perspective taking, compromise, and communication. It is solution-focused and is undertaken by individuals who are interested in coming to an agreement that is mutually acceptable and fair. Unlike other social happenings, bully/victim encounters are by nature not set up for resolution. They are characterized by an unequal distribution of power among the participants, with themes of domination and control being prominently expressed by one member over another (Olweus, 1993). The goals of such encounters differ among participants, with bullies creating their own opportunities to express dominance and reap perceived secondary social and interpersonal gains, while victims attempt to reduce the risks of being socially, emotionally, and physically injured.

Research has indicated that a variety of immediate and future consequences exist for bullies and victims. Children who are victimized are more likely to be depressed, develop low self-esteem (Austin & Joseph, 1996; Horne, Glaser, & Sayger, 1994; Olweus, 1992; 1993), experience a continuing loss of confidence, peer rejection, school absenteeism (Hazler, Carney, Green, Powell, & Jolly, 1997; Smith, Bowers, Binney, & Cowie, 1993), and anxiety (Besag, 1989). Children who are identified as bullies are more likely than the general population to have a criminal record by the time they are young adults (Huesmann, Eron, Lefkowitz, & Walder, 1984), and to abuse alcohol and engage in domestic violence (Olweus, 1993; Zarzour, 1994).

To make matters worse, bully and victim social roles tend to be relatively stable irrespective of changes in schools, teachers, classmates, and efforts by others to abolish bully and victim behaviors (Olweus, 1984). According to Olweus (1984), children rated as bullies and victims in grade 6 retained these roles at a 3-year follow-up. In a study by Boulton and Underwood (1992), it was found that by early middle school, children (11-12 years of age) who reported being bullied were the most likely to be bullied in the following terms, even though changes in classroom teachers had occurred.

GENDER DIFFERENCES

Boys and girls appear to differ in terms of the type of bullying that they engage in more often (Crick, Bigbee, & Howes, 1996). Bullying by girls tends to be relational (Crick and Bigbee, 1998) in that it includes behaviors such as malicious gossiping about the victim and group ostracism (Lagerspetz, Bjorkqvist, & Peltonen, 1988). Boys, on the other hand, are more likely to use direct forms of aggression such as, physical and verbal assaults. The large majority of research on bullying has focused on this direct form of aggression; however, it would be a mistake to assume that findings in this area do not apply to females. Girls do use direct forms of aggression, and in studies that have compared boys and girls who bully in this fashion, there does not appear to be a difference between the sexes on a variety of psychosocial and emotional characteristics.

Huesmann and Guerra (1997) explored the relation between beliefs about the appropriateness of aggression and peer nominations of aggression. They found that correlations between these beliefs and aggression were consistently lower for girls. However, the authors point out that although mean scores were lower for girls on beliefs and aggression, "the direction of the correlations were the same for both genders" (p. 414). Separate gender regressions did not produce any significantly different regression coefficients, indicating that aggression was similarly predicted by normative beliefs for boys and girls.

The majority of past research on bully and victim behavior has neglected to examine gender differences. Questions still remain with respect to whether those females that come to be identified as bullies and victims share similar characteristics to their male counterparts. In order to contribute to this area of research, the present study will examine gender differences across study variables.

COGNITIVE MEDIATION OF BEHAVIOR

The occurrence and stability of bully and victim behavior has been addressed by various theories and avenues of research. Some areas of focus have included the impact of external influences (i.e., the media's portrayal of violence; parenting style), predispositional factors (i.e., temperament), information processing variables (i.e., selective attention, recall and saliency issues), and interpretational biases (i.e., hostile misattributions), on later bully and victim social patterns. However, given the number of possible permutations of these factors together with the unique social experiences of any one individual, it remains difficult to ascertain how any given child will be affected by, or react to a particular experience. However, exploring commonalities among the internalized heuristics that have resulted from the unique consolidation of these various factors, might help in understanding what children are bringing with them into social situations that contribute to the maintenance of bully and victim behavior. The present study proposes a tripartite model of beliefs that might support or mitigate bully and victim behavior among elementary school children.

According to Piaget (as cited in Miller, 1989), external information affects behavior and future responding only in so much that it has been internalized into organizing heuristics known as schemata. Schemata represent an integration of the experiences that one has attended to and incorporated into a personal framework for understanding the world and include guiding beliefs and cognitions, which direct and shape how information is processed and abstracted (Guerra, Huesmann, & Hanish, 1995), and serve to reduce the amount energy required to deal with the continual barrage of new information (Huesmann & Guerra, 1997). Once schemata are developed, new information provides challenges to currently held schemata, and according to Piaget, this new information is responded to in one of two ways. Either the new information will be modified to fit currently held schemata (assimilation), or the schemata will be modified to better explain the new information (accommodation) (Miller, 1989). Therefore, what one derives from an experience depends on how s/he deals with the new information, which in turn is influenced by the strength of the current schemata.

Beliefs as Cognitive Mediators. Piaget's concept of assimilation could explain the characteristic styles of cross-situational responding and noted stability of bully and victim social roles. Social information might be filtered through and interpreted via specific beliefs that foster bully and victim reaction patterns. These beliefs act as cognitive mediators bridging the gap between external events and experiences, and actual behaviors. Three categories of beliefs considered to be relevant to bully and victim behavior are proposed. These are normative, self-efficacy, and outcome-expectancy beliefs.

Normative Beliefs. Normative beliefs refer to cognitions about the acceptability and appropriateness of certain behaviors and are assumed to play a role in the regulation of actual behavior (Guerra et al., 1995). In a model developed by Guerra and associates (1995), normative beliefs are posited to influence actual behavior by: affecting the relative salience and interpretation of situational cues; triggering specific behavioral scripts; and filtering out "unacceptable" information.

Huesmann, Guerra, Miller, and Zelli (1992) administered a 35-item normative beliefs survey to 293 second through fourth graders. Items were hypothetical situations involving an aggressive act that varied in terms of severity of provocation (i.e., being screamed at, hit, etc.), and response (i.e., screaming or hitting back). Moderate correlations were found between normative beliefs and self reports of aggression. However, weak correlations of normative beliefs with peer nominations, and non-significant correlations with teacher nominations, led the authors to conclude that there was little support for their measure as a predictor of aggressive behavior. Guerra and associates (1995) modified the Huesmann and associates (1992) measure, reducing it to a 20-item scale consisting of normative beliefs about aggression and retaliatory behavior. Two thousand thirty-five elementary school children (grades 1 to 4) were administered the scale, and a modest correlation ($r = .23$) between overall approval of aggression and peer-nominated reports of aggressive behavior was found. A subsample of children was reassessed one year later and it was found that children with more approving beliefs about aggression at time 1 were more aggressive and developed more approving beliefs about aggression at follow-up. This latter finding supports the notion that normative beliefs may serve as predictors of, and agents in, the development and maintenance of aggression. In a follow-up study, Huesmann and Guerra (1997) reported non significant correlations of beliefs with aggressive behaviors for 1st and 2nd graders but significant correlations for 4th graders. The authors note that this might be because children at this age are just beginning to develop stable beliefs about aggression, that are now starting to influence their behavior.

In a unique attempt to explore prevailing normative beliefs specific to bully and victim behavior, Rigby and Slee (1991) had 685 children from 6 to 16 years of age complete a 20-item questionnaire designed to assess attitudes toward victims of bullying. Children were asked to nominate classmates who they felt were "picked on a lot." Factor analyses revealed 3 factors including: (1) rejection of weak children, (2) approval of bullying, and (3) support for victims. Results indicated that most children disapproved of bullying and were supportive of victims although children became less supportive with age. There was a significant but small positive correlation between victimization scores and the support for victims. The Rigby and Slee (1991) study is a rare attempt to explore beliefs and attitudes specific to the bully and victim subculture. Items reflecting the malicious intent and lack of provocation of bullies, and the rejection of weakness and weak children such as victims, provide a starting point for the development of normative belief scales that might identify beliefs that contribute to the stability of bully and victim social roles.

Given the fact that bullies have also been found to be highly aggressive (Gottheil, 1995b), belief items that also reflect provocative aggression should also be included in a normative belief scale.

Although normative beliefs are likely a useful component in predicting behavior, the mere approval of a pattern of responding does not indicate whether an individual can then carry out the approved behavior, nor does it indicate whether it will be in the best interest of that person to even attempt such behavior. Therefore, normative beliefs alone may not be sufficient to predict and understand the stability of bully and victim behavior.

Self-Efficacy and Outcome-Expectancy Beliefs. Self-efficacy beliefs refer to the individual's beliefs about his/her ability to successfully carry out specific behaviors (Bandura, 1981, as cited in Perry, Perry, & Rasmussen, 1986). Outcome-expectancy beliefs refer to beliefs about the potential consequences for carrying out a particular action (Perry et al., 1986). An assumption within these research areas is that behavior is more likely to occur if the individual believes s/he is capable of performing the behavior, and that the production of the behavior will lead to positive outcomes (Boldizar, Perry, & Perry, 1989).

In a 1986 study, Perry and associates developed self-efficacy and outcome-expectancy measures related to aggression. Their self-efficacy measure is comprised of items describing various social situations that call for either an aggressive response or the inhibition of aggression. Children have to indicate their perceived ability either to use or inhibit aggressive behavior. Their outcome-expectancy measure is comprised of 6 categories of potential consequences of aggression: tangible rewards, adult approval, peer approval, reduction of aversive treatment by others, victim suffering, and self-reward. One hundred sixty children from the 4th through 7th grades received an aggression score based on peer nominations and were administered the self-efficacy and outcome-expectancy questionnaires. Aggressive children were found to be more confident than nonaggressive children in their ability to use aggression ($r = .15$) and less confident in their ability to inhibit aggression ($r = -.24$). Also, they were more likely to expect tangible rewards ($r = .18$), a reduction of aversive treatment from others ($r = -.25$), and to take pride in their aggression ($r = .15$; effect sizes were calculated from F scores following a procedure outlined by Rosnow & Rosenthal, 1988). The authors noted that self-efficacy and outcome-expectancy scores did not correlate with each other, suggesting that these are separate constructs.

In a study building upon the Perry et al. (1986) study, Boldizar and associates (1989) modified the outcome-expectancy measure to include 6 categories of consequences for aggression: tangible rewards, control of victim, suffering of the victim, retaliation from the victim, peer rejection, and negative self-evaluation. Various social situations were described in which children were asked to imagine performing an act of aggression in response to a frustrating or provocative child. Children were then asked to indicate how likely they believe a particular consequence would occur as a result of the aggression. One hundred sixty-five children from the 3rd through 6th grades received an aggression score based on peer nominations and were administered this revised outcome-expectancy measure. Results indicated that aggressive children tended to attach more value than nonaggressive children to the positive outcomes of aggression such as achieving control of their victim, and less value on negative outcomes such as victim suffering, retaliation, peer rejection, and negative self-evaluation. No significant differences were found between the groups on the tangible rewards subscale.

These modified outcome-expectancy subscales are relevant to bullies in that they focus on a number of victim related issues such as suffering and retaliation from, and control of victims. Given that bullies are more likely than other aggressive children to have identified victims that they repeatedly victimize, these victim-related consequences could be revealing in terms of the stability of bully behavior.

TRIPARTITE BELIEF MODEL

In the current study, a new model is proposed that is a melding of Huesmann and Guerra's work on normative beliefs with the work of Perry and associates on self-efficacy and outcome-expectancy beliefs, as these cognitions apply to bullies and victims. Accordingly, it is proposed that all three of these beliefs are necessary components in understanding the belief-behavior connections for victims and bullies. Normative beliefs, which refer to the individual's beliefs about the appropriateness of behavior, offer the direction that the individual will likely follow if s/he conjointly feels capable and motivated to do so. That is, one is more likely to carry out behavior that is consistent with one's beliefs about appropriateness (Egan, Monson, & Perry, in press). Self-efficacy beliefs are perceptions about whether the behavior can be carried out successfully. These beliefs provide the individual with a sense of readiness or capability to perform a given activity. Finally, outcome-expectancy beliefs provide the motivational component to the system in that individuals are more likely to carry out a course of action in which the positive or rewarding elements of the behavior outweigh the negative or punishing aspects. Therefore, the tripartite beliefs model proposes that a course of action or pattern of responding is most likely to occur when an individual believes it to be appropriate, doable, and rewarding.

In order to develop a beliefs model for bullies and victims, it is necessary to identify the unique characteristics of these subpopulations so as to derive relevant constructs for inquiry. Based on a review of the literature, noted bully and victim characteristics were used as a guide in the development and choice of the belief scales and subscales proposed in the current study.

With regard to bullies, some relevant findings include their noted tendency to be highly aggressive (Gottheil, 1995b) and that their aggression is often unprovoked, planned, and strategically used against weaker targets. Bully behavior is not an attempt to resolve conflict but to express power and control. Therefore, a feature of bullies that distinguishes them from other aggressive children is their willingness to use aggression even in unprovoked situations. Hence, beliefs about the appropriateness of aggression in unprovoked situations are relevant to understanding bully behavior. Beliefs about provoked aggression are also important to explore, given the bully's overall highly aggressive pattern of responding. Additionally, the planfulness and strategic use of aggression by bullies highlights the importance of exploring self-efficacy beliefs about control, such as beliefs about the capability to use and inhibit aggression. And, given that bully-victim conflicts usually involve an uneven distribution of power in favor of the bully, it is also important to explore beliefs that might allow bullies to justify their behavior toward weaker children. Therefore, normative beliefs about weakness and outcome expectancy beliefs about victim suffering are important to explore.

Victims of bullying also exhibit unique social, psychological, and physical characteristics that are relevant to model development considerations. Victims tend to express a fear of fighting, do not defend themselves, are physically weaker than their classmates, and have a negative attitude about aggression (Besag, 1989). Therefore, it is important to explore victim beliefs about the consequences of aggression, with the prediction that they will expect aggression to result in many negative and few positive outcomes. Additionally, the reported fear of fighting, lack of defending behavior, and physical weakness will likely contribute to low self-efficacy beliefs about the use of aggression and high self-efficacy for the inhibition of aggression. However, a fear of fighting, lack of defending behavior, etc., does not necessarily mean that victims disapprove of aggression. The fact that they are less capable of effectively using aggression, does not mean that they do not wish that they could. Therefore, it is important to explore their normative beliefs about provoked and unprovoked aggression. Their experiences of being recipients of unprovoked aggression, makes it more likely that victims will not approve of this behavior. However, it is less clear what their beliefs will be regarding provoked aggression, in that victims may have a desire to be able to defend themselves. It is additionally of interest to explore their beliefs about weakness. Given that victims have been found to have a low self-esteem and negative self-view, their beliefs about weakness may mirror their negative self-image, resulting in them being less accepting of weakness in others. However, it is likely that the suffering they experience in the face of unprovoked attacks would these children develop an advanced sense of empathy for other victims that would be reflected in a more pro-victim stance or acceptance of weakness (Rigby & Slee, 1991).

In the present study, it is hypothesized that indices of bully behavior will be positively related to a pattern of normative beliefs reflecting an approval of unprovoked and provoked aggression and a rejection of weakness. Additionally, higher bully scores are expected to be related to higher self-efficacy beliefs about the use and inhibition of aggression. Finally, bully scores are predicted to be related to patterns of outcome expectancy beliefs that reflect expectations for rewarding outcomes from the use of aggression (i.e., tangible rewards, feelings of control and power, positive self-evaluation, peer approval) and low expectations for negative outcomes (i.e., victim suffering, peer disapproval, fear of retaliation, negative self-evaluation).

Next, it is hypothesized that indices of victim behavior will be related to a pattern of normative beliefs reflecting the acceptance of weakness and the rejection of unprovoked aggression and provoked aggression. Additionally, higher victim scores are expected to be related to low self-efficacy beliefs about the use of aggression and high self-efficacy beliefs about the ability to inhibit aggression. Finally, victim scores are predicted to be related to a pattern of outcome-expectancy beliefs reflecting high expectations for negative outcomes resulting from the use of aggression (i.e., victim suffering, peer disapproval, fear of retaliation, negative self-evaluation), and low expectations for positive outcomes (i.e., tangible rewards, feelings of control and power, positive self-evaluation, peer approval). Gender differences will be examined for each of the current hypotheses.

METHOD

Subjects and Procedures

Data were collected on 180 elementary and middle school children in grades 5 and 6, comprising a 42% parent consent rate. Three children were dropped from further analyses because they obtained high scores on peer-nominated indices of both bully and victim behavior. Of the remaining 177 children, 57 did not complete all study measures and were only used for select analyses. The major reason for incomplete data was because 41 of the 57 children were not able to be assigned a peer nomination score because fewer than fifty percent of their classmates participated, and the remaining 16 children did not complete all the necessary measures. One hundred twenty children from grades 5 and 6 (55 males and 65 females) completed measures representing each of the belief categories (normative, self-efficacy, outcome-expectancy), as well as a peer nomination (Introducing My Classmates, IMC) and two self-derived indices of bully and victim behavior (Self Report Inventory of Bully and Victim Behavior, SRI; Perceived Peer Perspective Inventory, PPP). Seventeen classes from four different schools participated. All schools were located in areas whose residents were predominantly Caucasian and of low to moderate socioeconomic status.

Groups of children were administered two survey packages on two separate days, each lasting approximately 45 minutes. The first survey package included: (1) a basic demographics page; (2) a peer-nomination form used to obtain bully and victim behavior scores; (3) a self-report measure of bully and victim behavior and a self-report measure of perceived peer perception of bully and victim behavior; and (4) a normative beliefs survey. The second questionnaire package included a self-efficacy beliefs measure and an outcome-expectancy beliefs measure.

Measures

Beliefs and Attitudes Scale (BAS)

The BAS is an 18 item self-report survey of normative beliefs about bully and victim issues. Of the 18 BAS items, three items were selected and modified from Rigby and Slee (1991) and a few items were loosely based on the Aggression Approval Scale for Children–Form A, developed by Huesmann and associates (1992). The majority of items were original creations based on a review of the literature that pertained to the psychological and social characteristics of bullies and victims. Items describe situations that children may experience or have already experienced (e.g., "If someone yells at you it is okay to yell back"). Children completing the BAS respond on a 5-point Likert scale, as to how strongly they agree or disagree. (The items are shown in Table 1.)

The BAS was developed specifically to explore constructs thought to be relevant to the bully and victim subcultures. BAS items were developed and chosen to include beliefs about the appropriateness of unprovoked aggression (e.g., "It is okay to pick on certain kids, even if they don't do anything to deserve it"), provoked aggression (e.g., "If a kid hits you it is okay to hit him/her back"), and weakness (e.g., "It is not right to pick on kids who are weaker than you"). Each subscale contains 6 items whose scores are summed and can range

TABLE 1. Beliefs and Attitudes Scale (BAS) (Total Sample) and Highest Factor Loadings of Each Item

	I	II	III
Acceptance of Unprovoked Aggression			
3. It is okay to pick on certain kids, even if they don't do anything to deserve it.	.68		
6. It is okay to call kids nasty names for no good reason.	.65	.33	
9. If you want something from another kid it is okay to just grab it.	.66		−.35
12. It is okay to hit someone even if they are not bothering you.	.66		
15. It is okay to hit someone for no good reason.	.80		
18. If you don't like somebody it is okay to do mean things to them, even if they have done nothing wrong.	.63		
Acceptance of Provoked Aggression			
2. If a kid hits you it is okay to hit him/her back.		.78	
5. Kids shouldn't fight back even if they are being picked on **(reverse coded)**.		.64	
8. If someone yells at you it is okay to yell back.	.34	.75	
11. There is never a good reason to hurt someone, even if they deserve it **(reverse coded)**.		.42	−.47
14. It is only okay to call a kid a nasty name if he/she bothers you in some way.		.57	
17. If a kid pushes you during a game it is okay to push him/her back.	.34	.68	
Acceptance of Weakness			
1. Kids who get picked on a lot usually deserve it **(reverse coded)**.	−.30		.36
4. It is wrong to pick on kids who cannot defend themselves.			.46
7. Kids who are weak are just asking for trouble **(reverse coded)**.	−.39		.49
10. It is not right to pick on kids who are weaker than you.			.53
13. Kids who cannot defend themselves deserve what they get **(reverse coded)**.	−.49		.52
16. It is okay to pick on kids who don't stand up for themselves **(reverse coded)**.	−.53		.43

Note. This table reflects the results of Principal Axis factor analyses with Varimax rotation, requesting a 3-factor solution. Only factor loadings of |.30| and above are reported. Based on these items, alphas were .88 for the unprovoked aggression scale, .86 for the provoked aggression scale, and .77 for the weakness scale. N = 177.

from 6 to 30 per subscale. Higher scores reflect greater acceptance of weakness, provoked aggression, and unprovoked aggression.

A 3-factor solution, Principal Axis factor analysis with Varimax rotation, was computed for the total sample to correspond to the hypothesized constructs of approval for unprovoked aggression, provoked aggression, and weakness (Table 1). Factor 1 reflected an acceptance of Unprovoked Aggression factor, with an eigenvalue of 7.62 (42.3% explained unique variance); factor 2 reflected an acceptance of Provoked Aggression factor, with an eigenvalue of 1.79 (9.9% explained unique variance); and items loading highly on factor 3 reflected an acceptance of Weakness factor, with an eigenvalue of 1.21 (6.7% explained unique variance). Together, these three factors accounted for 59% of the variance.

Self-Efficacy Questionnaire–Modified (SEQM)

The SEQM consists of 16 items taken directly from the original 46-item survey developed by Perry and associates (1986). Items are descriptions of various social situations and subjects indicate their perceived ability either to use or inhibit aggression in these situations. Higher scores on either the use or inhibition subscales reflects the child's perceived self-efficacy for that behavioral domain. Scores on each subscale can range from 8 (lowest perceived self-efficacy) to 32 (highest perceived self-efficacy).

Based on a sample of 4th through 7th graders (mean age 11.3 years), Perry and associates (1986) reported internal consistencies of .86 and .73 for the perceived self-efficacy of aggression and inhibition subscales, respectively. As predicted, compared to nonaggressive children, aggressive children reported significantly higher self-efficacy for aggression and significantly lower self-efficacy for the inhibition of aggression. Both findings are consistent with the aggression research although as discussed above, one feature that distinguishes bullies from other aggressive children is the planful and controlled nature of their aggression. Therefore, one might expect that unlike other aggressive children, bullies might express high self-efficacy for the inhibition of aggression as well as its use.

Outcome Values Questionnaire. The outcome values questionnaire is a 40-item survey developed by Boldizar and associates (1989) that measures the values that children place on various outcome arising from the use of aggression. Presented with stories involving a frustrating or provocative peer, children indicate how concerned they are about a "specified consequence that might result" from their use of aggression (p. 574).

The outcome values questionnaire consists of 6 subscales containing 6 items each, and 4 filler items. For each item, subjects indicate the degree to which they devalue or value a given outcome along a 4 point scale, with higher subscale scores reflecting a greater perceived value of a particular outcome. The 6 subscales each tap a different potential consequence of the use of aggression and include: tangible rewards, feelings of control and power, victim suffering, retaliation from the victim, peer rejection, and negative self-evaluation. Based on a sample of 3rd through 6th graders (mean age 10.6 years), Boldizar and associates (1989) reported subscale alpha coefficients of .58, .74, .72, .81, .72, and .71, respectively (see Boldizar et al., 1989 for more in-depth subscale descriptions).

Behavioral Indices of Bully and Victim Behavior

Introducing My Classmates (IMC). The IMC is a peer-nomination form in which subjects are read a series of 4 stories about fictitious child characters and are asked to nominate all the classmates, that they feel are like the child in the story. Of the 4 stories, one describes a child exhibiting victim-like characteristics (e.g., "This boy Oscar, is picked on, made fun of, called names, and is hit and pushed by other kids. Kids do mean things to him and try to hurt his feelings."), one describes a child exhibiting bully-like characteristics (e.g., "This girl, Marianna, makes fun of people, says she can beat everyone up, hits and pushes others around, tries to pick fights with people, and if someone gets in her way she is likely to shove that person out of the way"), and two are filler items.

Bully and victim subscale scores were derived separately by adding up all the nominations that a given child received from his or her classmates on the respective bully and victim items. These scores were then divided by the total number of raters and multiplied by 100 in order to obtain a percentage score of peer nominated bully (Percent Bully Score, PBS) and victim (Percent Victim Score, PVS) behavior. Scores can range from 0 to 100 with higher scores reflecting a greater percentage of classmate nominations.

The distributions of PBS and PVS residuals were not normally distributed. As a result, a Log10 transformation was applied to both variables in order to pull in extreme scores, and increase normality in the distributions (Neter, Wasserman, & Kutner, 1990; Winer, 1971). Both transformed and non-transformed results are reported. The transformation did not appear to substantially affect the results in the current study.

Setting the Record Straight (SRS). The SRS is a survey that combines a previously developed self-report measure of bully and victim behavior (Self Report Inventory of Bully and Victim Behavior, SRI; Gottheil, 1994) with a newly developed measure of children's perceptions of how they are viewed by their peers (Perceived Peer Perspective Inventory, PPP). SRI items are self-referential true/false statements about bully and victim behaviors. Each SRI item (e.g., "I get beat up," "I hit and push others around") is preceded by a matching PPP item (e.g., "My classmates think that I get beat up," "My classmates think that I hit and push others around"). Fifteen of the original twenty SRI items were included in the SRS and were chosen based upon previous Principal Axis factor analyses with Varimax rotation, and internal consistency scores. Based on the current sample of 174 5th and 6th graders, alphas for the subscales of the SRI and PPP were as follows: .88 for the victim SRI, .72 for the bully SRI, .85 for the victim PPP, and .69 for the bully PPP.

SRI and PPP bully and victim scores were tabulated independently by taking an average of the bully and victim subscale scores and multiplying by 100 in order to obtain a percentage. Scores on each subscale can range from 0 to 100 with higher scores reflecting higher percentages of self-reported bully and victim behaviors, respectively.

RESULTS

Tripartite Beliefs Related to Bully Behavior

The pattern of significant correlations of the peer bully score (PBS) with belief subscale scores offers some support for the current hypothesis. Higher peer nominated bully behavior scores were related significantly to a higher level of acceptance of provoked aggression and a lower level of acceptance of weakness; the self-efficacy for the use of aggression variable; and four of the six outcome expectancy variables (victim suffering, negative self-evaluation, fear of retaliation, and peer disapproval). Significant correlations ranged from |.17| to |.32| for the PBS ($m = .21$); and |.20| to |.40| for the transformed PBS ($m = .27$) (see Table 2).

Both the bully self-report inventory (BSRI) and the bully perceived peer perspective (BPPP) measure, significantly correlated with all but one of the belief variables in the expected directions. Significant correlations ranged from |.22| to |.60| for the BSRI ($m = .47$); and |.16| to |.46| for the BPPP ($m = .33$). One consistent exception to the model, across peer and self derived behavioral measures of bully behavior, was the finding that bully scores were either negatively correlated with beliefs about self-efficacy to inhibit aggression or not related at all.

Support for the tripartite beliefs model of bully behavior was found across male (see Table 3) and female (see Table 4) subsamples when bully behavior was indexed by self-derived measures. In the female subsample, the beliefs model was also supported when peer derived bully scores were transformed to better normalize their distribution. In the male subsample no support was

TABLE 2. Correlations of Belief Subscale Scores with Peer and Self-Report Bully Scores (Total Sample)

		PBS	Transformed PBS	BSRI	BPPP
Normative Beliefs	Unprovoked	.05	.12	.48**	.27**
	Provoked	.18*	.32**	.58**	.44**
	Weakness	−.17*	−.21*	−.50**	−.24**
Self-Efficacy Beliefs	Aggression Eff.	.32**	.40**	.60**	.46**
	Inhibition Eff.	−.15	−.25**	−.41**	−.33**
Outcome Expectancy Beliefs	Victim Suffering	−.19*	−.22*	−.55**	−.38**
	Neg. Self Eval.	−.23**	−.26**	−.58**	−.39**
	Fear of Retaliation	−.24**	−.29**	−.41**	−.36**
	Power/Control	.04	.15	.47**	.31**
	Peer Disapproval	−.17*	−.20*	−.33**	−.30**
	Tangible Reward	.01	−.01	.22**	.16*

Note. PBS is total sample peer nomination percent bully score; Transformed PBS refers to a Log10 transformation of PBS scores; BSRI is bully self-report inventory score; and BPPP is bully perceived peer perspective score. Ns range from 131 to 177 due to missing data.
* p < .05, ** p < .01.

TABLE 3. Correlations of Belief Subscale Scores with Peer and Self-Report Bully Scores (Male Subsample)

		PBS	Transformed PBS	BSRI	BPPP
Normative Beliefs	Unprovoked	−.05	−.01	.45**	.19
	Provoked	.16	.32**	.51**	.34**
	Weakness	−.18	−.15	−.48**	−.25*
Self-Efficacy Beliefs	Aggression Eff.	.24	.35**	.59**	.40**
	Inhibition Eff.	−.12	−.22	−.43**	−.38**
Outcome Expectancy Beliefs	Victim Suffering	−.09	−.08	−.53**	−.30**
	Neg. Self Eval.	−.10	−.10	−.57**	−.29**
	Fear of Retaliation	−.21	−.26*	−.33**	−.20
	Power/Control	−.04	−.02	.44**	.26*
	Peer Disapproval	−.11	−.11	−.33**	−.25*
	Tangible Reward	.05	−.06	.19	.13

Note. PBS is total sample peer nomination percent bully score; Transformed PBS refers to a Log10 transformation of PBS scores; BSRI is bully self-report inventory score; and BPPP is bully perceived peer perspective score. Range of n = 62 - 93 due to missing data.
* p < .05, ** p < .01.

TABLE 4. Correlations of Belief Subscale Scores with Peer and Self-Report Bully Scores (Female Subsample)

		PBS	Transformed PBS	BSRI	BPPP
Normative Beliefs	Unprovoked	.18	.26*	.49**	.37**
	Provoked	.20	.29*	.62**	.52**
	Weakness	−.14	−.26*	−.48**	−.19
Self-Efficacy Beliefs	Aggression Eff.	.40**	.44**	.58**	.50**
	Inhibition Eff.	−.16	−.26*	−.30**	−.20
Outcome Expectancy Beliefs	Victim Suffering	−.29*	−.33**	−.53**	−.44**
	Neg. Self Eval.	−.38**	−.41**	−.52**	−.46**
	Fear of Retaliation	−.27*	−.29*	−.47**	−.48**
	Power/Control	.11	.28*	.45**	.33**
	Peer Disapproval	−.24*	−.27*	−.29**	−.35**
	Tangible Reward	−.02	.04	.30**	.20

Note. PBS is total sample peer nomination percent bully score; Transformed PBS refers to a Log10 transformation of PBS scores; BSRI is bully self-report inventory score; and BPPP is bully perceived peer perspective score. Range of n = 69 - 84 due to missing data.
* p < .05, ** p < .01.

found for the model when bully scores were indexed through peer nominations.

Tripartite Beliefs Related to Victim Behavior

The pattern of correlations of peer and self derived victim behavior scores with the belief subscale scores did not support the current study's hypothesis. Of the 132 possible correlations within the total sample, male and female subsamples, only 8 (6%) were significant and likely due to chance, although all significant findings were in the predicted direction.

DISCUSSION

Hypothesis 1: A Tripartite Beliefs Model of Bully Behavior

It was proposed that high bully behavior scores would be related to the endorsement of beliefs reflecting an approval of unprovoked and provoked aggression, and a rejection of weakness (normative beliefs); greater endorsement of self-efficacy beliefs about the use and inhibition of aggression (self-efficacy beliefs); and greater expectations of rewarding outcomes from the use of aggression such as tangible rewards, feelings of power and control, and the minimization of negative outcomes such as, victim suffering, peer disapproval, fear of retaliation, and negative self-evaluation (outcome-expectancy beliefs).

Based on the total sample, strong support was found for the tripartite beliefs model of bully behavior when such behavior was indexed by perceived peer perspective and self report measures. Moderate support of the model was found when behavior was indexed by peer nominations. In other words, children with higher bully behavior scores were more likely to endorse beliefs that were consistent with the tripartite beliefs model of bully behavior.

Breaking down the beliefs model into its component parts (normative, self-efficacy, and outcome-expectancy beliefs), an examination of the previous research offers support for the current findings. With regard to the research on normative beliefs, Huesmann and Guerra (1997) found a modest relation between approval of provoked aggression and peer nominations of aggressive behavior. Also, Huesmann and associates (1992) noted a moderate relation between normative beliefs about aggression and self-reports of aggressive behavior. The current study extends Huesmann's work by including beliefs about weakness and unprovoked aggression, and by exploring the relation of normative beliefs with indices of bullying rather than the broader category of aggressive behavior.

The current findings are also consistent with those found by Boldizar et al. (1989) and Perry et al. (1986) who examined the relation between outcome-expectancy and self-efficacy beliefs, respectively, with behavioral indices of aggression. Regarding outcome-expectancies, Boldizar and associates (1989) found that peer nominated aggressive children were more likely than their less aggressive peers to report believing that positive outcomes would arise from the use of aggression, and less likely to report believing that punishing consequences would result. The authors suggested that such a belief system allows aggressive children to "pursue their aggressive activities relatively unencumbered by devastating thoughts of inhibitory consequences" (p. 576), making it more likely that the behaviour would occur in the future. Perry and associates (1986) found that peer nominated aggressive children reported that they believed it would be easier for them to use aggression effectively and more difficult to inhibit the use of aggression in provoking situations, when compared with less aggressive peers. Although these results are consistent with the findings of the current study, one finding was counter to prediction. It was predicted that, children with higher bully scores would report greater self-efficacy to inhibit their aggressive impulses given the controlled nature of bullying. This was not found to be the case and is discussed below.

The tripartite beliefs model of bully behavior was proposed as a possible cognitive mediation explanation for the stability of bully behavior patterns. According to the model, one possible mechanism by which bully behaviors remain stable is through the presence of a series of beliefs that include: an acceptance or approval of bully behavior; a sense of efficacy to produce the behavior; and the belief that the production of such behavior would be worthwhile in some fashion. These beliefs might help to reduce cognitive dissonance by providing individuals with an internal environment that is supportive, encouraging, and justifying of bully behavior, and hence, increase the likelihood of its expression and stability. On the other hand, while beliefs might influence bully behavior, it is equally plausible that the expression of bully behavior might play a role in the development of one's beliefs. Beliefs are dynamic in that they are continuously being evaluated by the individual in terms of whether the beliefs effectively organize and explain one's experiences. Under such scrutiny, beliefs are either strengthened, weakened, or modified. Children who bully effectively might come to develop stronger beliefs that are more resistant to conflicting information. Hence, both beliefs about bullying and bully behavior might serve to affect each other, and account for part of the reason why such behavior is relatively stable across time and situations.

The current support for the tripartite beliefs model of bully behavior has potential prevention/intervention implications. Considering the likely influence of beliefs and behavior on each other, intervention approaches might need to strive toward promulgating inconsistency between beliefs and bully behavior. Therefore, challenging beliefs about the appropriateness of bully behavior by helping children develop perspective taking and empathy skills; educating students and school personnel about their role in openly disapproving of, and reporting children who bully; and constructing the environment so that bullying tends to result in negative outcomes, all might be steps that begin to challenge normative, self-efficacy, and outcome-expectancy beliefs that sustain bully behavior. Without direction, confidence, or positive outcomes, bully behavior might begin to starve as it is cognitively deprived of an internal rationale. However, one must assume that behaviors serve a purpose, and removing a behavior without finding a replacement could lead to the adoption of other maladaptive responses. Therefore, arranging opportunities for children to redirect their behavior along prosocial avenues, develop self-esteem and leadership skills, etc., might help when the utility and feasibility of using bully behavior is removed. An additional consideration is that once beliefs have been established or behavior has been long-standing, children will likely be more resistant to interventions (Huesmann & Guerra, 1997). This highlights the need to begin prevention/intervention efforts early. In a one-year longitudinal study by Huesmann and Guerra (1997), normative beliefs about aggression were found to become stable starting in the fourth grade. This may be a starting point, but further research that examines the developing stability of beliefs about bullying and aggression are needed.

Some notable exceptions to the tripartite beliefs model of bully behavior were the lack of relation of peer derived bully scores with beliefs about the approval of unprovoked aggression, and outcome-expectancy beliefs about the attainment of power/control and tangible rewards. However, these beliefs were all related, in the predicted direction, to self derived bully scores. This might be explained by the measurement issues regarding differences between peer and self derived indices of potentially reactive behaviors or ideas. That is, peer derived bully scores identify children both willing and unwilling to admit to engaging in bully behaviors on their own. Therefore, children with higher peer derived bully scores comprise a heterogeneous group with regard to levels of image management efforts. On the other hand, self derived reports only identify children willing to admit to engaging in bully behavior. Therefore, children with high bully scores comprise a more homogeneous group in terms of image management efforts. One might expect that children who are willing to admit to socially unacceptable behaviors such as bullying will be more likely to admit to some socially unacceptable beliefs, such as an approval of unprovoked aggression, or the beliefs that aggression can be used to obtain power or extort tangible rewards from others. This is supported in the current study and highlights the general limitation of self-report measures and the potential difficulties when attempting to make cross-rater inferences and interpretations.

Another notable exception to the tripartite beliefs model of bully behavior is the finding that higher bully behavior nominations are related to lower reported beliefs about being able to inhibit aggression if provoked. At first glance, this finding might appear to be contradictory to the bully research, which tends to support the notion that bully behavior is well within the control of the bully (Olweus, 1991,1993; Smith et al., 1993). In fact, Coie, Dodge, Terry, and Wright (1991) found that unlike reactive aggressors, bullies tended to stop aggressing after their victim submitted, demonstrating an ability to inhibit their aggressive activities.

The explanation for the current study finding might lie in the design of the measure used to explore beliefs about self-efficacy to inhibit aggression. Bully behavior has been found to be proactive in that it is usually unprovoked (Salmivalli, Karhunen, & Lagerspetz, 1996; Smith et al., 1993) and internally motivated by goals of domination and control (Batsche & Knoff, 1994; Besag, 1989; Gottheil, 1995a; Olweus, 1994, 1996). The index of self-efficacy to inhibit aggression used in the current study is exclusively made up of items occurring within a context of externally motivated/provoking situations (e.g., "While playing soccer a kid prevents you from making a goal. You really want to get the kid back by pushing the kid hard but you decide not to. Not pushing the kid back is _____ for you"), which is not the type of situation in which bullying typically occurs. Therefore, the finding that these children believe they will not be able to inhibit their aggression when provoked does not detract from the findings of previous research that indicate that these children are able to inhibit their aggression when they bully (Coie et al., 1991). To further explore this issue, there is a need for future research to compare children who primarily bully and those who are more reactive in their use of aggression. A new measure that includes items reflecting self-efficacy to inhibit aggression in the context of proactive/unprovoked situations might help to address the currently noted finding.

Hypothesis 2: A Tripartite Beliefs Model of Victim Behavior

It was proposed that victim behavior scores would be related to the endorsement of beliefs reflecting a disapproval of unprovoked and provoked aggression, and an acceptance of weakness (normative beliefs); a greater endorsement of self-efficacy beliefs about the inhibition of aggression and lower endorse-

·ments of self-efficacy beliefs regarding the use of aggression (self-efficacy beliefs); and greater expectations of negative outcomes from the use of aggression, such as, victim suffering, peer disapproval, fear of retaliation, and negative self-evaluation, and lower expectations of positive outcomes such as, tangible rewards and feelings of power and control (outcome-expectancy beliefs).

Based on the total sample and male and female subsamples, no support was found for the tripartite beliefs model of victim behavior. The lack of relations indicate that the beliefs explored in the current study were not related to the degree of indexed victim behavior, and therefore, do not provide an explanatory model for its stability. This might indicate that the belief categories examined in the current study were not well suited or representative of the cognitive environment of victims.

The reason for this lack of relation might lie in the fact that children tend to experience victim behavior rather than actively choose to engage in it. Victim behavior is passive in that it is ultimately determined by the behavior of victimizers, and therefore, might be less influenced by the beliefs of those being victimized. While beliefs might affect how children respond to bullying, the belief-victim behavior connection remains more indirect.

A cognitive mediation explanation that focuses on beliefs that can influence how children react to being victimized might better address a behavioral aspect of being a victim that is within a child's active control, and hence, might be more directly influenced by his/her beliefs. Children who passively submit to attacks by bullies may present as easy, non-threatening targets, and therefore, are more likely to be victimized in the future. Beliefs that support or increase the likelihood of submission might, in turn, be predictive of continued victimization. For example, beliefs about one's self-efficacy to defend against verbal and/or physical attacks, beliefs about one's power to affect changes in his/her environment, etc., might affect whether one will defend against or submit to being bullied. Outcome expectancies related to self-defense, such as beliefs about whether self-defense will lead to an escalation of abuse, more future attacks, injury, etc., might affect one's willingness to engage in such behavior. Additionally, beliefs about culpability for one's own victimization (i.e., believing that one deserves to be abused) might contribute to an acceptance of the victim status, reduce the likelihood for retaliation, and contribute to the stability of the victim role.

Nonetheless, one might still expect that some of the beliefs examined in the current study would have developed as a result of being victimized, such as beliefs about one's ability to aggress, victim suffering, etc., yet this was not the case. The lack of significant findings might be related to the composition of the group of children in the current study that were identified as experiencing victim behavior. Those who are victimized might derive different lessons and beliefs from their experiences. Some could come to identify with the pain they experience as victims and develop beliefs consistent with the tripartite beliefs model of victim behavior. For example, aggression might come to be viewed as unacceptable, be believed to result in negative outcomes, and be thought of as difficult to enact effectively. On the other hand, victims could come to identify with the aggressor, and instead, long for the ability to use aggression effectively, approve of its use, believe that it will result in positive outcomes for the user, and disapprove of weakness both in themselves and others. A heterogeneous group made up of children who identify with the victim and the aggressor, then, might be another explanation for the noted lack of relation between the beliefs proposed in the tripartite beliefs model and the indices of victim behavior.

CONCLUSION

Previous research has indicated that bully and victim social roles tend to be stable patterns of behavior. The tripartite beliefs models proposed in the current manuscript, were offered as potential cognitive mediation explanations for some of this noted stability. Strong support was found for the tripartite beliefs model of bully behavior, lending support to the notion that beliefs about aggression and bullying that are supportive, justifying, accepting, and encouraging of bullying, are related of its actual expression. No support was found for the tripartite beliefs model of victim behavior. The reason for this might lie in the fact that unlike bullies, victims are passive recipients of the aggression they receive, and hence, their social role may be imposed upon them regardless of their beliefs. Nonetheless, beliefs might contribute to the likelihood of being a victim in a more indirect fashion by affecting how one reacts to being bullied. Further research that addresses beliefs more representative of the internal environment of victims is warranted.

REFERENCES

Austin, S., & Joseph, S. (1996). Assessment of bully/victim problems in 8 to 11 year-olds. *British Journal of Educational Psychology*, *66*, 447-456.
Batsche, G. M., & Knoff, H. M. (1994). Bullies and their victims: Understanding a pervasive problem in the schools. *School Psychology Review*, *23* (2), 165-174.
Besag, V. (1989). *Bullies and victims in schools*. Philadelphia: Open University Press.
Boldizar, J. P., Perry, D. G., & Perry, L. C. (1989). Outcome values and aggression. *Child Development*, *60*, 571-579.

Boulton, M. J., & Underwood, K. (1992). Bully/victim problems among middle school children. *British Journal of Educational Psychology, 62*, 73-87.

Coie, J. D., Dodge, K. A., Terry, R., & Wright, V. (1991). The role of aggression in peer relations: An analysis of aggression episodes in boys' play groups. *Child Development, 62*, 812-826.

Crick, N. R., & Bigbee, M. A. (1998). Relational and overt forms of peer victimization: A multiinformant approach. *Journal of Consulting and Clinical Psychology, 66* (2), 337-347.

Crick, N. R., Bigbee, M. A., & Howes, C. (1996). Gender differences in children's normative beliefs about aggression: How do I hurt thee? Let me count the ways. *Child Development, 67*, 1003-1014.

Egan, S. K., Monson, T. C., & Perry, D. G. (in press). Social-cognitive influences on over-time changes in aggression. *Developmental Psychology.*

Gottheil, N. F. (1994). *Bullies and victims: Possible mechanisms of maintenance.* Unpublished master's thesis, Wayne State University, Detroit.

Gottheil, N. F. (1995a, March). *Bullies and victims: Lessons derived from actual conflicts as a possible mechanism for status maintenance.* Poster session presented at the meeting of the Society for Research in Child Development, Indianapolis, IN.

Gottheil, N. F. (1995b, March). *Bullies and victims: Patterns of the use and receipt of physical aggression as a possible mechanism for status maintenance.* Poster session presented at the meeting of the Society for Research in Child Development, Indianapolis, IN.

Guerra, N. G., Huessman, L. R., & Hanish, L. (1995). The role of normative beliefs in children's social behavior. In N. Eisenberg (Ed.), *Social Development* (pp. 140-158). California: Sage Publications.

Hazler, R. J., Carney, J. V., Green, S., Powell, R., & Jolly, L.S. (1997). Areas of expert agreement on identification of school bullies and victims. *School Psychology International, 18*, 5-14.

Horne, A. M., Glaser, B., & Sayger, T. V. (1994). Bullies. *Counseling and Human Development, 27* (3), 1-12.

Huesmann, L. R., Eron, L. D., Lefkowitz, M. M., & Walder, L. O. (1984). Stability of aggression over time and generations. *Developmental Psychology, 20* (6), 1120-1134.

Huesmann, L. R., & Guerra, N. G. (1997). Children's normative beliefs about aggression and aggressive behavior. *Journal of Personality and Social Psychology, 72* (2), 408-419.

Huesmann, L. R., Guerra, N. G., Miller, L. S., & Zelli, A. (1992). The role of social norms in the development of aggressive behavior. In H. Zumckly & A. Fraczek (Eds.), *Socialization and aggression* (pp. 139-152). New York: Springer-Verlag.

Lagerspetz, K. M. J., Bjorkqvist, K., & Peltonen, T. (1988). Is indirect aggression typical of females? Gender differences in aggressiveness in 11-to 12-year-old children. *Aggressive Behavior, 14*, 403-414.

Miller, P. H. (1989). *Theories of developmental psychology* (2nd ed.). New York: W. H. Freeman and Company.

Neter, J., Wasserman, W., & Kutner, M.H. (1990). *Applied linear statistical models: Regression, analysis of variance, and experimental designs* (3rd ed.). Boston: Richard D. Irwin, Inc.

Olweus, D. (1984). Aggressors and their victims: Bullying at school. In N. Frude & H. Gault (Eds.), *Disruptive behaviour in schools* (pp. 57-76). Chinchester: John Wiley & Sons, Ltd.

Olweus, D. (1991). Bully/victim problems among schoolchildren: Basic facts and effects of a school based intervention program. In D. J. Pepler & K. H. Rubin (Eds.), *The development and treatment of childhood aggression* (pp. 411-448). Hillsdale, N. J.: Erlbaum.

Olweus, D. (1992). Victimization by peers: Antecedents and long-term outcomes. In K. H. Rubin & J. B. Asendorf (Eds), *Social withdrawal, inhibition, and shyness in childhood* (pp. 315-341). Hillsdale, N. J.: Erlbaum.

Olweus, D. (1993). *Bullying at school: What we know and what we can do.* Oxford, UK: Blackwell Publishers Ltd.

Olweus, D. (1994). Annotation: Bullying at school: Basic facts and effects of a school based intervention program. *Journal of Child Psychology and Psychiatry, 35,* 1171-1190.

Olweus, D. (1996). Bully/victim problems in school. *Prospects, 26*(2), 331-359.

Perry, D. G., Perry, L. C., & Rasmussen, P. (1986). Cognitive social learning mediators of aggression. *Child Development, 57,* 700-711.

Rigby, K., and Slee, P. T. (1991). Bullying among Australian school children: Reported behavior and attitudes toward victims. *The Journal of Social Psychology, 131* (5), 615-627.

Rosnow, R. L., & Rosenthal, R. (1988). Focused tests of significance and effect size estimation in counseling psychology. *Journal of Counseling Psychology, 35* (2), 203-208.

Salmivalli, C., Karhunen, J., & Lagerspetz, K. M. J. (1996). How do the victims respond to bullying? *Aggressive Behavior, 22,* 99-109.

Smith, P. K., Bowers, L., Binney, V., & Cowie, H. (1993). Relationships of children involved in bully/victim problems at school. In S. Duck (Ed.), *Learning about relationships: Understanding relationship processes series volume 2* (pp. 184-212). Newbury Park, CA: Sage Publications, Inc.

Winer, B. J. (1971). *Statistical principles in experimental design* (2nd ed.). New York: McGraw-Hill, Inc.

Zarzour, K. (1994). *Battling the school-yard bully.* Toronto: HarperCollins Publishers Ltd.

Conversations with Middle School Students About Bullying and Victimization: Should We Be Concerned?

Dorothy L. Espelage
Christine S. Asidao

SUMMARY. An interview study was conducted with 89 middle school students (6th-8th grades) from three schools in mid-sized Midwestern towns. Students were asked to define bullying and were asked to describe their experiences with bullying. We elicited their opinions on why children harass each other, who are bullies and victims, how adults intervene and their thoughts on what should be done about the problem. The major themes elicited from the interviews support and expand previous research on bullying behavior and peer victimization conducted outside of the United States. Results provide important information needed for the de-

Dorothy L. Espelage, PhD, is Assistant Professor of Counseling Psychology, the University of Illinois, Urbana-Champaign. Christine S. Asidao, MA, is a doctoral candidate in the Counseling Psychology PhD program.

Address correspondence to: Dorothy L. Espelage, Department of Educational Psychology, University of Illinois, Urbana-Champaign, College of Education, 226 Education Building, 1310 South Sixth Street, Champaign, IL 61820-6990 (E-mail: espelage@uiuc.edu).

This research was supported in part by the University of Illinois Research Board Grant.

[Haworth co-indexing entry note]: "Conversations with Middle School Students About Bullying and Victimization: Should We Be Concerned?" Espelage, Dorothy L. and Christine S. Asidao. Co-published simultaneously in *Journal of Emotional Abuse* (The Haworth Maltreatment & Trauma Press, an imprint of The Haworth Press, Inc.) Vol. 2, No. 2/3, 2001, pp. 49-62; and: *Bullying Behavior: Current Issues, Research, and Interventions* (ed: Robert A. Geffner, Marti Loring, and Corinna Young) The Haworth Maltreatment & Trauma Press, an imprint of The Haworth Press, Inc., 2001, pp. 49-62. Single or multiple copies of this article are available for a fee from The Haworth Document Delivery Service [1-800-HAWORTH, 9:00 a.m. - 5:00 p.m. (EST). E-mail address: getinfo@haworthpressinc.com].

49

sign and implementation of future prevention and intervention programs to reduce bullying and victimization within the middle school environment. *[Article copies available for a fee from The Haworth Document Delivery Service: 1-800-HAWORTH. E-mail address: <getinfo@haworthpressinc.com> Website: <http://www.HaworthPress.com>* © *2001 by The Haworth Press, Inc. All rights reserved.]*

KEYWORDS. Bullying, middle school, victimization, interviews

INTRODUCTION

For too long bullying among American children and adolescents has been ignored. This is somewhat surprising given that almost every adult can recount some childhood experience with bullying, either as a perpetrator, victim, or witness. For several decades, many countries outside of the United States have documented the serious consequences associated with bullying and have, in some cases, implemented national campaigns to protect children from peer harassment (Olweus, 1994, 1997). Unfortunately, American scholars are only now beginning to recognize bullying as a serious concern for our youth. We are, therefore, a long way from a complete understanding of bullying and even further from instituting large scale prevention and intervention school programs.

Bullying has been identified and studied internationally with the earliest work in the field initiated in the late 1970s by Dan Olweus in Scandinavia. Other researchers in Great Britain (e.g., Boulton & Smith, 1994), Australia (Rigby & Slee, 1991), and in the United States (e.g., Hoover, Oliver, & Hazler, 1992) have contributed to the current understanding of the dynamics underlying bullying. Unfortunately, the question of whether research findings from international studies generalize to students in the U.S. remains unanswered.

Students are involved in normal, everyday conflicts with one another. However, conflict that involves bullying behavior is a cause for concern. Studies of American students have found nearly 80 to 90% of adolescents report some form of victimization from a bully at school and 10 to 15% of middle school students have been described as bullies (Boulton & Smith, 1994; Olweus, 1991, 1994). In a study by Hazler and colleagues (1992), 90% of the American students surveyed believed that bullying caused them problems such as loss of friendships, feelings of isolation, and academic difficulties.

Various definitions of bullying can be found in the literature with the majority of our knowledge stemming from studies utilizing international samples. Generally, behaviors defined as bullying are used to achieve and maintain social dominance through overt and covert aggressive means (Arora, 1987). However, these behaviors differ from aggression on three dimensions. First, bullying behaviors are more systematic and self-initiated as students who bully carefully select their victims and create encounters in which they can control others. Second, unlike other aggressive youth, students who bully tend to repeatedly attack their victims. Third, these behaviors often include a variety of hurtful actions in addition to physical attacks, such as name calling, social exclusion, taking and damaging belongings, extortion, nasty rumors, and verbal threats (Sharp & Smith, 1991).

The extant literature in the area of bullying and peer victimization has several limitations that preclude definitive statements about the types of bullying behavior that occurs in our schools and how we should proceed to intervene. First, physical aggression has been the focus of much research with very few empirical investigations on low-level aggression, such as bullying. This is in part due to a lack of consensus on what constitutes bullying behavior and how it differs from more aggressive behaviors such as fighting (Boulton & Underwood, 1992). Second, as stated earlier in this document, the majority of the studies have been conducted at the international level and not in the U.S. It is possible that the type and frequency of bullying in U.S. schools might differ from the behaviors seen in other countries. Third, of those studies conducted with U.S. samples, the majority of them have examined bullying behavior among elementary school children and have failed to explore bullying during the middle school years. Given these limitations it is imperative that researchers learn more about the type, frequency, and location of bullying in middle schools across the U.S.

The goal of the current study was to investigate the experiences of middle school students had with bullying and victimization through individual interviews. Study objectives included: (1) identifying and clarifying how students define bullying; (2) investigating personal accounts of bullying and victimization; and (3) eliciting student's suggestions on how to decrease future bullying and peer victimization. The interview format allowed students to express their thoughts without being constrained to previous conceptualizations of bullying. Thus, the open-ended nature of the interview provided students with the opportunity to tell their story about what they saw in their particular school. Our intention in this paper was not to make definitive statements about bullying in our schools, but instead, our goal was to present the pertinent issues through the voice of students themselves.

METHOD

Participants

Eighty-nine middle school students (grades 6th-8th) in three schools located in three mid-sized Midwestern towns were participants in this study. Participants were identified by their teachers as bullies, victims, or neither bullies nor victims. Students' ages ranged from 11 to 14 years ($M = 12.40$). The sample included 55 (62.6%) males and 34 (37.4%) females. The racial composition was as follows: 68 (76.4%) European-American, 13 (14.3%) African-American, 4 (4.4%) Asian-American, 1 (1.1%) Hispanic-American, and 3 (3.3%) Biracial.

Procedure

Once teachers identified students as potential study participants, permission forms were sent to the parent/guardian of each child. Only those students who returned a signed permission form and agreed to participate were included in the study. Because this study was part of a pilot investigation to evaluate the psychometric properties of bullying measures, students first completed a 30-minute survey in small groups during a free period. The survey was read to the students by the principal investigator and a graduate research assistant monitored student progress. During the month following the survey administration, the research team returned to the school to conduct in-depth interviews with each study participant. Interviews ranged in length from 30 to 60 minutes and were audiotaped for the purposes of transcription. Students were asked to define bullying, to identify where bullying takes place in their school, to explain why some students bullied their peers and why other students were targets of bullying, to discuss how teachers and administrators managed bullying in the classroom and in the school, and to suggest some useful strategies for addressing bullying and victimization in the school.

RESULTS

What Is Bullying?

According to the children we interviewed, their definition of bullying was relatively consistent. Students' major responses included both verbal (e.g., teasing) and physical aggression (e.g., hitting, pushing), as well as threats, manipulation, spreading rumors, destroying others' property, taking other people's property, seeking revenge or retaliation, and seeking power. The vast majority of children defined bullying as acts of teasing or picking on others (i.e., name-calling, making fun of others) that were intentional and designed to hurt the other's feelings. Some children did not consider teasing as bullying behavior, but when probed, agreed that teasing was bullying under certain conditions. Many students shared the same comment as this 6th grade student:

"Bullying is pushing someone around and making them feel like a failure . . . like if you are beating someone up, that is bullying, and also if you are black-mailing or threatening them, that is bullying. . . . If it is playful teasing, no, but if you are hurting someone's feelings, yes."

Students clearly recognized a difference between teasing that involved joking amongst friends and teasing that was designed to hurt another's feelings. However, it was found that many of the teacher-nominated bullies were often quick to add that teasing should not be taken seriously and in fact they thought that students should be able to handle some teasing. One male student provided the following definition of bullying, "My definition of bullying is when you hit somebody and they're younger or smaller than you . . . making fun of somebody is not bullying, you can just brush that off, that ain't nothing . . . I mean if you can't take that, it's stupid."

Consistent with previous research, gender differences in the types of bullying described emerged throughout the interviews (Eron, Huesmann, Dubow, Romanoff, & Yarmel, 1987). Boys committed the majority of physical acts of bullying, whereas girls engaged in more relational forms of aggression. Research on relational aggression (Crick, 1995) found that the aggressive behaviors most characteristic of girls tend to focus on damaging or manipulating peers' relationships. One female bully described how she teased other students, "I don't usually hit other students, but sometimes in band class we will get bored and talk about a girl's hairstyle or what she is wearing that day. And one time at track practice me and some of my friends pulled a girl's pants down in front of the entire boys track team to make other students laugh."

It was evident that a wide range of behaviors can be included as bullying and it is not uncommon for victims to experience different forms of harassment. An 11-year old male victim described a common day at school: "I've been flicked in the ear and thrown into lockers. In the locker room, I've been thrown up on the bench and pushed into walls. I've been picked up and turned around into the air . . . they've jumped on me, they kick me, shoot rubber bands at me, call me names, . . . Yeah, most of them just keep on doing it almost every day."

Why Do Students Bully Others?

The typical bully is usually characterized by having a positive attitude toward violence, impulsivity, a strong need to dominate others, and little empathy for victims. They are average or slightly below average in popularity, are surrounded by a small group of peers, and are usually physically stronger than their victims (if male). They are usually motivated by a need for power, are rewarded by their aggression with both positive and negative attention from their

·peers and teachers, and are more likely to grow up in hostile family environments (Olweus, 1991).

When we asked students why they bullied their peers, many of these characteristics were evident in their responses. Bullies' reasons for why they pick on students ranged from being provoked, because they did not like the victim, and many indicated that they harassed other students when they themselves were feeling upset or angry. As a result, many of them express feeling good or happy when they engage in the act of bullying.

Responses from all participants to the question of why students bully their classmates yielded a remarkable understanding of the motivation behind such acts. Participants indicated that students bully: to feel superior and to make victims feel inferior, to be "cool" or popular, to succumb to peer pressure, to seek attention, to demonstrate a general dislike for the victim, to manipulate the victim, to just have fun, and to get revenge. One 7th grade male comments on the decision to bully, "Students bully so they can be a part of a group and they do it so the group will respect them more. I used to do it with my friends, but now I don't because it hurts people. People just want to be cool and fit in."

Why Are Some Students Bullied More Than Others?

When children were asked why certain kids were teased more than others, the vast majority of children described victims as appearing physically different in some way. Participants believed that some students were teased more than others because of the way they looked and behaved. Others mentioned that some students were victims of bullying because they were weaker, did not have much money, were unpopular, were too smart or because the bully felt inadequate or was simply jealous of the victim. Many children cited that they were or knew victims who were teased because of wearing glasses, were too fat or too skinny, did not wear fashionable clothes or hairstyles, were in a different clique, or behaved in ways that irritated others (i.e., distracted others in the classroom, talked incessantly, or did annoying things). An 11-year old victim explained "There was this one kid who would not leave me alone and he kept on pushing me and I fell down and stuff and I told my mom that I did not want to go to school the next day. But, I still went . . . I have had tons of kids push me around before . . . they push me around and call me lots of names because they don't like the way I look." This comment from a 7th grade female explains the situation at her school: "Like they wear glasses or something like that or they are smarter. They could be different religions or races . . . In this school, Asians get picked on."

Several students also thought that students who were often teased contributed to their own victimization. A 8th grade female explained "Because they (victims) say stuff to get kids to think, 'Oh this kid can be teased.' I mean I think that some kids are easier targets, and they just let teasing get to them, and that is like saying to bullies, 'I am like the perfect target, I am really easy to bully.' " Another 8th grade male argues that "They are nerdy. If you got someone who you know who will fight, and you have someone who won't do anything, who would you pick on?"

Consistent with our large-scale survey studies, the age of the child also seemed to be related to whether they were at more risk of engaging in bullying behavior or becoming the target of it (Bosworth, Espelage, & Simon, 1999; Espelage & Holt, in press). In these three middle schools, the 6th graders tended to be the victims of bullying, while the 8th graders were the ones who did the bullying. Seventh grade appeared to be a time where children did not experience as much victimization or engage in much bullying. It was interesting to find that the 6th graders who were exempt from bullying tended to be friends with the 8th graders.

What Are Your Experiences with Bullying?

Student's experiences ranged from being the victim of teasing, experiencing social exclusion and physical attacks to initiating, reinforcing, or joining in on bullying that was already in progress. Students also mentioned either trying to stop the bullying or attempting to comfort the victim of a bullying episode. Others have tried to stay completely out of the bullying situation.

As expected, children who were nominated victims shared similar stories of an individual child or a group of children teasing, excluding, picking fights with, and threatening them. It was also found that several of the children who were bullies in the present were also victims in the past. A common comment from these participants included, "I started making fun of them because somebody else was making fun of me so I was mad and I just started making fun of somebody else and pushed them around." One female student recalled how she was often the butt of jokes and was very unpopular when she lived in another town, but when she moved she became a friend with children who were bullies and became one herself. Currently, she enjoys having power, whereas in the past, she had none. Clearly, understanding the association between prior victimization and the tendency to bully others would be a fruitful area of study.

On a positive note, there were also children who told stories of being bullied when they were younger, but were not anymore and were strongly opposed to any sort of bullying. These children stressed the fact that they knew what it felt like to be bullied and this is the reason why they do not tolerate bullying now. These children were also more likely to try and stop bullying behavior when they saw it.

Again, participants indicated that they often teased other students to go along with the crowd or to fit in but also recognized that they were upsetting their targets. An 8th grade female teacher-nominated bully recalled a recent situation, "I was talking about someone just to fit in with the group and then later on they were crying and I would be like, 'Why did I do that?' " Despite the insight that name-calling and taunting does have the potential to hurt other students, they continue to join in to support their friends in the act of bullying in order to gain acceptance by their peers. Sometimes students resist the temptation to join in, but also do not intervene either; one 8th grade male remarked "I have been with a group of people who have went up and started messing with someone but I haven't messed with them."

Where Does Bullying Occur?

Playgrounds and classrooms are often sites for bullying among elementary school children (Craig, Pepler, & Atlas, 2000; Craig & Pepler, 1997). However, less is known about where bullying occurs in middle schools. Participants recounted stories of witnessing bullying in the hallways, cafeteria, locker rooms, bathrooms, during recess, in class, during passing periods, and outside the school. Many students mentioned that bullying took place out of the sight and hearing distance of teachers. One 6th grade male student explained, "Bullying takes place mostly in places where the teacher is not in hearing range." Another 6th grade male further elaborated, "Well it goes on all around. It is not in one spot. . . . Somewhere where the teacher is not going to look." Who do you or other students talk to about bully/victim situations and what do they suggest?

Given preliminary evidence that many students are victimized by their peers (Bosworth et al., 1999; Hoover et al., 1992; Limber et al., 1997), we explored whether the students talked to adults about these experiences. Most of the victims had people with whom they could talk to about their problems. People included parents, teachers, principals, friends, siblings, social workers, and counselors. Suggestions to deal with bullying situations included trying to ignore the bully, walking away, asking the bully to leave them alone, reporting the incident to a teacher or principal, and fighting back. Some students reported people providing them with mixed messages of peaceful conflict resolution and fighting. Thus, these victims found that the advice they received from adults was not always helpful. For example, parents gave advice such as "ignore the person" or "go tell a teacher." However, many of the victims were too scared to tell a teacher because they were afraid that the bully would find out. Others felt that ignoring the person did not help because the bullying behavior continued.

There was a mixed review of the staff and faculty. Some of the children felt that faculty and staff did very little about the bullying in the school. Many of the students complained of teachers seeing the bullying going on, but ignoring it. Children also complained of the lack of confidentiality when seeking out the help of a teacher or principal. This supports Hazler, Hoover, and Oliver's (1992) finding that students do not feel that school personnel protect victims or deal effectively with bullies. However, other children felt that when they told teachers or principals about bullying incidents, their problems ceased. It is unclear as to why some children found staff helpful and effective and why others did not. One 12-year old student explained how a teacher deals with bullying in her classroom, "She's the nicest teacher I know. She doesn't yell at her students . . . she just goes off and talks to them and they, I don't know how she does it, but they always come back with a smile. And they are all nice for the rest of the day. She's just nice like that, and she'll listen to you if you want to talk to her."

In contrast, several students who had been victims for many years appeared helpless about getting assistance with their situation. They further explained that they did not want to burden their parents with their problems at school. What was evident from these interviews with these students was their acceptance of their situation and their desire to just survive school every day. One victim explained, "Everyday I say to myself 'I hope this is a day when they will leave me alone.' Some days they do leave me alone and they are good days, but others days I am not so lucky."

What Will Help Decrease Bullying Behavior?

Children were quite creative in their responses to the question of how we might decrease bullying during early adolescence. There were a few children who could not think of any suggestions for a future prevention/intervention program, but the majority of the children were quite thoughtful in their responses. Suggestions to decrease bullying behavior included involving the bully in extra-curricular activities, providing them with positive attention, sending them away, establishing a reward system for good behavior, and administering consequences for negative behavior. Consistently, kids felt that it was crucial to have confidentiality when it came to telling a teacher or principal about a bullying incident. These kids felt that the reason why children did not report bullying behavior more often was because those kids who were victimized were afraid of someone finding out that they told. Therefore, their suggestion was to make reporting a confidential matter. Other children, mainly victims, felt that bullies should learn what it is like to be bullied. They felt that if a bully knew what it felt like to get bullied, then maybe they would stop.

Some kids felt that support groups, individual counseling, or peer mediation would be helpful for students who bully. An 8th grade female who was sometimes seen standing up for victims explained,

> I think that bullies need to raise their self-esteem. They need to learn to get along with kids at school in a positive manner and they need to learn to control their anger, mainly I think that it comes from the family or some other problem that is in school and they just want to take it out on someone. I think that a mentor for them would also be a really good idea. Get them in positive activities and get them to know the people that they are bullying better so that they don't bully them as much. Possibly try to get them to be friends.

Students also mentioned providing supportive peer groups for victims, establishing confidentiality for victims so that they feel safe reporting bullying incidents, helping victims change themselves, be it physically or socially, providing counseling, help them understand why bullying occurs, fighting back, asking them to ignore bullying, and having them communicate with bullies. Many students would agree with the following statement made by a 7th grade male "You see a lot of times those students who are picked on, they don't really like to tell on the person . . . Because they don't want other people to call them a tattletale . . . Yeah, so if you could figure out some way to neutralize that, I think that would be one thing right there." Although these students need to feel safe when they do report their victimization, more work needs to be done to repair the damage of victimization. A 7th grade female explained "Well, first of all, try to build up their self-esteem because that might be low after all the name calling. Another thing, you might want to try to get them a mentor. Get them involved in positive activities so that they know they are not this person that other people claim them to be."

DISCUSSION

In this study, middle school students participated in individual interviews about bullying and victimization. Student responses supported many of the already existing research findings on bullying and victimization. We found that bullying is a complex phenomenon that is quite salient in the lives of middle school students. All of the children contributed personal experiences in reference to bullying and/or victimization. Their answers helped clarify and expand many of the existing information found in the bully literature. The students were very open and responsive to the questions and appeared quite engaged during the interviews. The unstructured nature of the interviews was a wonderful method of exploring real-life experiences students have had with bullying and victimization during the middle school years.

Consistent with previous research, students described bullying as a wide range of behaviors (from verbal teasing to physical aggression). Our study lends support to the definition proposed by Dan Olweus (1978), the most influential researcher in this area. He argued that a person is being bullied or victimized when he or she is exposed, repeatedly and over time, to negative actions on the part of one or more other persons. This negative action can cause physical or psychological discomfort. We found further support for Olweus' delineation between direct and indirect bullying (Olweus, 1978). Students in this investigation defined bullying to include both direct bullying (e.g., physical attacks, verbal teasing) and indirect bullying (e.g., exclusion, rumor spreading).

Results from this study support the stereotype of the victim as younger and physically different (Boulton & Underwood, 1992; Olweus, 1991). In each of the three schools, 6th graders were most frequently the targets of name-calling and teasing, but 8th graders were at less risk for such victimization. In addition, ethnic minority students were often the targets of harassment, in three schools with a primarily Caucasian student body. While age and ethnicity were significant risk factors for victimization, other individual differences were consistently reported by students as a cause for ridicule from classmates. More specifically, during early adolescence having less money and fewer fashionable clothes, wearing glasses, and being overweight could lead to teasing and harassment.

As expected, students told us that kids who bully others do so for a variety of reasons, including trying to feel superior, to make the victim feel inferior, and to look cool in front of other kids. A somewhat surprising finding in each of the schools was the significant percentage of students–not necessarily identified as bullies by teachers–who reported teasing others to go along with the crowd. While these students expressed some guilt after participating in the harassment, very few went against the crowd to stop the bullying. The more conversations we had with students, the more apparent it was that middle school targets of bullying were often harassed, teased, and threatened by groups of students, not necessarily by one "school yard bully." This finding was consistent with the few studies that have found that bullying is a peer group process (Espelage & Holt, in press; Pellegrini, Bartini, & Brooks, 1999; Rodkin, Farmer, Pearl, & VanArcher, 2000; Salmivalli, Lagerspetz, Bjorkqvist, Osterman, & Kaukiainen, 1996). Together these studies suggest that further research that explicates the various roles of peers and bullying should be conducted so that we can consider how to intervene at the peer group level.

Previous research on bullying has yielded a group of kids that have been called bully-victims, who report being victimized while at the same time report bullying other students (Craig, 1998). From our conversations with several of the teacher nominated bullies, they reported a history of victimization and felt that they harassed other students because it was their turn to be the bully. This finding suggests that we need to learn more about how this bully-victim subtype differs from bullies who report no history of victimization or from those victims who are not aggressive toward others. In fact, these students might be similar to the provocative-victims that have been discussed in several studies of elementary school children. Provocative-victims are usually characterized by a combination of both anxious and aggressive reaction patterns (Olweus, 1978; Perry, Kusel, & Perry, 1988).

In summary, this interview study with American middle school students provides some direction for prevention and intervention efforts. This is certainly not an exhaustive list of things to consider as we try to reduce bullying in our schools, but are recommendations that teachers, administrators, and parents might find helpful when working with bullies and victims. What was quite clear from our conversations with students is that interventions to prevent and minimize victimization in middle school students should include a module on understanding and appreciating individual differences. These interventions should also consider bullying as a group process rather than bully-victim dyadic interactions; students are participating in teasing other students to go along with the crowd and might not have the skills to go against the pressure to join in. Teachers and parents need to continue to be supportive of students who are victimized; many students find this support invaluable. However, teachers and parents should not assume that victimization has ceased when students stop talking about being teased. Although victims report significant distress, they still believe that they need to be strong and manage the harassment without adult intervention. As such, parents need to have frequent conversations with their children about the way in which they are treated at school. With respect to future research, we need to continue to explore differences between physical aggression and bullying (teasing, humiliation, rumor spreading). Finally, research on the impact of prior victimization on students' tendency to bully others warrants further research attention.

REFERENCES

Arora, C.M. (1987). Defining bullying for a secondary school. *Educational and Child Psychology, 3-4*, 110-120.

Bosworth, K., Espelage, D.L., & Simon, T. (1999). Factors associated with bullying behavior among early adolescents. *Journal of Early Adolescence, 19*, 341-362.

Boulton, M.J., & Smith, P.K. (1994). Bully/victim problems in middle school children: Stability, self-perceived competence, peer perceptions, and peer acceptance. *British Journal of Developmental Psychology, 12,* 315-329.

Boulton, J. J., & Underwood, K. (1992). Bully/victim problems among middle school children. *British Journal of Educational Psychology, 62,* 73-87.

Craig, W.M. (1998). The relationship among bullying, victimization, depression, anxiety, and aggression in elementary children. *Personality and Individual Differences, 24,* 123-130.

Craig, W.M., & Pepler, D.J. (1997). Observations of bullying and victimization in the school yard. *Canadian Journal of School Psychology, 13,* 41-59.

Craig, W.M., Pepler, D.J., & Atlas, R. (2000). Observations of bullying in the playground and in the classroom. *School Psychology International, 21,* 22-36.

Crick, N.R. (1995). Relational aggression: The role of intent attributions, feelings of distress, and provocation type. *Development and Psychopathology, 7,* 313-322.

Eron, L. D., Huesmann, R. L., Dubow, E., Romanoff, R., & Yarmel, P. W. (1987). Aggression and its correlates over 22 years. In D. Cromwell, I.M. Evans, & C.R. O'Donnell (Eds.), *Childhood aggression and violence.* New York: Plenum.

Espelage, D.L., & Holt, M.K. (2001). Bullying and victimization during early adolescence: Peer influences and psychosocial correlates. *Journal of Emotional Abuse.*

Hoover, J.H., Oliver, R., & Hazler, R.J. (1992). Bullying: Perceptions of adolescent victims in the midwestern USA. *School Psychology International, 13,* 5-16.

Limber, S.P., Cummingham, P., Florx, V., Ivey, J., Nation, M., Chai, S., & Melton, G. (1997, June/July). *Bullying among school children: Preliminary findings from a school-based intervention program.* Paper presented at the Fifth International Family Violence Research Conference, Durham, NH.

Olweus, D. (1978). *Aggression in the schools: Bullies and whipping boys.* New York: Wiley.

Olweus, D. (1991). Bully/victim problems among school children: Basic facts and effects of a school based intervention program. In I. Rubin & D. Pepler (Eds.), *The development and treatment of childhood aggression* (pp.411-447). New Jersey: Erlbaum.

Olweus, D. (1994). Bullying at school: Long-term outcomes for the victims and an effective school-based intervention program. In L. R. Huesmann (Ed.), *Aggressive behavior: Current perspectives.* (pp. 97-130). New York: Plenum.

Olweus, D. (1997). Tackling peer victimization with a school-based intervention program. In D. P. Fry & K. Bjorkqirst, *Cultural variation in conflict resolution: Alternative to violence.* (pp. 215-231). New Jersey: Laurence Erlbaum.

Pellegrini, A.D., Bartini, M., & Brooks, F. (1999). School bullies, victims, and aggressive victims: Factors relating to group affiliation and victimization in early adolescence. *Journal of Educational Psychology, 91,* 216-224.

Perry, D. G., Kusel, S. J., & Perry, L. C. (1988). Victims of peer aggression. *Developmental Psychology, 24,* 807-814.

Rigby, K., & Slee, P.T. (1991). Bullying among Australian school children: Reported behavior and attitudes towards victims. *Journal of Social Psychology, 131,* 615-627.

Rodkin, P.C., Farmer, T.W., Pearl, R., & Van Acker, R. (2000). Heterogeneity of popular boys: Antisocial and prosocial configurations. *Developmental Psychology, 36,* 14-24.

Salmivalli, C., Lagerspetz, K., Bjorkqvist, K., Osterman, K., & Kaukiainen, A. (1996). Bullying as a group process: Participant roles and their relations to social status within the group. *Aggressive Behavior, 22,* 1-15.

Sharp, S. & Smith, P.K. (1991). Bullying in UK schools: The DES Sheffield Bullying Project. *Early Childhood Development and Care, 77,* 47-55.

The Roles of Dominance and Bullying in the Development of Early Heterosexual Relationships

Anthony D. Pellegrini

SUMMARY. In this article, we suggest that school-level and peer-level factors predict bullying, negative attitudes toward bullying, and ultimately sexual harassment during late adolescence. Our theoretical orientation leads us to hypothesize that aggression and social dominance play important roles in heterosexual relationships as adolescents are maturing sexually. We also outline the ways in which early heterosexual contact and dating develops. Suggestions are made for future research. *[Article copies available for a fee from The Haworth Document Delivery Service: 1-800-HAWORTH. E-mail address: <getinfo@haworthpressinc.com> Website: <http://www.HaworthPress.com> © 2001 by The Haworth Press, Inc. All rights reserved.]*

KEYWORDS. Dominance, bullying, heterosexual relationships, sexual harrassment

Anthony D. Pellegrini, PhD, is affiliated with the Department of Educational Psychology, University of Minnesota–Twin Cities Campus.

Address correspondence to: Anthony D. Pellegrini, PhD, Department of Education Psychology, 214 Burton Hall, University of Minnesota, Minneapolis, MN 55455 (E-mail: pelle013@umn.edu).

Work on this project was supported by a grant from the W. T. Grant Foundation.

[Haworth co-indexing entry note]: "The Roles of Dominance and Bullying in the Development of Early Heterosexual Relationships." Pellegrini, Anthony D. Co-published simultaneously in *Journal of Emotional Abuse* (The Haworth Maltreatment & Trauma Press, an imprint of The Haworth Press, Inc.) Vol. 2, No. 2/3, 2001, pp. 63-73; and: *Bullying Behavior: Current Issues, Research, and Interventions* (ed: Robert A. Geffner, Marti Loring, and Corinna Young) The Haworth Maltreatment & Trauma Press, an imprint of The Haworth Press, Inc., 2001, pp. 63-73. Single or multiple copies of this article are available for a fee from The Haworth Document Delivery Service [1-800-HAWORTH, 9:00 a.m. - 5:00 p.m. (EST). E-mail address: getinfo@haworthpressinc.com].

Bullying can involve either reactive or proactive aggression (Schwartz, Dodge, & Coie, 1993). Aggressive victims tend to use aggression reactively (Pellegrini, Bartini, & Brooks, 1999): Their aggression is typically emotionally laden and in response to some provocation. Most cases of bullying involve deliberate and proactive aggression that persists over time. Bullying is characterized by a power differential between the bully and the victim. Further, bullying can be either direct and physical, based on physical intimidation (e.g., hitting or threatening to hit) or indirect and based on relational aggression (e.g., using rumors or innuendo to damage a peer's reputation). Bullying, then, is a form of instrumental aggression that is motivated to achieve some outcome (Pellegrini et al.,1999; Pellegrini & Bartini, in press). In adolescence, bullying is associated with social dominance and often motivated by issues associated with peer status, generally, and heterosexual relationships, specifically.

Our earlier research demonstrated that a combination of bullying and prosocial behavioral strategies were used to establish and maintain dominance as youngsters made the transition to middle school (Pellegrini & Bartini, in press). More specifically, we found that during the transition from primary to middle school, bullying initially increased, and when dominance relationships were established, aggression decreased.

This dominance argument is consistent with cross-national data (Smith, Madsen, & Moody, 1999) showing a secular decrease in bullying during adolescence, except in cases where youngsters moved from primary to middle or junior high schools. As with our data (Pellegrini & Bartini, in press), transitions witnessed increases, followed by decreases during the first year of middle/junior high school. The logic of dominance hierarchies has it that aggression is used to order individuals for access to resources. This order is established through a series of agonistic encounters where individuals know their status in relation to their peers.

Dominance is typically defined in terms of agonistic exchanges with winners and losers, and agonistic dimensions of dominance are often apparent in the initial phases of group formation. Recently, however, some ethologists and developmental psychologists have defined it in terms of the co-occurrence of both physically aversive (e.g., bullying peers) and affiliative (leadership, reconciliation) dimensions (e.g., Hawley, 1999; Pellegrini & Bartini, in press; Vaughn, 1999; Vaughn & Waters, 1981). As a result of a series of aversive and affiliative exchanges, as well as other factors, such as kin status, dominance relationships between individuals are formed. Dominant individuals, relative to subordinates, then have prioritized access to resources; (Bernstein, 1981; Strayer, 1980). Resources vary with development and might include access to toys for preschoolers, place in a queue for older children, and attractive opposite sex friends during adolescence.

Once dominance is established, aggression between individuals is minimized as they recognize their dominance status in relation to others. Consequently, less dominant individuals do not usually challenge more dominant individuals because of the associated high costs (e.g., high likelihood of defeat) relative to possible benefits. If one challenges an individual of higher status the subordinate usually loses (Boulton & Smith, 1990). High status individuals have little reason to challenge subordinants as they have little to gain and only risk injury. The stability of relationships between individuals, such as alliances and friendships, also supports subsequent cooperation and inhibits aggression among group members (e.g., Chapais, 1996).

Abrupt changes in children' s ecology can disrupt the dominance structure of a group (Pellegrini & Bartini, in press; Strayer, 1980). Changes in resource availability and in social relationships, such as networks and friendships, often occur when children change schools or group members mature at rapid rates. For example, when youngsters move from primary to middle school and from middle to high school, they must renegotiate their place in a large and more diverse peer group (e.g., being liked by a target group) and form new relationships with peers (e.g., friendships). These changes should have corresponding effects on individuals' dominance in new social groups.

Access to resources is a central variable in the study of social dominance (deWaal, 1989). Resources, however, have not been widely addressed in the child developmental literature on dominance (for recent exceptions see Hawley, 1999; Vaughn, 1999). Consideration of dominance in terms of access to resources, further helps to identify possible proximal and distal functions of dominance. At the proximal level, resources for individuals vary with development. Preschool and primary school children, for example, often compete for access to toys and other play related materials (Smith & Connolly, 1980). Resources for adolescents should be related to heterosexual relationships as this period marks the beginning of sexual maturity and activity (Bjorklund & Pellegrini, 2000; Brooks-Gunn & Furstenberg, 1989). More distally, something or someone is a resource, if they are related to "fitness," where fitness is used in the biological sense of reproductive fitness (Archer, 1992). Natural selection favors those individuals, and their kin, who gain access to resources at costs which are less than accrued benefits (Wilson, 1975).

Consistent with this view, we suggest that for some youngsters, bullying manifests itself in heterosexual relationships and sexual harassment during the period of late adolescence as they compete for access to resources (e.g., dates). That is, aggressive and quasi-aggressive strategies may be used as part of heterosexual relationships. These patterns, in turn, may be related to sexual harassment. Sexual harassment is defined as any deliberate and repeated physical or verbal sexual behaviors that are not welcomed by and deleterious to the recipients (American Association of University Women [AAUW], 1993; Fitzgerald, 1993). In school settings, perpetrators can be either students or adults (AAUW, 1993). In close to 50% of the cases, sexual harassment is proactive (e.g., to get a date, to exhibit power) (AAUW, 1993). From this view sexual harassment resembles bullying.

More specifically, sexual harassment, according to a recent national survey sponsored by the American Association of University Women (AAUW, 1993), found that a surprising number of boys and girls were sexually harassed in high school, many of whom were harassed by adult school personnel. This inexcusable practice leads to both psychological and academic problems, such as frequent absences, dropping out of school, and in extreme cases, suicide attempts. The persistence and seriousness of sexual harassment has recently led the U.S. Supreme Court (1999) to rule that schools were liable for damages to students associated with victimization and sexual harassment. Justice Sandra Day O' Connor noted that sexual harassment in school can be so severe that it denies victims equal access to education (Davis v. Forsyth Co., GA Board of Education).

DOMINANCE AND BULLYING IN EARLY ADOLESCENCE

In our work with middle school students we found that bullies and perpetrators of aggression were more frequently boys than girls, and after an initial rise during the first year of middle school, it decreased over time. Not surprisingly, we find that boys aggressed against other boys more than against girls. Physical aggression is mostly the purview of boys and used against each other in male groups (Maccoby, 1998).

At the school-level, it has been suggested that the stress on competition between peers and teachers' attitudes towards bullying (e.g., It' s part of life and kids have to learn to deal with it) characteristic of many secondary schools are partially responsible for bullying and sexual harassment (Eccles, Wigfield, & Schiefele, 1999). Lack of a cooperative school community can encourage subtle forms of bullying peers (e.g., denigrating a peer's efforts or honesty) and sexual harassment because it is indicative that students do not support each other.

In addition, and as indicated by the AAUW survey, sexual harassment is perpetrated by adults in the school. Thus, perceived school community and teacher modeled bullying and sexual harassment in high school should predict frequency of bullying and sexual harassment. That is, bullying and sexual harassment should be stable from middle to high school. However, the developmental continuity in bullying and sexual harassment from middle to high school should be mediated by school climate (e.g., competition vs. cooperation, adults' attitudes toward bullying). For example, reducing adult modeled bullying and sexual harassment should also reduce bullying and sexual harassment in school.

At the level of the peer group, bullying and sexually harassing peers are ways in which some youngsters increase their status and social dominance with peers (Pellegrini et al., 1999; Pellegrini & Bartini, in press). Access to peers of the opposite sex represents a particularly important status resource for which adolescents compete (Bjorklund & Pellegrini, 2000). Thus, the relative scarcity of either boys and girls in a school population (the operational sex ratio) may affect the use proactive physical and relational (using aggression to manipulate peer relations [Crick & Grotpeter, 1995]) in high school. As females become scarce, rates of male dominance-related aggression should increase. Similarly, as males are scarce, dominance related aggression by females should increase.

DIFFERENT PERCEPTIONS

Extant research has shown that teachers and students have different perceptions of bullying and of the factors contributing to bullying and sexual harassment. Regarding bullying, teachers, especially in secondary school, tend to underestimate its occurrence and do little to discourage it (Olweus, 1993). In extreme cases, they actually model these aversive behaviors. Most troubling, some students suggest that school personnel are sometimes actively involved in sexual harassment; for example, they may use sexual innuendo. Our own work with middle school teachers suggested that they did not see either bullying or sexual harassment as problems (Pellegrini & Bartini, in press). Further, teachers' rating of youngsters' aggression seemed biased relative to ratings of research associates who observed students (Pellegrini & Bartini, 2000). If teachers do see bullying and sexual harassment as a school-wide problem, they may be reluctant to report negative practices for fear of recrimination, despite assurances of anonymity from researchers. Given this divergence in perspectives, it is important for future research to utilize a multi-informant, multi-method research strategy, where constructs are defined by different individuals. For example, bullying and sexual harassment and factors relating to each should be defined from different points of view: individual students (through self-report measures) and school personnel (through teacher checklists). Further, the perceived sense of community and instances of adult sexual harassment should be examined from the perspectives of different informants (teachers and students) and the

.role of these factors in predicting bullying and sexual harassment during the transition from middle to high school.

HETEROSEXUAL RELATIONSHIPS

For reasons of both biology and socialization, boys and girls segregate themselves into groups of like-sex peers. Prior to adolescence, segregated groups are modal (Maccoby, 1998). Things begin to change in adolescence. In our research with middle school students we found that during the first two years of middle school, heterosexual contact increased. Specifically, boys initiated cooperative interaction with girls, and girls initiated cooperative interaction with boys across all school venues (i.e., cafeteria, hallways, free time, school dances).

These data suggest that as youngsters enter an institution designed for adolescents, their behaviors change accordingly. Entry into secondary school represents a change from childhood to adolescence. The initial increases in cross-sex cooperative interaction for both boys and girls represent youngsters' attempts to accommodate to the role expectations associated with this developmental hallmark (Collins & Sroufe, 1999).

This is not to say that youngsters spend a majority of time in across sex groups. Rather, this is a period which should witness a gradual, yet significant, increase in cross-sex contact. Consequently, we should witness an increase in cross-sex cooperative interaction being initiated by both boys and girls with the progression of time.

Initial cross-sex contacts are, however, quite risky to initiate in that they break well-established patterns of sex segregation, entrenched since early childhood (Maccoby, 1998; Serbin et al., 1977). Further, there is a real likelihood that one's overtures to an opposite sex peer will be publically rejected. One way in which youngsters can minimize these risks is to use overtures that are playful and ambiguous in their intent. Specifically, youngsters of this age sometimes resort to "pushing and poking" courtship behaviors (e.g., playfully hitting, pushing, grabbing, and teasing an opposite sex peer) (Maccoby, 1998). These behaviors can be interpreted as "courting" or affiliative overtures by the recipient and reciprocated. Alternatively, they can be rejected. In the former cases, cross-sex contact has been successfully initiated and in the latter case, the initiator saves faces for an unsuccessful attempt because the bout can be dismissed as playful and not serious.

Rough play is one form of pushing and poking courtship, and yet it is typically the purview of males. Males, cross-culturally, engage in rough play more than girls, and it is typically done with other males (Pellegrini & Smith, 1998).

Additionally, male rough play decreases during the period of early adolescence as mixed gender interaction increases. In our middle school research we found that males engaged in more rough play with males than with females, and it decreased with time. However, boys initiated more rough play with girls, with time, as part of pushing and poking courtship. That cross-sex rough play increased for both boys and girls may be indicative of the more general increases in cross-sex interaction, including cooperative interaction, during this period.

It was probably the case that boys used these relatively immature and low risk behaviors as initial strategies to broach cross-sex contact. For example, during one free time break a group of six youngsters (four girls and two boys) were sitting in bleachers in the gym (boys together in one row, and girls together in the next lower row). One boy poked a specific girl with an accompanying laugh; she reciprocated, by laughing as well. These trends suggest that in the first year of middle school, 6th grade boys are using a strategy reminiscent of same-sex play during childhood.

Teasing can be another form of pushing and poking courtships as it, like rough play, is a relatively safe and ambiguous way in which to interact with peers of the opposite sex. Boys also used teasing as a way in which to interact with girls, and this trend also increased across the first year of middle school. The rate of boys teasing girls in the second half of the year was also greater than the rate of rough play during that period. It may be that boys recognized girls' dislike of rough play and used teasing as a form of pushing and poking courting. In 7th grade, both boys and girls alike indicated that they had changed, relative to 6th grade, to a more conventional strategy for cross-sex interaction during adolescence dating.

The use of these rough, but playful, routines seems to be implicated in dating during the first two years of middle school. Our research implicates bullying and dominance during this period in subsequent dating and sexual harassment (Pellegrini, in press; Pellegrini & Bartini, in press). For example, bullying at the start of middle school, mediated by interest in heterosexual relationships, predicted sexual harassment at the end of middle school (Pellegrini, in press). More specifically, boys who had been bullies at the start of middle school and had high self-expressed interests in dating became sexual harassers at the end of middle school.

Relatedly, at the end of middle school, girls nominated "dominant boys" as dates to a hypothetical party (Pellegrini & Bartini, in press a). Importantly, proactive aggression/bullying predicted unique variance in the hypothetical dating measure, beyond the variance associated with boys' physical attractiveness and prosocial behavior. A similar finding with young adolescents (where girls find aggressive boys attractive) has been reported by Bukowski, Sippola, and Newcomb (2000).

We explained this finding in the following way. Dating during the period of early adolescence is a peer group activity, not an intimate, close relationship (Connolly & Goldberg, 1999). Girls may be attracted to these boys because they are dominant and leaders of their peer group (Bjorklund & Pellegrini, 2000). Further, girls of this age are also exploring different roles and independence from parental norms and these boys may represent an experiment with different, and non-normative, roles (Moffitt, 1993).

Of course, there is a real danger that youngsters will continue to find aggressive peers attractive and that aggression will characterize their adult relationship. Specifically, origins of aggressive adult relationships may begin in the context of adolescent heterosexual relationships and increase into adulthood (Roscoe & Callahan, 1985). In our work we have found, however, that aggression was more frequently initiated with peers of the same sex, compared to opposite sex peers. On the surface it appears that girls were victimized by other girls more than by boys, at least in places where they could be observed publically. Similarly, we found that both boys and girls were perpetrators of sexual harassment.

More research, however, is needed to explore the developmental trajectories of youngsters during the transition into and across the high school years. To our knowledge the question of bullying, heterosexual relationships, and sexual harassment has not been addressed with this age group. Extant theory and research suggest that the incidence of bullying and sexual harassment in high school may be related to both school-level and peer-level variables.

The increase in heterosexual relationships during secondary school corresponds to increases in sexual harassment, a time when both bullying and sexual harassment peak. Sexual harassment of members of the opposite sex may be one way in which some individuals engage in heterosexual relationships. Further, some females find aggressive boys attractive, at least at a hypothetical level (Bukowski et al., 2000; Pellegrini & Bartini, in press).

In our middle school sample we found that boys' proactive aggression was viewed positively by females in terms of their being nominated to a hypothetical party. Things may change in high school, however. Aggression should not predict dating during this period as the nature of dating becomes less peer group oriented and more romantic and dyadic. From this view, aggressive dates should be viewed as more dangerous and less attractive.

Future research should examine two extreme groups of girls (1 SD above and below the mean, respectively) who nominate aggressive boys for dates. Girls who frequently, relative to those who less frequently, nominate aggressive boys should be characterized as having less secure relationships with their peers and their parents during middle school and should be less popular with their male and female peers alike during high school.

CONCLUSION

In conclusion, we have documented the role of bullying and dominance in heterosexual relations and sexual harassment during the period of adolescence. Much more research in this area is clearly needed. It is especially important to understand the reasons for the relation between bullying and proactive aggression and dating. This relation seems to be part of a more general phenomenon where bullying is viewed less negatively by peers, and in some cases, positively during adolescence than during childhood (Graham & Juvonen, 1998; Pellegrini et al., 1999). While some of the attraction to aggressive boys may be part of "pushing and poking" courtship and girls' exploring new roles, there is reason for concern. Some of these bullies also become sexual harassers, and this sort of behavior is clearly evident in society at large, as evidenced by the Tailhook scandal where male Navy officers were harassing female officers, and more recently, the 1999 case of Davis vs. the Forsyth Co. Board of Education, where schools were seen as tolerating sexual harassment.

REFERENCES

American Association of University Women (1993). *Hostile hallways: The AAUW survey on sexual harassment in America's schools*. Washington, DC: Author.

Archer, J. (1992). *Ethology and human development*. Hemel Hempstead (UK): Harvester Wheatsheaf.

Bernstein, I. (1981). Dominance: The baby and the bathwater. *The Behavioral and Brain Sciences, 4*, 419-457.

Bjorklund, D. F., & Pellegrini, A. D. (2000). Child development and evolutionary psychology. *Child Development, 71*, 1687-1708.

Boulton, M. J., & Smith, P. K. (1990). Affective biases in children's perceptions of dominance relationships. *Child Development, 61*, 221-229.

Brooks-Gunn, J., & Furstenberg, F. F. (1989). Adolescent sexual behavior. *American Psychologist, 44*, 249-257.

Bukowski, W. M., Sipploa, L. K., & Newcomb, A. F. (2000). Variations in patterns of attraction to same-and other-sex peers during early adolescence. *Developmental Psychology, 36*, 147-154.

Chapais, B. (1996). Competing through co-operation in nonhuman primates: Developmental aspects of matrilinear dominance. *International Journal of Behavioral Development, 19*, 7-23.

Collins, W. A., & Sroufe, L. A. (1999). Capacity for intimate relationships: A developmental perspective. In W. Furman, B. B. Brown, & C. Feiring (Eds.), *The develop-*

ment of romantic relationships in adolescence (pp. 125-147). New York: Cambridge University Press.

Connolly, J., & Goldberg, A. (1999). Romantic relationships in adolescence: The role of friends and peers in their emergence and development. In W. Furman, B. B. Brown, & C. Feiring (Eds.), *The development of romantic relationships in adolescence* (pp. 266-290). New York: Cambridge University Press.

Crick, N. R., & Grotpeter, J. K. (1995). Relational aggression, gender, and social-psychological adjustment. *Child Development, 66,* 710-722.

Davis vs Forsyth, GA Board of Education (1999).

deWaal, F. B. M. (1989). *Peacemaking among primates*. Cambridge, MA: Harvard University Press.

Eccles, J. S., Wigfield, A., & Schiefele, U. (1998), Motivation to succeed. In N. Eisenberg (Ed.), *Handbook of child psychology, Vol. 3* (pp. 1017-1096). New York: Wiley.

Fitzgerald, L. F. (1993). Sexual harassment-Violence against women in the workplace. *American Psychologist, 48,* 1070-1076.

Graham, S., & Juvonen, J. (1998). Self blame and peer victimization in middle school: An attributional analysis. *Developmental Psychology, 34,* 587-599.

Hawley, P. H. (1999). The ontogenesis of social dominance: A strategy-based evolutionary perspective. *Developmental Review, 19,* 97-132.

Maccoby, E. E. (1998). *The two sexes: Growing up apart, coming together.* Cambridge, MA: Harvard University Press.

Moffitt, T. E. (1993). Adolescence-limited and life-course-persistent antisocial behavior: A developmental taxonomy. *Psychological Review, 100,* 674-701.

Olweus, D. (1993). *Bullying at school.* Cambridge, MA: Blackwell.

Pellegrini, A. D. (in press). Aggression, dominance, and sexual harassment during the transition to middle school. *Journal of Applied Developmental Psychology.*

Pellegrini, A. D., Bartini, M & Brooks, F. (1999). School bullies, victims, and aggressive victims: Factors relating top group affiliation and victimization in early adolescence. *Journal of Educational Psychology, 91,* 216-224.

Pellegrini, A. D., & Bartini, M. (2000). An empirical comparison of methods of sampling aggression and victimization in school settings. *Journal of Educational Psychology, 92,* 360-366.

Pellegrini, A. D., Bartini, M. (in Press a). Dominance in early adolescent boys': Affiliative and aggressive dimensions and possible functions. *Merrill-Palmer Quarterly.*

Pellegrini, A. D., Bartini, M. (in Press b). A longitudinal study of bullying, victimization, and peer affiliation during the transition from primary to middle school. *American Educational Research Journal.*

Pellegrini, A. D., & Smith, P. K. (1998). Physical activity play: The nature and function of a neglected aspect of play. *Child Development, 69,* 577-598.

Roscoe, B., & Callahan, J. E. (1985). Adolescents' self-report of violence in families and dating relations. *Adolescence, 79,* 545-553.

Schwartz, D., Dodge, K. A., & Coie, J. D. (1993). The emergence of chronic peer victimization. *Child Development, 64,* 1755-1772.

Serbin, L. A., Tonick, I. J., & Sternglanz, S. H. (1977). Shaping cooperative cross-sex play. *Child Development, 48*, 924-929.

Smith, P. K., & Connolly, K. (1980). *The ecology of preschool behavior*. London: Cambridge University Press.

Smith, P. K., Madsen, K. C., & Moody, J. C. (1999). What causes the age decline in reports of being bullied at school? Toward a developmental analysis of risks of being bullied. *Educational Research, 41*, 267-285.

Strayer, F. F. (1980). Social ecology of the preschool peer group. In W. A. Collins Ed.), *Minnesota symposium on child development, Vol. 13* (pp. 165-196). Hillsdale, NJ: Erlbaum.

Vaughn, B. E. (1999). Power is knowledge (and vice versa): A commentary on *Winning some and losing some: A social relations approach to social dominance in toddlers. Merrill-Palmer Quarterly, 45*, 215-225.

Vaughn, B. E., & Waters, E. (1981). Attention structure, sociometric status, and dominance: Interrelations, behavioral correlates, and relationships to social competence. *Developmental Psychology, 17*, 275-288.

Wilson, E. O. (1975). *Sociobiology: The new synthesis*. Cambridge, MA: Harvard University Press.

DYNAMICS OF BULLYING BEHAVIOR: CLINICAL RESEARCH

The Interrelationships of Behavioral Indices of Bully and Victim Behavior

Neil F. Gottheil
Eric F. Dubow

SUMMARY. The interrelations of three behavioral indices of bully and victim behavior were examined. Each measure is assumed to represent a different reporting perspective of the bully and victim experience: a peer derived point of view, a self-referential report, and a newly developed self-report measure of one's perceptions of how he/she is perceived by his/her peers, specifically with regard to bully and victim behavior. As a part of a larger study, 120 children from grades 5 and 6 completed all three behavioral indices of bully and victim behavior. The interrelations among the *victim* behavior indices supported the notion that victimized children tended to both recognize how they were perceived by others and

Neil F. Gottheil, PhD, is Clinical Psychologist, Children's Hospital of Eastern Ontario and an associate in a private practice. Eric F. Dubow, PhD, is Professor, Department of Psychology, Bowling Green State University.
Address correspondence to: Neil F. Gottheil, PhD, 2249 Carling Avenue, Suite 314, Ottawa, Ontario, Canada, K2B 7E9 (E-mail: Ngottheil@ home.com).

[Haworth co-indexing entry note]: "The Interrelationships of Behavioral Indices of Bully and Victim Behavior." Gottheil, Neil F., and Eric F. Dubow. Co-published simultaneously in *Journal of Emotional Abuse* (The Haworth Maltreatment & Trauma Press, an imprint of The Haworth Press, Inc.) Vol. 2, No. 2/3, 2001, pp. 75-93; and: *Bullying Behavior: Current Issues, Research, and Interventions* (ed: Robert A. Geffner, Marti Loring, and Corinna Young) The Haworth Maltreatment & Trauma Press, an imprint of The Haworth Press, Inc., 2001, pp. 75-93. Single or multiple copies of this article are available for a fee from The Haworth Document Delivery Service [1-800-HAWORTH, 9:00 a.m. - 5:00 p.m. (EST). E-mail address: getinfo@haworthpressinc.com].

agree with the perceptions of their peer group. The interrelations among the *bully* behavior indices suggested that bullies were somewhat aware of how they were perceived by their peer group and yet disagreed with or disregarded this characterization. The additional descriptive information, provided by including a measure of children's perceived peer perspective, and the clinical implications of using all three behavioral indices in concert are discussed. *[Article copies available for a fee from The Haworth Document Delivery Service: 1-800-HAWORTH. E-mail address: <getinfo@haworthpressinc.com> Website: <http://www.HaworthPress.com> © 2001 by The Haworth Press, Inc. All rights reserved.]*

KEYWORDS. Bullying, peer victimization, aggression, behavioral measures, self-report, peer perspective, peer nomination, scale development, identification

Bullying and the chronic victimization of children in today's schools remain a significant problem with longstanding clinical implications. Recent media coverage of retaliatory violence, reportedly by children who have been victimized by their peers, has contributed to a new found awareness of, and sense of urgency about, a problem that has been as common in our schools as the 3 r's. In a United States based study, Perry, Kusel, and Perry (1988) found that 10% of their sample (N = 165) of 3rd through 6th graders were classified as "extremely victimized" (p. 807). Using retrospective data from adolescent students, Hoover, Oliver, and Hazler (1992) found that 76.8% of respondents reported having experienced some form of bullying during their school careers, with 14% reporting that they had been severely victimized. In a Canadian based survey of children aged 4 to 14 years, Charach, Pepler, and Ziegler (1995) found that 8% of children reported being bullied on at least a weekly basis and 15% of students admitted to frequently bullying others.

Research has indicated that a variety of immediate and future consequences exist for bullies and victims. Children who are victimized are more likely to be depressed, develop low self-esteem (Austin & Joseph, 1996; Horne, Glaser, & Sayger, 1994; Olweus, 1992; 1993), experience a continuing loss of confidence, peer rejection, school absenteeism (Hazler, Carney, Green, Powell, & Jolly, 1997; Smith, Bowers, Binney, & Cowie, 1993), and anxiety (Besag, 1989). In severe cases of victimization, children have been known to attempt suicide (Olweus, 1991; Smith et al., 1993), and child victims tend to be at a greater risk for developing depressive symptomatology as adults (Olweus, 1992). Based on a survey of 631 5th through 7th graders, Slee (1993) found that 65% of bullied subjects reported feeling worse about themselves after being bullied, and 15% of the sample reported feeling unsafe at school.

The research indicates that child bullies are more likely than the general population to have a criminal record by the time they are young adults, and to abuse alcohol and engage in domestic violence (Olweus, 1993; Zarzour, 1994). In a 22-year longitudinal study by Huesmann, Eron, Lefkowitz, and Walder (1984), aggressive children appeared to carry their aggression with them into adulthood. Subjects initially rated as highly aggressive were significantly more likely than less aggressive peers to have committed a criminal act, been convicted of a criminal act, been caught driving while intoxicated, and have more traffic violations by age 30. Eron's (cited in Roberts, 1988) research has indicated that 8-year-old bullies have a 1 in 4 chance of having a criminal record by the age of 30, as compared to a 1 in 20 chance for non-bullies.

Bully and victim social roles tend to be relatively stable irrespective of changes in schools, teachers, classmates, and efforts by others to abolish bully and victim behaviors (Olweus, 1984). According to Olweus (1984), children rated as bullies and victims in grade 6 retained these roles at a 3-year follow-up. In a study by Boulton and Underwood (1992), it was found that by early middle school, children (11-12 years of age) who reported being bullied were the most likely to be bullied in the following terms, even though changes in classroom teachers had occurred. Boulton and Smith (1990, as cited in Boulton & Underwood, 1992) found that based on peer nominations, both victim and bully statuses remained stable throughout the school year and into the next. In a study by Craig and Pepler (1993), 6 to 12 year old children involved in bullying during the winter school term were found to continue to engage in this behavior during the spring term.

The enduring quality, social ramifications, and future consequences of being a bully or victim, highlight the need to discover the mechanisms responsible for the maintenance of these social positions. Such information can help in the design of more effective prevention/intervention programs that might contribute to a reduction in the likelihood of children adopting or remaining in these social roles.

In the current study, three different social information perspectives were examined through the use of behavioral indices of bully and victim behavior. One such perspective is that of the peer group. Peer-nomination inventories involve having a number of children rate an individual child on a set of characteristics. The scores obtained are a composite of multiple rater judgments and therefore offer greater reliability and validity than single-rater inventories (Achenbach, McConaughy, & Howell, 1987; Kane & Lawler, 1978). Given the social nature of bully-victim encounters, the peer group has often been used as the informant of choice in identifying bullies and victims.

The individual is another source that has been used to classify children as bullies or victims. A problem with self-referential data is that self-serving biases and selective recall might be operating, and can result in inaccurate reporting (Ledingham, Younger, Schwartzman, & Bergeron, 1982; Wayment & Zetlin, 1989). In a study by Hymel, Bowker, and Woody (1993), peer-identified aggressive children tended to overestimate their competencies on self-report measures. Ledingham and associates (1982) found that children's self-reports were lowest when asked to identify aggressive and withdrawal behaviors, and highest on likability. These findings support the notion that self-referential data might be vulnerable to some form of image management, particularly when individuals are asked to self-report on controversial areas, such as bully and victim behavior.

Another important consideration with respect to self-referential reports is whether a single individual can offer useful information about an inherently social phenomenon. A consistent finding in the literature is that self-ratings do not tend to correlate well with other measures, and therefore should not be used alone when evaluating social phenomena (Ledingham & Younger, 1985; Ledingham et al., 1982). Nonetheless, self-report data offer insight into the cognitions, feelings, and goals of the individual that cannot be easily obtained from other sources (Hymel & Franke, 1985). How one perceives him/herself in the social world will likely influence future interpersonal behavior, and therefore needs to be accounted for in order to understand the individual within a social context.

In addition to peer nomination and self-referential report inventories, the current study also includes a newly developed self-report measure of children's awareness, regarding how they are viewed by their peers. The Perceived Peer Perspective (PPP) Inventory is a self-report measure in which children are presented with statements about bully and victim behaviors and are asked to take the perspective of their classmates in rating themselves.

Therefore, in the current study three behavioral indices of bully and victim behavior were administered in order to gather information about: (1) how one is seen by others (peer nominations); (2) how one sees him/herself (self-referential, self-report data); and (3) how one thinks he/she is perceived by others (perceived peer perspective data). With this information, discrepancies between peer and self-derived behavioral descriptions can provide information about one's ability to accept and/or recognize his/her social persona.

METHOD

Subjects and Procedures

Data were collected on 180 elementary and middle school children in grades 5 and 6, comprising a 42% parent consent rate. Three children were dropped from further analyses because they obtained high scores on peer-nominated indices of both bully and victim behavior. Of the remaining 177 children, 57 did not complete all study measures and were only used for select analyses. The major reason for incomplete data was because 41 of the 57 children were not able to be assigned a peer nomination score because fewer than fifty percent of their classmates participated and the remaining 16 children did not complete all the necessary measures. One hundred and twenty children from grades 5 and 6 (55 boys and 65 girls) completed self-referential and perceived peer perspective measures of bully and victim behavior and received peer nomination bully and victim behavior scores. Seventeen classes from four different schools participated. All schools were located in areas whose residents were predominantly Caucasian and of low to moderate socioeconomic status.

Groups of children were administered two survey packages as a part of a larger study, on two separate days, each lasting approximately 45 minutes. Data for the current project were collected on the first administration day and included: (1) a basic demographics page; (2) a peer-nomination form; (3) a self-report measure of bully and victim behavior; and (4) a self-report measure of perceived peer perception of bully and victim behavior.

Measures

Introducing My Classmates (IMC). The IMC is a peer nomination form in which subjects are read a series of stories about fictitious child characters and are asked to nominate all the classmates, on provided lists, that they feel are like the child in the story (i.e., "This girl Loraine is picked on, made fun of, called names, and is hit and pushed by other kids. Kids do mean things to her and try to hurt her feelings. Write the code numbers for all the girls on your list that you feel are like Loraine"; "This boy, Johnny, makes fun of people, says he can beat everyone up, hits and pushes others around, tries to pick fights, and if a someone gets in his way he is likely to shove that person out of the way. Write the code numbers for all the boys on your list that you feel are like Johnny"). Children are read four stories about different boys and four stories about different girls. The two versions of stories are identical except for the described child's name, which is gender specific. Of the four stories, one describes a child exhibiting victim-like characteristics, one describes a child exhibiting bully-like characteristics and two are filler items. Bully and victim items were adapted from a previously developed peer nomination inventory (PNI-R; Gottheil, 1994). Based on principal axis factor analyses and tests of internal consistency, derived bully and victim subscale items were separately combined into single story formats.

IMC nominations on any given child were made by both boys and girls, regardless of the nominee's gender. This allowed for more raters, therefore reducing the effects of any individually biased ratings. The decision to have both genders rate each other is supported by research, in that bullying is most likely to occur during times when boys and girls are in close vicinity of each other, such as in the classroom (when the teacher is not looking), on the playground, or during recess and lunch. Because boys and girls are likely to observe and be knowledgeable of the ongoing bully and victim behaviors of their peers, it was believed that both should be included as nominators. Additionally, the use of both boys and girls as raters allows for a greater representation of the overall social impression of a given child who is being evaluated by the standards of both male and female subcultures.

Bully and victim subscale scores were derived separately by adding up all the nominations that a given child received from his or her classmates on the respective bully and victim items. These scores were then divided by the total number of raters and multiplied by 100 in order to obtain a percentage score of peer nominated bully (Percent Bully Score, PBS) and victim (Percent Victim Score, PVS) behavior. Scores can range from 0 to 100 with higher scores reflecting a greater percentage of classmate nominations.

Setting the Record Straight (SRS). The SRS is a survey containing true/false statements that combines a previously developed self-referential self-report measure of bully and victim behavior (Self Report Inventory of Bully and Victim Behavior (SRI); Gottheil, 1994) with the newly developed measure of children's perceptions of how they are viewed by their peers (Perceived Peer Perspective Inventory; PPP).

Fifteen of the original twenty SRI items were included in the SRS and were chosen based upon previous principal axis factor analyses and indices of internal consistency. Based on a sample of 218 fourth and fifth graders, the internal consistencies for bully and victim subscales derived from the SRI were .63 and .89, respectively.

Each SRI item (e.g., "I get beat up") was preceded by a matching PPP item (e.g., "My classmates think that I get beat up"). The format of the survey was such that pairings of SRI and PPP items were clearly recognizable to subjects. This was done in order to reduce the reactivity of items by allowing children to admit to being "perceived" as engaging in potentially inappropriate or embarrassing behaviors (bully and victim behavior) while providing them with the opportunity to present their perspective through the SRI items. Of the 15 SRI/PPP pairings, 10 are victim item pairs and 5 are bully item pairs (see Table 1).

SRI and PPP bully and victim scores were tabulated independently. Scores were derived by adding up the respective bully and victim subscale items responded to by the subject as true for them. Bully scores included the number of true responses that a child endorsed for the bully subscale items divided by the total number of bully items and multiplied by 100, in order to obtain a percentage. The derivation of victim scores followed the same procedure except that they were divided by the total number of victim items. Scores on each subscale can range from 0 to 100 with higher scores reflecting higher percentages of self-reported bully and/or victim behaviors.

RESULTS

Scale Refinement Analyses for the Perceived Peer Perspective (PPP) and Self-Report Inventory of Bullying and Victimization (SRI)

Because the SRI and PPP were developed for the present study, it was important to determine whether the factor structure conformed to the conceptualization of bully and victim behavior. For the total sample, two separate 2-factor solution, Principal Axis factor analyses with Varimax rotation were computed, one with PPP items and one with SRI items. The same analyses were computed for male and female subsamples, in order to compare factor structures across gender.

Total sample PPP and SRI factor analyses (Table 1). For the PPP, factor 1 was determined to be a victim factor, with an eigenvalue of 4.48 (29.8% explained unique variance); and factor 2 was determined to be a bully factor, with an eigenvalue of 2.49 (16.6% explained unique variance). Together, these two factors accounted for 46.4% of the variance.

Nine of the ten "expected" victim PPP items loaded highest and exclusively on the Victim PPP factor (factor loadings ranged from .31 to .79). One of the "expected" victim items (item 21; "My classmates probably think that when I get picked on I don't like to fight back") originally loaded negatively on the bully factor, and was reverse coded and included with the five original "expected" bully items. All five "expected" bully items and the reverse coded victim item 21, loaded highest and exclusively on the Bully PPP factor (factor loadings ranged from .30 to .80).

For the SRI, factor 1 was determined to be a victim factor, with an eigenvalue of 4.46 (29.7% explained unique variance); and factor 2 was deter-

.TABLE 1. Setting the Record Straight (SRS) (Total Sample) and Highest Factor Loadings of Each Item

Victim Perceived Peer Perspective	I	II
1. My classmates probably think that kids make fun of me.	.68	
3. My classmates probably think that I get beat up.	.38	
5. My classmates probably think that I get called names by other kids.	.68	
9. My classmates probably think that kids do mean things to me.	.71	
13. My classmates probably think that I get picked on by other kids.	.79	
15. My classmates probably think that I get hit and pushed by other kids.	.57	
17. My classmates probably think that kids try to hurt my feelings.	.74	
23. My classmates probably think that I get teased a lot.	.77	
29. My classmates probably think that I don't defend myself.	.31	
Bully Perceived Peer Perspective		
7. My classmates probably think that I make fun of people.		.69
11. My classmates probably think that I hit and push others around.		.80
19. My classmates probably think that if someone gets in my way I will shove them out of the way.		.63
25. My classmates probably think that there are certain kids I like to bother.		.48
21. My classmates probably think that when I get picked on I don't like to fight back **(reverse coded)**.		.30
27. My classmates probably think that I can beat everyone up.		.30

Victim Self-Report Inventory		
2. Kids make fun of me.	.80	
4. I get beat up.	.30	
6. I get called names by other kids.	.67	
10. Kids do mean things to me.	.80	
14. I get picked on by other kids.	.80	
16. I get hit and pushed by other kids.	.60	
18. Kids try to hurt my feelings.	.68	
24. I get teased a lot.	.75	
30. I don't defend myself (dropped).		
Bully Self-Report Inventory		
8. I make fun of people.		.66
12. I hit and push others around.		.68
20. If someone gets in my way I will shove them out of the way.		.63
22. When I get picked on I don't like to fight back **(reverse coded)**.		.45
26. There are certain kids I like to bother.		.67
28. I can beat everyone up (dropped).		

Note. This table reflects the results of Principal Axis factor analyses with Varimax rotation. Only factor loadings of |.30| and above are reported. Based on these items, alphas were .85 for the victim PPP scale, .69 for the bully PPP scale, .88 for the victim SRI scale, and .72 for the bully SRI scale. N = 174 for PPP section and N = 175 for SRI section of table.

mined to be a bully factor, with an eigenvalue of 2.60 (17.3% explained unique variance). Together, these two factors accounted for 47% of the variance.

Eight of the ten "expected" victim SRI items loaded highest and exclusively on the Victim SRI factor (factor loadings ranged from .30 to .80). One of the "expected" victim items (item 22; When I get picked on I don't like to fight back) originally loaded negatively on the bully factor, and was reverse coded and included with the five original "expected" bully items. One item (item 30; I don't defend myself) did not meet the inclusion criteria (loading |.30| or above) for either victim or bully factors, and was dropped from further analyses. Four of the five "expected" bully items and the reverse coded victim item 22, loaded highest and exclusively on the Bully SRI factor (factor loadings ranged from .45 to .68). One of the "expected" bully items (item 28; I can beat everyone up) did not meet the inclusion criteria for either victim or bully factors and was dropped from further analyses.

Male sample PPP and SRI factor analyses (Table 2). For the PPP, factor 1 was determined to be a victim factor, with an eigenvalue of 5.08 (33.9% explained unique variance); and factor 2 was determined to be a bully factor, with an eigenvalue of 2.25 (15% explained unique variance). Together, these two factors accounted for 48.9% of the variance.

As with the total sample, the same nine of the ten "expected" victim PPP items loaded highest and almost exclusively on the Victim PPP factor (factor loadings ranged from .38 to .82). Item 21 did not meet inclusion criteria for either victim or bully factors. Four of the five "expected" bully items loaded highest and exclusively on the Bully PPP factor (factor loadings ranged from .56 to .78). Item 27 ("My classmates probably think that I can beat everyone up") did not meet inclusion criteria for either victim or bully factors.

For the SRI, factor 1 was determined to be a victim factor, with an eigenvalue of 4.96 (33.1% explained unique variance); and factor 2 was determined to be a bully factor, with an eigenvalue of 2.62 (17.4% explained unique variance). Together, these two factors accounted for 50.5% of the variance.

Eight of the ten "expected" victim SRI items loaded highest and exclusively on the Victim SRI factor (factor loadings ranged from .36 to .87). One of the "expected" victim items (item 22; "When I get picked on I don't like to fight back") loaded negatively on the bully factor, and was reverse coded and included with the five original "expected" bully items. One item (item 30; "I don't defend myself") did not meet the inclusion criteria for either victim or bully factors. Four of the five "expected" bully items and the reverse coded victim item 22, loaded highest and exclusively on the Bully SRI factor (factor loadings ranged from .41 to .81). One of the "expected" bully items (item 28; "I can beat everyone up") did not meet the inclusion criteria for either victim or bully factors.

Female sample PPP and SRI factor analyses (Table 3). For the PPP, factor 1 was determined to be a victim factor, with an eigenvalue of 3.80 (25.3% explained unique variance); and factor 2 was determined to be a bully factor, with an eigenvalue of 2.74 (18.3% explained unique variance). Together, these two factors accounted for 43.6% of the variance.

Seven of the ten "expected" victim PPP items loaded highest and exclusively on the Victim PPP factor (factor loadings ranged from .34 to .72). Item 3 ("My classmates probably think that I get beat up") and item 29 ("My classmates probably think that I don't defend myself") did not meet inclusion crite-

TABLE 2. Setting the Record Straight (SRS) (Male Sample) and Highest Factor Loadings of Each Item

Victim Perceived Peer Perspective	I	II
1. My classmates probably think that kids make fun of me.	.69	
3. My classmates probably think that I get beat up.	.42	.32
5. My classmates probably think that I get called names by other kids.	.69	
9. My classmates probably think that kids do mean things to me.	.71	
13. My classmates probably think that I get picked on by other kids.	.82	
15. My classmates probably think that I get hit and pushed by other kids.	.65	
17. My classmates probably think that kids try to hurt my feelings.	.78	
23. My classmates probably think that I get teased a lot.	.81	
29. My classmates probably think that I don't defend myself.	.38	
Bully Perceived Peer Perspective		
7. My classmates probably think that I make fun of people.		.71
11. My classmates probably think that I hit and push others around.		.78
19. My classmates probably think that if someone gets in my way I will shove them out of the way.		.62
25. My classmates probably think that there are certain kids I like to bother.		.56
21. My classmates probably think that when I get picked on I don't like to fight back **(reverse coded)**.		
27. My classmates probably think that I can beat everyone up.		

Victim Self-Report Inventory		
2. Kids make fun of me.	.87	
4. I get beat up.	.36	
6. I get called names by other kids.	.72	
10. Kids do mean things to me.	.85	
14. I get picked on by other kids.	.81	
16. I get hit and pushed by other kids.	.67	
18. Kids try to hurt my feelings.	.71	
24. I get teased a lot.	.78	
30. I don't defend myself (dropped).		
Bully Self Report Inventory		
8. I make fun of people.		.71
12. I hit and push others around.		.60
20. If someone gets in my way I will shove them out of the way.		.60
22. When I get picked on I don't like to fight back **(reverse coded).**		.41
26. There are certain kids I like to bother.		.81
28. I can beat everyone up. (dropped)		

Note. This table reflects the results of Principal Axis factor analyses with Varimax rotation. Only factor loadings of |.30| and above are reported. Alphas were computed using items from total sample refinements. Based on these items, alphas were .88 for the victim PPP scale, .63 for the bully PPP scale, .90 for the victim SRI scale, and .75 for the bully SRI scale. n = 91.

ria for either victim or bully factors. Item 21 ("My classmates probably think that when I get picked on I don't like to fight back") loaded negatively on the bully factor, and was reverse coded and included with the "expected" bully items. All five of the "expected" bully items, and the reverse coded victim item 21, loaded highest and exclusively on the Bully PPP factor (factor loadings ranged from .40 to .80).

For the SRI, factor 1 was determined to be a victim factor, with an eigenvalue of 3.91 (27.9% explained unique variance); and factor 2 was deter-

TABLE 3. Setting the Record Straight (SRS) (Female Sample) and Highest Factor Loadings of Each

Victim Perceived Peer Perspective	I	II
1. My classmates probably think that kids make fun of me.	.68	
3. My classmates probably think that I get beat up.		
5. My classmates probably think that I get called names by other kids.	.56	
9. My classmates probably think that kids do mean things to me.	.68	
13. My classmates probably think that I get picked on by other kids.	.72	
15. My classmates probably think that I get hit and pushed by other kids.	.34	
17. My classmates probably think that kids try to hurt my feelings.	.71	
23. My classmates probably think that I get teased a lot.	.71	
29. My classmates probably think that I don't defend myself.		
Bully Perceived Peer Perspective		
7. My classmates probably think that I make fun of people.		.71
11. My classmates probably think that I hit and push others around.		.80
19. My classmates probably think that if someone gets in my way I will shove them out of the way.		.64
25. My classmates probably think that there are certain kids I like to bother.		.40
21. My classmates probably think that when I get picked on I don't like to fight back **(reverse coded)**.		.42
27. My classmates probably think that I can beat everyone up.		.61

Victim Self-Report Inventory		
2. Kids make fun of me.	.72	
4. I get beat up (dropped due to lack of variance)		
6. I get called names by other kids.	.61	
10. Kids do mean things to me.	.73	
14. I get picked on by other kids.	.78	
16. I get hit and pushed by other kids.	.47	
18. Kids try to hurt my feelings.	.71	
24. I get teased a lot.	.72	
30. I don't defend myself (dropped).		
Bully Self-Report Inventory		
8. I make fun of people.		.58
12. I hit and push others around.		.79
20. If someone gets in my way I will shove them out of the way.		.71
22. When I get picked on I don't like to fight back **(reverse coded)**.		.41
26. There are certain kids I like to bother.		.49
28. I can beat everyone up.		.34

Note. This table reflects the results of Principal Axis factor analyses with Varimax rotation. Only factor loadings of |.30| and above are reported. Alphas were computed using items from total sample refinements. Based on these items, alphas were .78 for the victim PPP scale, .75 for the bully PPP scale, .85 for the victim SRI scale, and .67 for the bully SRI scale. n = 83 for PPP section and n = 84 for SRI section of table.

mined to be a bully factor, with an eigenvalue of 2.68 (19.2% explained unique variance). Together, these two factors accounted for 47.1% of the variance.

Seven of the ten "expected" victim SRI items loaded highest and exclusively on the Victim SRI factor (factor loadings ranged from .47 to .78). Item 22 ("When I get picked on I don't like to fight back") loaded negatively on the bully factor, and was reverse coded and included with the five original "expected" bully items. Item 4 ("I get beat up") did not vary and therefore, could not be included in the factor analysis. Item 30 ("I don't defend myself") did not meet the inclusion criteria for either victim or bully factors. All five of the "expected" bully items and the reverse coded victim item 22, loaded highest and exclusively on the Bully SRI factor (factor loadings ranged from .34 to .79).

Summary and decisions about subscale formation. The factor analyses based on the total sample supported a priori predictions of scale item composition (i.e., bully behavior, victim behavior). The factor structure remained relatively stable across gender with some exceptions. This might be partly accounted for by the lowered sample size resulting from dividing the total sample along gender lines. Therefore, it was decided that scale items based on the total sample would be retained for all further analyses involving the PPP and SRI.

Internal consistencies for PPP and SRI subscales. Based on the results of the total sample factor analysis, Cronbach's alphas were computed for the total sample, and male and female subsamples, for each PPP and SRI subscale. For the victim PPP subscale items, alpha levels were .85 for the total sample, .88 for the male subsample, and .78 for the female subsample. For the bully PPP subscale items, alpha levels were .69 for the total sample, .63 for the male subsample, and .75 for the female subsample. For the victim SRI subscale items, alpha levels were .88 for the total sample, .90 for the male subsample, and .85 for the female subsample. For the bully SRI subscale items, alpha levels were .72 for the total sample, .75 for the male subsample, and .67 for the female subsample.

Intercorrelations of Behavioral Indices

The distributions of peer-derived Percent Bully Score (PBS) and Percent Victim Score (PVS) residuals were not normally distributed. As a result, a Log10 transformation was applied to both variables in order to pull in extreme scores, and increase normality in the distributions (Neter, Wasserman, & Kutner, 1990; Winer, 1971). Both transformed and non-transformed results are reported. The transformation did not appear to substantially affect the results in the current study.

The intercorrelations of all variables were computed and are presented in Table 4. All self derived-(VPPP and VSRI) and peer-report (PVS and Transformed PVS) measures of victim behavior were significantly and positively correlated with one another for the total sample (range = .50 to .82, M = .63), male subsample (range = .49 to .82, m = .62), and female subsample (range = .45 to 82, m = .55). With few exceptions, self derived-(BPPP and BSRI) and peer-report (PBS and Transformed PBS) measures of bully behavior were significantly and positively correlated with one another for the total sample (range = .38 to .79, M = .53), male subsample (range = .28 to .75, m = .44), and

TABLE 4. Intercorrelations of Dependent Variables

Total Sample

	BSRI	PBS	TransPBS	VPPP	VSRI	PVS	TransPVS
BPPP	.55**	.38**	.41**	.04	.06	−.15	−.19*
BSRI		.10	.20*	−.04	−.11	−.13	−.06
PBS			.79**	−.03	−.17	−.17	−.15
TransPBS				−.08	−.19*	−.18*	−.17
VPPP					.68**	.52**	.50**
VSRI						.63**	.60**
PVS							.82**

Male Subsample

	BSRI	PBS	TransPBS	VPPP	VSRI	PVS	TransPVS
BPPP	.44**	.29*	.28*	.26*	.12	−.03	−.11
BSRI		.05	.17	.03	−.14	−.18	−.14
PBS			.75**	−.08	−.16	−.21	−.17
TransPBS				−.12	−.17	−.26*	−.24
VPPP					.70**	.53**	.49**
VSRI						.75**	.70**
PVS							.82**

Female Subsample

	BSRI	PBS	TransPBS	VPPP	VSRI	PVS	TransPVS
BPPP	.57**	.45**	.47**	−.09	.05	−.20	−.24*
BSRI		.14**	.17	−.25*	−.11	−.16	−.14
PBS			.85**	.09	−.19	−.12	−.16
TransPBS				.02	−.23	−.12	−.14
VPPP					.64**	.46**	.45**
VSRI						.48**	.47**
PVS							.82**

Note. BPPP refers to Bully Perceived Peer Perspective score; BSRI refers to Bully Self Report Inventory score; PBS refers to peer derived Percent Bully Score; TransPBS refers to Log10 transformed peer derived Percent Bully Score; VPPP refers to Victim Perceived Peer Perspective score; VSRI refers to Victim Self Report Inventory score; PVS refers to peer derived Percent Victim Score; and TransPVS refers to Log10 transformed peer derived Percent Victim Score.
*$p < .05$; **$p < .001$

female subsample (range = .14 to .85, m = .50). The Bully Self Report Inventory score did not significantly correlate with the peer nomination Percent Bully Score (PBS) for the total sample, with the PBS or Transformed PBS for the male subsample, nor with the Transformed PBS for the female subsample. The Bully Self Report Inventory score was modestly correlated with the peer nomination Percent Bully Score for the female subsample ($r = .14, p < .001$)

and the Transformed PBS for the total sample ($r = .20, p < .05$). Interestingly, and in contrast to the Bully Self Report Inventory scores, the Bully Perceived Peer Perspective scores consistently and significantly correlated with peer-report measures for the total sample (PBS: $r = .38, p < .001$; Transformed PBS: $r = .41, p < .001$) and male (PBS: $r = .29, p < .05$; Transformed PBS: $r = .28, p < .05$) and female (PBS: $r = .45, p < .001$; Transformed PBS: $r = .47, p < .001$) subsamples. All means and ranges reported above are of the significant correlations.

With few exceptions, self derived and peer-report measures of bully behavior did not correlate with measures of victim behavior. Of the few exceptions (7 of 48), bully and victim indices were negatively correlated, except for one instance in the male subsample, in which the BPPP and VPPP was positively correlated. Also noteworthy is the moderate to high, significant correlations of VSRI with PVS and Transformed PVS, in contrast to the largely nonsignificant, low correlations of BSRI with PBS and Transformed PBS.

DISCUSSION

By using three indices of bully and victim behavior (peer, perceived peer perspective, and self-report), the results offer descriptive information beyond any single measure and allow for speculation about possible mechanisms contributing to the maintenance of bully and victim behaviors. The pattern of behavioral indices of bullying and victimization, and the potential implications, will be discussed separately, and in turn. In the current study, peer, perceived peer perspective, and self-referential self-report measures of bullying and victimization will be discussed as though they represent actual perceptions. However, caution is necessary given that bully and victim behaviors represent a controversial social phenomenon and hence, might be susceptible to image management efforts, selective recall, etc. (Hymel et al., 1993; Ledingham et al., 1982), potentially resulting in an under or over report of bully and victim behavior.

Pattern of Interrelations Among Bully Behavior Indices

Based on the total sample, bully scores obtained through peer nominations were not significantly related to those derived from the bully self-report inventory, but were moderately related to measures of perceived peer perspectives on bullying. Previous research in the area of bullying has tended to note an absence of, or minimal relations between peer and self reports (Ledingham & Younger, 1985; Ledingham et al., 1982). In a study by Gottheil (1995), bully behavior scores derived from peer nomination and self-report measures were only minimally related ($r = .18$). However, the moderate relations between peer nominations and perceived peer perceptions of bullying, provides support to the notion that the lack of relations between conventional bully self-report indices with peer nominations might simply reflect children's disagreement with, rather than a lack of recognition about, how they are being perceived by their peers.

Each of the three measures of bullying used in the current study provides a different perspective on the bully phenomenon. Given the social nature of bullying, the peer nomination method is the only measure of the three that provides a social perspective, by virtue of having each child's social classification determined by his/her peers. Additionally, the peer nomination method has tended to be regarded in the literature as the method of choice in identifying bully behavior, and has been the standard by which other measures have been compared (e.g., Hymel et al., 1993; Ledingham & Younger, 1985). However, if, as in the current study, the objective is to learn about the factors that serve to maintain bully behavior, it becomes important to gather information about children's understanding about their own behavior, and the degree to which they are aware of how they present themselves on the social stage. Hence, peer nominations, alone, do not provide enough information about bullying, beyond mere classification.

In order to explore potential social information processing factors as possible contributors to the durability of bully behavior, three reporting perspectives are useful, and in the current study, include information about: (1) how one is seen by others; (2) how one sees him/herself; and (3) how one thinks he/she is perceived by others. With this information, discrepancies between peer and self behavioral descriptions can provide information about one's ability to accept and/or recognize his/her social persona.

In the current study, the pattern of relations among the behavioral indices of bully behavior suggests that bullies are somewhat aware of how they are perceived by their peer group and yet disagree with or disregard this characterization. The use of an *index* of perceived peer perspectives, together with peer and self-report indices, provides additional information that sheds new light on the commonly noted minimal relations between self and peer indices of bully behavior. Such a pattern of findings lends support to the notion that children with higher peer bully scores are more likely to process this information in a way described by Piaget (as cited in Miller, 1989) as assimilation. Assimilation is the process of taking information and making it fit into one's "current cognitive organizations" or schemata (p. 74). Rather than modifying one's way of thinking (accommodation), contradictory information is modified to better fit already present schemata. The tendency of these children to be aware of yet discount social information about their bully behavior, is possibly an example of this process.

Children who disagree with or simply disregard the opinions of others are less inclined to benefit from social information and likely lack the motivation necessary to change their behavior. Therefore, an assimilation cognitive style has implications regarding the focus and prognosis of treatment interventions. Based on this conceptualization, the goal of treatment will be to help these children begin to modify their beliefs about their bully behavior so that their beliefs are more consistent with the social information being provided to them. The objective is to provide these children with the necessary motivation to give up bully behavior patterns. The development of perspective-taking and empathy skills might help these children better recognize the full impact of their behaviors on others, and possibly move them toward obtaining the above-mentioned goal. However, the noted stability of bully behavior and the lack of acceptance of peer feedback present a treatment challenge. Information about the beliefs that these children hold might be helpful in designing more effective treatment interventions.

With regard to male and female subsamples, the same set of relations among behavioral indices was noted with one exception in the female subsample. For the female subsample, there was a minimal but significant relationship between self and peer reports. Therefore, girls tend to somewhat agree with their peer group's perceptions. The fact that girls continue to engage in behavior that they recognize as being a social and personal phenomenon, might indicate that they either lack the skills to change this behavior, lack understanding of the serious impact of this behavior on others, do not care about peer opinions, or possibly have beliefs about bully behavior that encourage its continuation. The latter will be explored more fully below.

Pattern of Interrelations Among Victim Behavior Indices

The pattern of indices of victim behavior was consistent across the total sample, and male and female subsamples. Victim scores derived from peer nominations were significantly related to scores derived from the self-reports of victim behavior, and perceived peer perspectives on victim behavior.

Therefore, unlike the pattern noted for indices of bully behavior, children reporting on victim behavior tended to both recognize how they were perceived by others and agreed with the perceptions of their peer group. Therefore, children tended to have somewhat "accurate" perceptions of their social standing with regard to victim behavior and yet, having this social information did not serve to change their social standing. Such a pattern of responding might indicate that children with high levels of victim behaviors lack the necessary skills to break free from their difficult social position. One can surmise that children who are aware that they are victims and remain so, despite this awareness, might also be dealing with feelings of helplessness and hopelessness regarding their social situation.

With regard to treatment implications, given that these children appear to be aware of their social standing, increasing social awareness of this general fact is not necessary. However, interventions that focus on social and problem solving skills development might be useful. Given the likely initial feelings of helplessness and hopelessness, maintaining motivation and increasing self-confidence in the use of newly developed skills likely will be crucial. Therefore, interventions should be designed to promote successes by providing the necessary structure to make the skill acquisition and employment process feel safe.

Limitations and Future Research

There is an important consideration regarding the peer and self-report behavioral indices used in the current study, in terms of their ability to identify accurately the children who engage in bully and victim behaviors. The peer reports presumably identify those children who engage in bully and victim behaviors, regardless of whether the children being identified would be willing to admit to this behavior themselves. However, the self-referential self-report measure identifies those children who are willing to admit to bully or victim behavior. This is relevant when interpreting results from self-report data, in that scores only represent the different degrees of bully or victim behavior among those children who are willing to admit to engaging in this behavior. And even then, one must consider the fact that people might be willing only to admit to certain degrees of "truth" about their behavior. While it has been proposed that the commonly noted minimal relations between peer and self-report indices of bully behavior could reflect a disagreement between peer and self perceptions, it is also possible that this finding is explainable by the reactivity of the construct being measured, and the limitations of the measurement tools.

This issue might have been somewhat addressed through the design and presentation of the three behavioral measures used in the current study. The fact that children were made aware that peer reports would be used could have contributed to a sense of having to acknowledge these reports, such as through the perceived peer perspective measure, while still being able to disagree with these ratings through their self-reports. It is possible that without the peer ratings children might have been less inclined to admit to being perceived by their peers as engaging in bully behaviors. Future research that manipulates the timing of when subjects become aware that peer ratings will be used could help to examine the influence of the inclusion of peer ratings on self and perceived peer perspective scores.

In light of the various treatment implications based on the different behavioral indices profiles, an additional area for future research is to look at treatment successes and effective interventions for children belonging to different behavioral indices profile groups.

REFERENCES

Achenbach, T. M., McConaughy, S. H., & Howell, C. T. (1987). Child/adolescent behavioral and emotional problems: Implications of cross-informant correlations for situational specificity. *Psychological Bulletin, 101* (2), 213-232.

Austin, S., & Joseph, S. (1996). Assessment of bully/victim problems in 8 to 11 year-olds. *British Journal of Educational Psychology, 66,* 447-456.

Batsche, G. M., & Knoff, H. M. (1994). Bullies and their victims: Understanding a pervasive problem in the schools. *School Psychology Review, 23* (2), 165-174.

Besag, V. (1989). *Bullies and victims in schools.* Philadelphia: Open University Press.

Boulton, M. J., & Underwood, K. (1992). Bully/victim problems among middle school children. *British Journal of Educational Psychology, 62,* 73-87.

Charach, A., Pepler, D., & Ziegler, S. (1995). Bullying at school: A Canadian Perspective. *Education Canada, 35,* 12-18.

Craig, W., & Pepler, D. (1993, March). *Bullies and victims.* Poster presented at the meeting of the Society for Research in Child Development, New Orleans, LA.

Gottheil, N. F. (1994). *Bullies and victims: Possible mechanisms of maintenance.* Unpublished master's thesis, Wayne State University, Detroit.

Gottheil, N. F. (1995, March). *Bullies and victims: Patterns of the use and receipt of physical aggression as a possible mechanism for status maintenance.* Poster session presented at the meeting of the Society for Research in Child Development, Indianapolis, IN.

Hazler, R. J., Carney, J. V., Green, S., Powell, R., & Jolly, L.S. (1997). Areas of expert agreement on identification of school bullies and victims. *School Psychology International, 18,* 5-14.

Hoover, J. H., Oliver, R., & Hazler, R. J. (1992). Bullying: Perceptions of adolescent victims in the midwestern USA. *School Psychology International, 13,* 5-16.

Horne, A. M., Glaser, B., & Sayger, T. V. (1994). Bullies. *Counseling and Human Development, 27* (3), 1-12.

Huesmann, L. R., Eron, L. D., Lefkowitz, M. M., & Walder, L. O. (1984). Stability of aggression over time and generations. *Developmental Psychology, 20* (6), 1120-1134.

Hymel, S., Bowker, A., & Woody, E. (1993). Aggressive versus withdrawn unpopular children: Variations in peer and self-perceptions in multiple domains. *Child Development, 64,* 879-896.

Hymel, S., & Franke, S. (1985). Children's peer relations: Assessing self-perceptions. In B. H. Schneider, K. H. Rubin, & J. E. Ledingham (Eds.), *Children's peer relations: Issues in assessment and intervention* (pp. 75-91). New York: Springer-Verlag New York, Inc.

Kane, J. S., & Lawler, E. E. (1978). Methods of peer assessment. *Psychological Bulletin, 85* (3), 555-586.

Ledingham, J. E., & Younger, A. J. (1985). The influence of the evaluator on assessments of children's social skills. In B. H. Schneider, K. H. Rubin, & J. E. Ledingham (Eds.), *Children's peer relations: Issues in assessment and intervention* (pp. 75-91). New York: Springer-Verlag New York, Inc.

Ledingham, J. E., Younger, A., Schwartzman, A., & Bergeron, G. (1982). Agreement among teacher, peer, and self-ratings of children's aggression, withdrawal, an likability. *Journal of Abnormal Child Psychology, 10* (3), 363-372.

Miller, P. H. (1989). *Theories of developmental psychology* (2nd ed.). New York: W. H. Freeman and Company.

Neter, J., Wasserman, W., & Kutner, M.H. (1990). *Applied linear statistical models: Regression, analysis of variance, and experimental designs* (3rd ed.). Boston: Richard D. Irwin, Inc.

Olweus, D. (1984). Aggressors and their victims: Bullying at school. In N. Frude & H. Gault (Eds.), *Disruptive behaviour in schools* (pp. 57-76). Chinchester: John Wiley & Sons, Ltd.

Olweus, D. (1991). Bully/victim problems among schoolchildren: Basic facts and effects of a school based intervention program. In D. J. Pepler & K. H. Rubin (Eds.), *The development and treatment of childhood aggression* (pp. 411-448). Hillsdale, N. J.: Erlbaum.

Olweus, D. (1992). Victimization by peers: Antecedents and long-term outcomes. In K. H. Rubin & J. B. Asendorf (Eds), *Social withdrawal, inhibition, and shyness in childhood* (pp. 315-341). Hillsdale, N. J.: Erlbaum.

Olweus, D. (1993). *Bullying at school: What we know and what we can do*. Oxford, UK: Blackwell Publishers Ltd.

Perry, D. G., Kusel, S. J., & Perry, L. C. (1988). Victims of peer aggression. *Developmental Psychology, 24* (6), 807-814.

Roberts, M. (1988, February). School yard menace. *Psychology Today*, pp. 52-56.

Slee, P. T. (1993). Bullying: A preliminary investigation of its nature and the effects of social cognition. *Early Child Development and Care, 87*, 47-57.

Smith, P. K., Bowers, L., Binney, V., & Cowie, H. (1993). Relationships of children involved in bully/victim problems at school. In S. Duck (Ed.), *Learning about relationships: Understanding relationship processes series volume 2* (pp. 184-212). Newbury Park, CA: Sage Publications, Inc.

Wayment, H., & Zetlin, A. G. (1989). Theoretical and methodological considerations of self-concept measurement. *Adolescence, 24* (94), 339-348.

Winer, B. J. (1971). *Statistical principles in experimental design* (2nd ed.). New York: McGraw-Hill, Inc.

Zarzour, K. (1994). *Battling the school-yard bully*. Toronto: HarperCollins Publishers Ltd.

Psychosocial Correlates in Bullying and Victimization: The Relationship Between Depression, Anxiety, and Bully/Victim Status

Susan M. Swearer
Samuel Y. Song
Paulette Tam Cary
John W. Eagle
William T. Mickelson

Susan M. Swearer, PhD, is Assistant Professor of School Psychology, Department of Educational Psychology; Samuel Y. Song, MEd, is a doctoral student, School Psychology Program; Paulette Tam Cary, MA, is a doctoral student, School Psychology Program; John W. Eagle, MSW, is a doctoral student, School Psychology Program, University of Nebraska-Lincoln; and William T. Mickelson, PhD, is Assistant Professor of Quantitative and Qualitative Methods in Education, Department of Educational Psychology. All authors are affiliated with the University of Nebraska-Lincoln.

Address correspondence to: Susan M. Swearer, PhD, Department of Educational Psychology, The University of Nebraska-Lincoln, 130B Bancroft Hall, Lincoln, NE 68588-0345 (Email: sswearer@unlserve.unl.edu).

The authors wish to thank the school personnel and the students who participated in this research.

This research was supported by a grant from the University of Nebraska Foundation to Susan M. Swearer.

[Haworth co-indexing entry note]: "Psychosocial Correlates in Bullying and Victimization: The Relationship Between Depression, Anxiety, and Bully/Victim Status." Swearer, Susan M. et al. Co-published simultaneously in *Journal of Emotional Abuse* (The Haworth Maltreatment & Trauma Press, an imprint of The Haworth Press, Inc.) Vol. 2, No. 2/3, 2001, pp. 95-121; and: *Bullying Behavior: Current Issues, Research, and Interventions* (ed: Robert A. Geffner, Marti Loring, and Corinna Young) The Haworth Maltreatment & Trauma Press, an imprint of The Haworth Press, Inc., 2001, pp. 95-121. Single or multiple copies of this article are available for a fee from The Haworth Document Delivery Service [1-800-HAWORTH, 9:00 a.m. - 5:00 p.m. (EST). E-mail address: getinfo@haworthpressinc.com].

95

SUMMARY. Examined differences between bullies, victims, and bully-victims on internalizing psychopathology (depression and anxiety). Participants included 133 (66 male and 67 female) sixth-grade students from a Midwestern middle school, ages ranging from 11 to 13 years old. The data presented are from the first two years of a five-year longitudinal study that began January of 1999. Initial results indicate differences between bullies, victims, bully-victims, and students without bully/victim problems (no status) in terms of depression and anxiety. Specifically, bully-victims and bullies were more likely to be depressed than victims and no status students. Bully-victims and victims were more likely to experience anxious symptoms than bullies and no status students. Thus, an interesting pattern emerged with respect to internalizing psychopathology along the bully/victim continuum. Bully-victims may be the most impaired subtype with respect to depression and anxiety. Implications for prevention and intervention programs are discussed. *[Article copies available for a fee from The Haworth Document Delivery Service: 1-800-HAWORTH. E-mail address: <getinfo@haworthpressinc.com> Website: <http://www.HaworthPress.com> © 2001 by The Haworth Press, Inc. All rights reserved.]*

KEYWORDS. Bullying, victimization, depression, anxiety, early adolescence

Bullying may be the most prevalent form of school violence with approximately 15% to 20% of students experiencing bullying during their elementary, middle, and/or high school years (Batsche, 1997). Worldwide incidence rates of bullying range from 5% (Whitney & Smith, 1993) to 23% (Stephenson & Smith, 1989). Studies in the United States have yielded higher rates of bullying; ranging from a low of 10% (Perry, Kusel, & Perry, 1988) to a high of 75% of school-aged children who reported being bullied at least one time during their school years (Hoover, Oliver, & Hazler, 1992). Recently, the Centers for Disease Control and Prevention Youth Risk Behavior Surveillance survey data indicate that 7.4% of American youth were threatened or injured with a weapon on school grounds one or more times within the past year and 4% have missed school within the last 30 days because they fear being intimidated or bullied (Kann, Kinchen, Williams, Ross, Lowry, Hill, Grunbaum, Blumson, Collins, & Kolbe, 1998). A study by Olweus and Alsaker (1991) suggests that present day bullying occurs more frequently and with greater lethality than it did in the previous two decades. Clearly, in light of these statistics, meeting the goals, established by the National Education Goals Panel of 1993, that every school in America will be free of violence and the school environment will be conducive to learning (Johnston, O'Malley, & Bachman, 1993) is a formidable task.

Previous studies have used various definitions of bullying. One of the most common definitions of bullying is: "A person is being bullied when he or she is exposed, repeatedly and over time, to negative actions on the part of one or more other persons" (Olweus, 1993, p. 9). Other researchers have delineated three aspects of bullying: "imbalance of strength (whether physical or psychological), repeated negative action against an individual, and a deliberate intention to hurt the other where the aggression is largely unprovoked" (Slee, 1995, p. 57). Hoover, Oliver, and Hazler (1992) define bullying as "the physical or psychological abuse of an individual by one or a group of students" (p. 76). Bullying may take the form of direct and open attacks on the victim, or social isolation and intentional exclusion from a group (Olweus, 1994). Thus, bullying can manifest in both verbal and physical behaviors (Bosworth, Espelage, & Simon, 1999).

Researchers have suggested that the construct of bullying should be viewed as a continuum ranging between "bully" and "victim" (Olweus, 1994; Slee, 1995; Smith, 1991). Based on the existing empirical literature, Olweus (1994) delineated bullies, passive bullies, passive/submissive victims, and provocative victims along the continuum. According to Olweus, bullies are aggressive, have positive attitudes towards violence, are impulsive, need to dominate others, have little anxiety, are average to slightly below average in popularity, and do not suffer from low self-esteem. Passive bullies (or followers) are individuals who participate in bullying (usually in groups), but do not initiate the bullying. Passive/submissive victims are anxious, rejected by their peers, physically weaker than their peers, and do not retaliate when bullied. Provocative victims are anxious, aggressive, have concentration problems, may be hyperactive, and retaliate when bullied. Although Smith (1991) distinguished between bullies, anxious bullies, victims, provocative victims, and bully-victims, these subtypes were not empirically-based. While the majority of studies make distinctions between bullies, victims, and bully-victims, little empirical work has examined psychological processes behind these subtypes of bullies and victims. Bully-victims are the individuals who are bullied and who, in turn, bully others.

Several studies have reported negative effects of being involved in bullying during childhood and adolescence (Bosworth et al., 1999; Craig, 1988; Juvonen, Nishina, & Graham, 2000; Olweus, 1994; Pellegrini, Bartini, & Brooks, 1999; Rigby, 1998; Slee, 1995; Smith, 1991). Recent evidence in particular has emerged that underscores the association between bullying and mental health. Psychosocial difficulties have been found to affect not only victims, but also bully-victims and bullies. Victims exhibit poor mental and physical health (Rigby, 1999); high incidence of emotional distress and more perceived adverse health effects (Rigby, 1998); internalizing behavior, psychosomatic symptoms, and anhedonia (Kumpulainen et al., 1998). Bully-victims exhibit psychological distress (Duncan, 1999a); anxiety (Craig, 1998); loneliness (Forero, McLellan, Rissel, & Bauman, 1999); and depression (Craig, 1998; Kaltiala-Heino, Rimpela, Marttunen, Rimpela, & Rantanen, 1999). Bullies report feelings of depression (Kaltiala-Heino et al., 1999), suicidal ideation (Kaltiala-Heino et al., 1999); and suicidal behavior (Bailey, 1994).

THE RELATIONSHIP BETWEEN DEPRESSION, BULLYING, AND VICTIMIZATION

Previous research indicates that victims of bullying tend to display unique characteristics and behaviors. Victims typically possess lower self-esteem and experience more feelings of loneliness, anxiety and depression than nonvictimized individuals (Callaghan & Joseph, 1995; Hodges & Perry, 1996; Slee, 1994). This is not surprising considering children with low self-esteem are more vulnerable to signs of depression (Harter, 1993; Lewinsohn, Roberts, Seeley, Rohde, Gotlib, & Hops, 1994). Egan and Perry (1998) investigated the characteristics of third- and seventh-grade students that made them vulnerable to victimization. They found that low self-esteem over time contributed to victimization by peers. Behavioral characteristics such as weakness, manifest anxiety, and poor social skills, also contributed to the victimization of children with low self-regard. The authors discussed how children with low self-regard may contribute to their victimization by failing to assert themselves during conflict. Behaviors such as sadness, fear, and social withdrawal exhibited by these children may actually invite aggressive behavior from bullies. Egan and Perry (1998) also found that victimization led to decreased self-esteem over time. Therefore, a vicious cycle may exist that perpetuates and exacerbates a child's victim status.

Graham and Juvonen (1998) found that middle school children who identified themselves as victims possessed "characterological" self-blame. The self-blaming attributions mediated the relationship between self-perceived victimization and adjustment problems such as loneliness, social anxiety, and low self-worth. That is, victims with self-blaming tendencies were particularly vulnerable to adjustment problems. The repeated cycle of "victimization–self-blame–maladjustment" supports Egan and Perry's (1998) findings that low self-regard leads to victimization, and that over time, victimization leads to decreases in self-regard (Graham & Juvonen, 1998, p. 596). Graham and Juvonen (1998) explained that "children who view themselves as socially incompetent behave in ways that promote abuse by others (the antecedent function of low self-worth) and they feel worse about themselves as victimization escalates over the school year (the consequence function)" (p. 596).

Research has found that victimization is not only related to low self-worth, but also higher rates of depression (Biggam & Power, 1999; Callaghan & Joseph, 1995; Neary & Joseph, 1994; Olweus, 1995). In a study of 75 Scottish youth offenders (ages 16-21), Biggam and Power (1999) found that victims possessed higher levels of both anxiety and depression. While the Hospital Anxiety and Depression Scale (HADS) ratings for both bullies and the control group were in the normal range, victims' ratings were in the mild depression and moderate anxiety range. Neary and Joseph (1994) studied 60 schoolgirls in Ireland, ranging in age from 10 to 12 years. Both self- and peer-identified victims scored significantly higher on the Peer Victimization Scale and the Birleson Depression Inventory. In addition, these girls scored significantly lower on the social acceptance scale and the global self-worth scale. Callaghan and Joseph (1995) replicated these findings in their study of both boys and girls in two schools in Northern Ireland. They noted that boys who were bullied scored slightly higher than girls on the Peer Victimization Scale. This is consistent with research that has identified increased bullying behaviors among boys versus girls (Boulton & Underwood, 1992; Craig, 1998; Kumpulainen et al., 1998).

Most research in the area of bullying and depression has focused on the relationship between victimization and depression. However, several researchers have identified relationships between bullying and depression as well. Slee (1995) investigated the relationship between victims and depression, as well as bullies and depression. For both boys and girls, victimization was significantly related to higher levels of depression and unhappiness at school. The tendency to bully was also significantly related to higher levels of depression for both boys and girls. These students reported significantly greater unhappiness at school. Craig (1998) investigated the effects of bullying and victimization on depression, anxiety, and aggression in elementary school children. Victims reported more depression than comparison children. In contrast to Slee's (1995) findings, Craig discovered gender differences in the amount of depression reported. She found that females reported more depression than males. Further, older children reported more depression than younger children. Austin and Joseph (1996) investigated the similarities and differences among victims, bullies, and bully-victims. They found that both victims and bully-victims scored higher on the Birleson Depression Inventory than bullies. This finding could provide further support for Slee's (1995) finding that a relationship between bullying and depression exists. Slee's study did not account for bully-victims. Possibly, some of the bullies in his study with higher depression ratings were actually bully-victims, rather than just bullies.

The effects of depression due to bullying and victimization can be understood within a developmental context. Over time, the anxiety and depression experienced by children involved in the bullying interaction, may lead to physical manifestations (e.g., increased somatic complaints and more illnesses) (Rigby, 1996). These difficulties may result in increased absences and/or a passive style of coping (i.e., learned helplessness).

The child who is bullied may further stand out from his or her peers, which may result in increased bullying. This supports the notion of a vicious cycle in bullying interactions (Salmivalli, Karhunen, & Lagerspetz, 1996). That is, victims' behaviors and emotional states may make them vulnerable to bullying. The bullying behavior towards them may perpetuate their issues with low self-esteem, depression, anxiety, and loneliness, which may make them increasingly vulnerable to bullying. This underscores the importance of examining depression and anxiety in bullying and victimization in longitudinal studies.

THE RELATIONSHIP BETWEEN ANXIETY, BULLYING, AND VICTIMIZATION

Anxiety disorders may be one of the most prevalent disorders among children, with prevalence rates ranging from 8.7% to 17.2% of community samples (Kashan et al., 1987; Costello et al., 1988; Fersusson, Horwood, & Lynskey, 1993; Kessler et al., 1994). One of the most critical aspects of anxiety disorders in children is that they are often comorbid with other difficulties, including depression and conduct problems (Costello et al., 1988; Strauss, Last, Hersen, & Kazdin, 1988; Brady & Kendall, 1992; Fersusson et al., 1993).

Anxious children often have difficulty initiating and maintaining social and peer relations, which may be the result of, or have an impact upon, other internalizing factors. Although not all children suffering from anxiety disorders present significant deficits in peer social status (Strauss, Lahey, Frick, Frame, & Hynd, 1988), several studies have reported that anxious children are perceived by their peers as withdrawn or neglected by their peers. Strauss et al. (1988), found that anxious children were more likely to be peer nominated into a socially neglected group, rather than groups that were socially accepted or rejected by their peers. Children who were considered "highly anxious" were also more likely to be characterized by their peers as shy and socially withdrawn (Strauss, Frame, & Forehand, 1987).

While there is a paucity of studies specifically identifying the role of anxiety with bullying, a great deal of literature exists that examines the role of anxiety with aggression and with victimization. This literature will be reviewed and the connection between anxiety and bullying will be made.

The research demonstrating the relationship between anxiety and aggression has followed an interesting and contradictory progression. It was first hypothesized that anxiety lessened levels of aggression. This hypothesis primarily stemmed from research that examined comorbid states of anxiety and conduct disorder among children. Conduct disordered boys with a comorbid anxiety disorder were less likely to be peer nominated for aggression ("fight most" and "meanest") in comparison to children with conduct disorder alone (Walker et al., 1991). These authors hypothesized, in accordance with Gray's model (1987), that boys with comorbid anxiety disorder were more in tune with perceiving and reasoning about consequences of their behavior and thus less likely to exhibit aggressive behavior in the future.

Later research produced a contradictory hypothesis. Kashani, Dueser, and Reid (1991) found a positive relationship between anxiety and aggression, among a sample of 210 eight, twelve, and seventeen year old males and females. They reported significantly higher levels of anxiety in subjects that demonstrated "high verbal" and high physical aggression.

Ialonogo, Edelsohn, Werthamer-Larsson, Crockett, and Kelam (1996) found a positive relationship between anxiety in the fall of first grade children with comorbid anxiety disorder and aggression in the spring of first grade. Children suffering from comorbid symptoms were more likely to be situated among the top twenty-five percent of students identified as aggressive in the spring than were children with aggressive symptoms alone. These results were true for both boys and girls according to teacher ratings but only true for boys according to peer nominations. Children suffering from anxious only symptoms were less likely to demonstrate future aggression than children suffering from aggressive only symptoms. The authors hypothesized that comorbid anxiety may "have a dampening effect on predatory or proactive aggression than on defensive aggression, where the fight/flight system is activated" (Ialonogo et al., 1996). It was also hypothesized that anxious children were more likely to misinterpret environmental stimuli and thus exhibit aggressive behavior due to their anxiety. This hypothesis is in accord with Barret, Rappee, Dadds, and Ryan (1996) who concluded that anxious children are more likely to interpret ambiguous situations as being threatening.

Several studies examining the relationship between anxiety and victimization have reported that victims are more anxious than nonvictims (Olweus,

·1978; Hodges & Perry, 1996; Olweus 1995). Graham and Juvonen (1998) reported differential relationships between anxiety levels of children who identified themselves as victims and those whom peers identified as victims. Self-perceived victimization was related to higher levels of social anxiety, loneliness, and low self-worth; peer-perceived victimization was not related to high levels of social anxiety although it was predictive of peer acceptance and rejection. Middle school students who viewed themselves as victims (whether they were or were not) reported higher scores in social anxiety than students who viewed themselves as non-victims (whether they were or were not) (Graham & Juvonen, 1998).

Studies specifically examining bullying have also concurred that victims of bullying have higher rates of anxiety than children who bully (Olweus, 1994; Perry et al., 1988; Slee, 1994). Bernstein and Watson (1997) reported findings that both passive and aggressive victims tend to show greater levels of anxiety and insecurity than bullies. Olweus (1994) also found that bullies report little anxiety.

According to the results of study of 546 males and females in the fifth through eighth grades, Craig (1998) reported a significant association with anxiety and children who self-reported to engage in verbal aggressive behavior and indirect aggressive behavior (e.g., behaviors that harm others by damaging or threatening existing peer relationships) and children who self-reported to be the victims of verbal, physical, and indirect aggressive acts. Consistent with previous research, Craig (1998) found that victims self-reported greater degrees of anxiety than bullies when comparisons between groups were made.

Recently, however, there has been some indication that these previous findings may be in question. Duncan (1999b) reported results from a study of 375 seventh and eighth grade students that found that peer bullies and victims reported similar levels of anxiety. However, children who were classified as bully-victims, according to their responses on a self-report questionnaire, reported significantly higher levels of anxiety than bullies or victims alone. Duncan (1999b) also found that children who were associated with bullying activities (e.g., were classified as bullies, victims, or bully-victims) reported significantly higher levels of anxiety than children who were not associated with bullying.

The current study examines the association between depression and anxiety in middle school bullies and victims. While previous research has drawn attention to the problem of internalizing psychopathology in bullies and victims, the relationship between depression and anxiety in students who are both bullies and victims (i.e., bully-victims) has yet to be fully understood. In contrast to previous studies, this study specifically examines internalizing symptoms in students who are bully-victims in addition to students who are bullies, victims, and students who do not identify as a bully or a victim (no status students). We hypothesized that bully-victims would experience the greatest internal distress and would be the most impaired subtype along the continuum. The data presented are from the first two years of a five-year longitudinal study following three cohorts of middle school students. The data presented in this study are from the first two cohorts of students.

METHOD

Participants

Participants included 133 (66 male and 67 female) sixth-grade students from a Midwestern middle school. Their ages ranged from 11-13 years old ($M =$ 11.52; $SD = 1.38$). The group's racial distribution consisted of 63.2% Caucasian, 14.3% African-American, 9% Asian, 6.8% Hispanic, 5% Mixed Minority, .8% Native American, and .8% Middle Eastern. Among the participants, 52.3% live with both parents; 39.4% live with mother only; 6.8% live with father only; and 1.5% live with another relative.

Participants were grouped according to status based on their responses on the Bully Survey (Swearer & Paulk, 1998). That is, students who completed the section on being bullied were classified as victims ($n = 52$); students who completed the section on bullying others were classified as bullies ($n = 7$); and students who completed both sections were classified as bully-victims ($n =$ 40). Students who did not complete either section were classified as no status students ($n = 34$). Thus, 39.1% of the sample were victims; 30.1% were bully-victims; 25.6% were no status; and 5.3% were bullies.

Instrumentation

The Bully Survey (Swearer & Paulk, 1998). Students completed The Bully Survey, a three-part, 17-page survey that queried students regarding the nature of bullying, motivations for bullying, and how bullying was handled by school personnel. In Part A of the survey, students answered questions about when they were victims of bullying. If students were not bullied at school within the school year, they were instructed to skip Part A and move to the next section of the survey. Part B of the survey addressed questions about observations the individual has made of bullying behavior among his or her peers. If students did not observe any bullying during the school year, they were instructed to move to the next section of the survey. Part C of the survey requested information from students about when they bullied others. Students did not complete this section unless they bullied others during the school year. Thus, students self-identified as bullies, victims, or both (bully-victim status) by endorsing the appropriate separate sections on this survey. At the end of Part C, a final section (two pages) contained a scale that measures attitudes (positive and negative) toward bullying (e.g., "Being bullied is no big deal") and two items that assess educational aspirations (i.e., "How far do you hope to go in school?" and "How far do you think you will go in school?").

The Children's Depression Inventory (CDI; Kovacs, 1992). This instrument is the most commonly used self-report measure of depression for children 7 to 17 years of age. Based on the Beck Depression Inventory, the CDI consists of 27 items designed to assess the overt symptoms of childhood depression. The CDI measures five highly-correlated factors: Negative Mood, Interpersonal Problems, Ineffectiveness, Anhedonia, and Negative Self Esteem. These five factors are combined to yield one higher-order factor of childhood depression. Each item refers to one factor and assesses its presence and severity during the two weeks prior to testing. A three-alternative choice format is used; the choices are scored from 0 to 2 with total scores of 19 and higher considered to be indicative of significant levels of depression (Kovacs, 1992). Overall, the CDI has demonstrated acceptable internal consistency and test-retest reliability as well as convergent validity (Kovacs, 1992). Cronbach's alpha for the CDI in a normative sample was found to be equal .86 and alpha coefficients for the factors range from .59 to .68, which are acceptable for short factor subscales (Kovacs, 1985). In the present study, the internal consistency reliability using coefficient alpha was .91 for the total score.

The Multidimensional Anxiety Scale for Children (MASC; March, 1997). The MASC consists of 39 items, which are distributed across four major scales: physical symptoms, social anxiety, harm avoidance, and separation anxiety. These four scales comprise a single higher-order scale called the MASC Total Anxiety. The physical symptoms scale, the social anxiety scale, and the harm avoidance scale may further be divided into subscales which represent tense/restless and somatic/autonomic, humiliation/rejection and public performance fears, and perfectionism and anxious coping, respectively. The scale has demonstrated high internal reliability as well as high test-retest reliability at 3 weeks and 3 months. Internal reliability for the MASC Total Anxiety scale was reported to be .88 for females and .89 for males (March, Parker, Sullivan, Stallings, & Conners, 1997). Test-retest reliability for a 3 month time period was reported to be .93 for the MASC Total Anxiety scale (March et al., 1997). In the present sample, the internal consistency reliability using coefficient alpha was .93 for the MASC Total Anxiety scale.

Procedure

Data were collected in April 1999 and April 2000 for two cohorts of students entering the 6th grade. All students in the sixth grade were given a consent form to take home to their parents that explained the nature of the study. Parents were informed that results would be confidential, that their child would not be personally identified to school personnel as a bully or victim, and that they could withdraw their child from the study at any time without penalty. Parents received a follow-up call to confirm receipt of the consent form and study description. Parents without a copy of the consent form and study description were sent a copy via the postal service if they wished to consider having their child participate in the study.

All students with parental consent to participate in the study ($N = 133$) were administered a series of instruments in April 1999 (Cohort 1) and April 2000 (Cohort 2) as part of a five-year longitudinal study on bullying and victimization. It was explained to students that they were not required to participate despite parental consent and that they could leave the study at any time without penalty. One student in Cohort 1 chose not to participate despite parental consent. Students were required to read and sign a youth assent form in order to participate in the study. The instruments included The Bully Survey (Swearer, & Paulk, 1998), a modified Peer Nomination Inventory (Perry, Williard, & Perry, 1990), a modified Teacher Nomination Inventory (Perry, et al., 1990), the Children's Depression Inventory (Kovacs, 1992) and the Multidimensional Anxiety Scale for Children (March, 1997). Students were pulled from morning classes and completed the instruments in small groups. Students required approximately one-and-a-half hours to complete the instruments.

RESULTS

Analyses were run to determine whether cohort effects existed for the depression and anxiety variables across group status. No cohort effect for any category and response variable existed except the victim group with the depression response variable. A comparison of group means found that cohort 2 experienced less depression than cohort 1 (F (1, 132) = 7.83, $p < .001$). This is most likely due to sampling issues in cohort 2, as parents seemed reluctant to allow their child to participate in research on bullying in the Spring of 2000. This reluctance may be due to the increased visibility of school violence and the concern that parents might have regarding participation in research on bullying. Thus, on the depression measure, cohort 2 is more similar to the no status students than cohort 1. This acts as a lower bound estimate for depression

·for the victim group in cohort 2 and dampens the effect of the victim category in the depression analysis. However, given that cohort 2 was equivalent to cohort 1 on the other variables and that the depression score for the cohort 1 victim group was a lower bound estimate (versus upper bound), the authors decided to pool the groups across cohorts.

The results will be presented in three sections. The first section will review the results between the groups (bully, victim, bully-victim, and no status) on the depression measure, the second section will review the results on the anxiety measure, while the final section will examine the multivariate nature of anxiety and depression.

Depression

Table 1 presents summary statistics on the total depression score (CDIsum) for the four groups. One-way ANOVA revealed a statistically significant relationship between group membership and total depression scores (F (3, 133) = 8.34, $p < .001$). Unequal sample sizes and variances paired inversely (see Table 1) call this statistically significant F-test result into question.[1] Therefore, the analysis proceeded by examining confidence intervals on mean depression scores for each group. Figure 1 presents the confidence intervals for depression. From this figure it is clear that the bully-victims scored highest on the measure of depression, bullies had the next highest scores, followed by the victims and then the no status students. From the confidence interval graph, it is clear that no status students are significantly different from the victims and bully/victims.[2]

Given that all mean scores were below the clinical cut-off suggested for moderate depression (> 19; Kovacs, 1992), we created a clinical score for students who scored above 19 raw score points on the CDI. Thus, students were categorized into two groups based on the cut-off score of 19: not depressed and depressed. Cross tabulation procedures revealed an interesting pattern between the groups. Specifically, 42.9% of the bullies were depressed, 30% of the bully-victims were depressed, 13.5% of the victims were depressed, and 0% of the no-status students were depressed (see Figure 2).

Anxiety

Table 2 presents summary statistics on the total anxiety score (MASCsum) for the four groups. One-way ANOVA revealed a significant relationship between group membership and the total anxiety score (F (3, 131) = 3.82, $p < .01$). Unequal sample sizes and direct pairing of variances (see Table 2) cause the F-test to be conservative. Here, the null hypothesis is still rejected. Due to

FIGURE 1. Confidence Intervals for Depression Scores by Group Membership

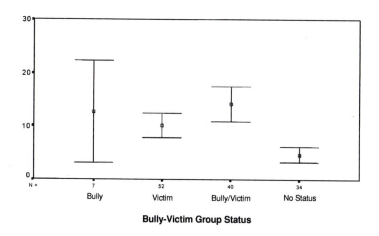

FIGURE 2. Percent of Students Scoring ≥ 19 on the CDI

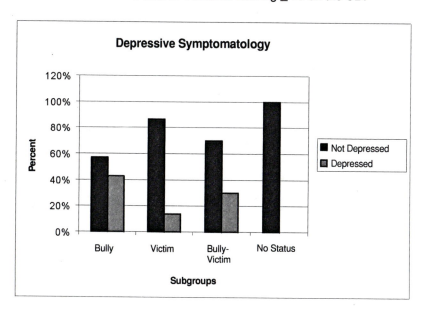

TABLE 1. Summary Statistics for Depression Score and Groups

Group	n	Mean CDIsum	Std. Dev.	Std. Error
Bully	7	12.71	10.33	3.90
Victim	52	10.07	8.15	1.13
Bully-Victim	40	14.15	10.26	1.62
No Status	34	4.70	4.16	.71
Total	133	10.06	8.88	.77

Note. CDIsum = total score from Children's Depression Inventory ; Std. Dev. = standard deviation.

TABLE 2. Summary Statistics for Anxiety Total Score and Groups

Group	n	Mean MASCsum	Std. Dev.	Std. Error
Bully	7	24.28	9.16	3.46
Victim	51	44.58	22.88	3.20
Bully-Victim	40	44.80	17.77	2.80
No Status	34	34.73	18.67	3.20
Total	132	41.03	20.49	1.78

Note. MASCsum = total score from Multidimensional Anxiety Scale for Children; Std. Dev. = standard deviation.

the conservative nature of the test, mean differences are considered to exist. Therefore, the analysis proceeded by examining confidence intervals on mean anxiety scores for each group. Figure 3 presents the confidence intervals for anxiety. From this figure, it is clear that the bully-victims and victims scored highest on the total anxiety score, followed by the no status students, and the bullies. Bullies were significantly different from victims and bully-victims but were not different from the no status students on total anxiety scores.[3]

Given that all mean scores were below the cut-off suggested for significant symptoms of anxiety (T score > 65; March, 1997), we created a clinical score for students who scored at or above a T score of 65 on the MASC. Thus, students were categorized into two groups based on the cut-off T score of 65: not anxious and anxious. Cross tabulation procedures revealed an interesting pattern between the groups. Specifically, 0% of the bullies were anxious, 19.2%

FIGURE 3. Confidence Intervals for Anxiety Scores by Group Membership

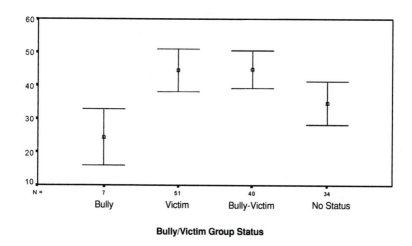

of the victims were anxious, 17.5% of the bully-victims were anxious, and 5.9% of the no-status students were anxious (see Figure 4).

Multivariate Examination of Depression and Anxiety

A correlation matrix between the depression and anxiety total scores revealed a moderate correlation between the two constructs ($r = .36, p = .001$). This suggests that the two measures may not be completely independent constructs and may reflect the on-going discussion regarding the comorbidity of depression and anxiety (Brady & Kendall, 1992; Kovacs & Devlin, 1998). However, a correlational analysis of the subscales of the MASC and the CDI reveal an interesting pattern (Table 3). Specifically, the physical symptom subscale of the MASC is more highly correlated with the CDI than the remaining subscales. This may be due to somatic complaints that are characteristic of both depression and anxiety (i.e., headache, irritability, etc.). Additionally, the harm avoidance subscale has a low, negative correlation with the CDI that is not statistically significant. Thus, there is not a connection between being depressed and perfectionism or anxious coping. There is a correlational structure between depression and the anxiety subscales and there are differences between groups along the bully/victim continuum. In order to further understand the differences between groups, we examined

FIGURE 4. Percent of Student Scoring ≥ T-Score of 65 on the MASC

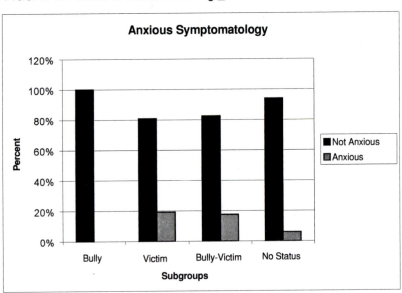

TABLE 3. Correlation Matrix Between Depression and Anxiety Subscale Scores

	CDIsum	MASCsoc	MASCphys	MASCsep	MASCharm
CDIsum	1.00				
MASCsoc	.31**	1.00			
MASCphys	.53**	.61**	1.00		
MASCsep	.25**	.55**	.58**	1.00	
MASCharm	−.03	.56**	.43**	.56**	1.00

Note. **p < .001; CDIsum = total score from the Children's Depression Inventory; MASCsoc = social anxiety scale; MASCphys = physical symptoms scale; MASCsep = separation/ panic scale; MASCharm = harm avoidance scale.

those differences relative to the correlational structure through multivariate procedures.

Exploratory Discriminant Function Analysis

Exploratory discriminant function analysis was used to best differentiate between the bully/victim groups across the depression and anxiety measures taking into account their correlational structure. As recommended, equal prior probabilities for group membership were set for the discriminant analyses (Stevens, 1996). The decision criteria for each variable was set for F-to-enter the function at 1.0 or larger.

Results from the discriminant function analysis are presented in Tables 4 and 5. Two discriminant functions are interpreted in this analysis. The eigenvalues canonical correlations, Wilks' Lamdba, and significance test results are presented in Table 4. The standardized function coefficients and pooled within-group correlation between discriminant functions and discriminating variables (i.e., structure matrix) are presented in Table 5. From the structure coefficients, we have interpreted the first discriminant function as depression with somatic symptomatology. The second discriminant function we have interpreted as reflective of general anxiety, represented by social anxiety and harm avoidance. Researchers typically recommend coefficients of the structure matrix to exhibit correlations of approximately .30 or higher for inclusion in the interpretation of the functions (Hair, Anderson, Tatham, & Black, 1992; Tabachnick & Fidell, 1989). In the analysis of the function-variable correlations in the current study, correlations of .30 or less were not interpreted.

The centroids for the groups suggest that the two functions maximally separate the four groups and are displayed in Figure 5. The centroids represent means of standard scores on the two discriminant functions, Depression/Somatic (Function 1) and Anxiety–Social/Worry (Function 2). These means can be interpreted as standard deviation scores. From Figure 5, it is clear that bullies scored at least one standard deviation below the other groups on anxiety. Bullies scored almost half a standard deviation above the victims and no status students on depression. Bully-victims scored half a standard deviation above the victims and no status students on depression and physical symptoms of anxiety. Victims also had elevated anxiety scores when compared with the bullies and the no status students. As predicted, the no status students did not endorse depressive or anxious symptomatology.

TABLE 4. Results of Discriminant Function Analysis

Function	Eigenvalue	Canonical Correlation	Wilks' Lambda	Chi-Square	df	p
1	.23	.43	.71	41.89	15	.00
2	.10	.30	.88	15.43	8	.05

TABLE 5. Discriminant Function Coefficients and Correlation

| Variable | Standardized Canonical Discriminant Function Coefficients | | Structure Matrix | |
	Function 1	Function 2	Function 1	Function 2
CDISUM	0.770	0.122	0.091	0.302
MASCSOC	−0.337	0.790	0.067	0.952
MASCHARM	−0.234	0.396	−0.221	0.748
MASCSEP	−0.070	−0.011	0.112	0.584
MASCPHYS	0.524	−0.136	0.543	0.581

Note. CDISUM = total score from the Children's Depression Inventory; MASCsoc = social anxiety scale; MASCharm = harm avoidance scale; MASCsep = separation/panic scale; MASCphys = physical symptoms scale.

FIGURE 5. Discriminant Function Centroids

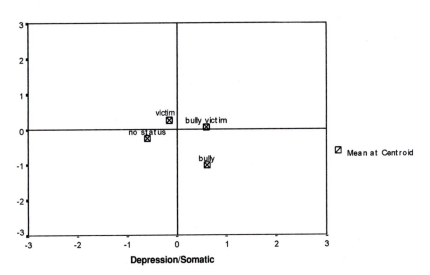

DISCUSSION

Results from this study suggest that bully-victims may be the most impaired group in terms of internalizing psychopathology along the bully/victim continuum. Specifically, the bully-victims were both more depressed and experienced greater physical symptoms of anxiety than the other subgroups. This is consistent with previous research, which has found that the bully-victim subgroup is the most impaired psychologically (Kumpulainen et al., 1998). While bully-victims endorse greater internalizing psychopathology, some interesting patterns also emerged in the other subtypes. The results will be discussed below and implications for the development of effective intervention and prevention programs will be addressed.

Interestingly, in this study, the bully-victim subtype was the second largest group (following the victim subtype). Previous research has defined this group as "aggressive victims" and has found that this group represents only about 5% of most school populations (Pellegrini et al., 1999). However, other research has found that the bully-victim subtype is larger, with almost 15% (Austin & Joseph, 1996) to 25% (Forero et al., 1999) of students being categorized as bully-victims. Given the psychosocial difficulties expressed by this group of students, it is important for future research to examine this subtype in more detail.

While much of the research on bullying and depression has focused on the relationship between being victimized and depression, the bullies and bully-victims in this sample endorsed the highest levels of depression when compared with the other groups. This suggests that in terms of depression, the bullies may be more like bully-victims than the victims and no status students. This finding supports previous research which has found that bullies reported feelings of depression and suicidal ideation (Kaltiala-Heino et al., 1999).

Slee (1995) investigated the relationship between being a victim or a bully and depression. He found that both bullies and victims were likely to experience depressive symptoms. However, Slee's study did not account for the bully-victim subgroup. Possibly, some of the bullies in his study with higher depression ratings were actually bully-victims, rather than just bullies. Craig (1998) also investigated the effects of bullying and victimization on depression, anxiety, and aggression in elementary children and found that victims reported more depression than comparison children. Austin and Joseph (1996) investigated the similarities and differences among victims, bullies, and bully/victims. They found that both victims and bully-victims had higher levels of depression than bullies. Results from this study suggest that bullies also experience depressive symptomatology.

Interestingly, the variability of the bullies on the depression measure was extreme. The bully subtype seems to endorse both extremes (depressed and not depressed). This finding is consistent with the literature on the comorbidity of depression and conduct disorder which suggests there is a subgroup of aggressive children with comorbid depression (Anderson, Williams, McGee, & Silva, 1987; Angold, 1988; Harrington, Fudge, Rutter, Pickles, & Hill, 1991; Kovacs, Paulauskas, Gatsonis, & Richards, 1988; Petersen et al., 1993; Rey,

1994; Zoccolillo, 1992). This may be the case in this sample, however, this issue needs to be further explored with a larger cell size.

The effects of depression due to bullying and victimization can be understood within a developmental context. Over time, the anxiety and depression experienced by children involved in the bullying interaction, may lead to physical manifestations (e.g., increased somatic complaints and more illnesses) (Rigby, 1996). These difficulties may result in increased absences and/or a passive style of coping (i.e., learned helplessness). The child who is bullied may further stand out from his or her peers, which may result in increased bullying. This supports the notion of a vicious cycle in bullying interactions (Salmivalli et al., 1996). That is, victims' behaviors and emotional states may make them vulnerable to bullying. The bullying behavior towards them may perpetuate their issues with low self-esteem, depression, anxiety, and loneliness, which may make them increasingly vulnerable to bullying. This underscores the importance of examining depression and anxiety in bullying and victimization in longitudinal studies.

The no status students in this study reported low anxiety and depression, which was predicted, as these students did not endorse bullying or victimization difficulties. This group provides a valuable comparison point for understanding bullying and victimization. As bullying has been characterized as a normative experience (Limber & Small, 2000), it is important to include students who do not experience these difficulties.

The bully-victims and victims appear similar in terms of anxiety in this sample. Both groups reported higher levels of anxiety. These findings are supported by previous research, which has found that victims were more anxious than nonvictims (Olweus, 1978; Hodges & Perry, 1996). Graham and Juvonen (1998) found that self-perceived victimization was related to higher levels of social anxiety, loneliness, and low self-worth. Peer-perceived victimization was not related to high levels of social anxiety although it was predictive of peer acceptance and rejection. Middle school students who viewed themselves as victims (whether they were or were not) reported higher scores in social anxiety than students who viewed themselves as non-victims (whether they were or were not).

Some interesting differences emerged with respect to anxiety in this sample. Specifically, the bullies did not endorse feelings of anxiety. This is consistent with previous research which has that bullies exhibit little to no anxiety (Olweus, 1995). Previous research examining comorbid anxiety in aggressive children has found that anxiety may strengthen the presence of aggression in first graders (Ialongo et al., 1996). These authors hypothesize that anxiety in aggressive children may serve to activate the fight/flight system, thus a bully-victim may be more likely to respond to bullying in an aggressive fashion because he or she is responding defensively. It has also been hypothesized that there are two subgroups of anxious children: youth who fear social evaluation and youth who fear physical harm (Campbell & Rapee, 1994).

In the present study, levels of anxious symptoms were highest in the victim subgroup. Additionally, bullies reported the lowest levels of anxiety. Studies specifically examining victimization have also concurred that victims of bullying have higher rates of anxiety than children who bully (Olweus, 1994; Perry et al., 1988; Slee, 1994). Bernstein and Watson (1997) reported findings that both passive and aggressive victims tend to show greater levels of anxiety and insecurity than bullies. Olweus (1994) also found that bullies report little anxiety. Consistent with previous research, Craig (1998) found that victims self-reported greater degrees of anxiety than bullies when comparisons between groups were made.

Recently, however, there have been some contradictory findings with respect to bullying, victimization, and anxiety. Duncan (1999b) reported results from a study of 375 seventh and eighth grade students that found that bullies and victims reported similar levels of anxiety. Additionally, children who were classified as bully-victims, reported significantly higher levels of anxiety than bullies or victims alone. Thus, the bully-victims were the more impaired group in terms of anxious symptomatology. Duncan (1999b) also found that children who were associated with bullying activities (e.g., were classified as bullies, victims, or bully-victims) reported significantly higher levels of anxiety than children who were not associated with bullying. This research suggests that the relationship between anxiety, bullying, and victimization may be more complex than previously thought.

While this study contributes to the literature by examining depression and anxiety along the bully-victim continuum, several limitations must be noted. First, the cell size in the bully subgroup ($n = 7$) is small. However, given that this is the second year of a five-year longitudinal study, it is anticipated that this cell size will increase. Also, the small cell size could be reflective of the suggestion that many bullies may also view themselves as victims. Previous research has found that bullies under-report their status when compared with peer and teacher nominations (Paulk, Swearer, Song, & Cary, 1999). Thus, the self-perception of bullies is important to assess in research on bullying. Additionally, self-report measures were the only measures utilized in this study. Thus, common method variance might be affecting the results of this study. Research on bullying and victimization suggests that multi-method procedures (self-report, peer nomination, teacher nomination, observations, self-monitoring) are important to utilize in a comprehensive assessment of bullying and victimization. This study only used self-report as the grouping variable.

The differences between internalizing symptoms along the bully/victim continuum are important to elucidate as comorbidity may impact the success of bullying prevention and intervention programs. Bully-victims may be the most common subgroup along the bully-victim continuum. Bully-victims are the individuals who are bullied and who, in turn, bully others. This vicious cycle of bullying behavior has direct implications for prevention and intervention programs. If a student feels justified in his or her actions (i.e., "She called me a name, so I can call her one back"), then it may be difficult for that individual to change his or her views about bullying.

Additionally, the finding that bullies reported higher levels of depression than the other groups has implications for prevention and intervention programs. Increasingly, researchers are finding that high levels of comorbidity between depression and conduct disorder exists (Kovacs et al., 1988; Petersen et al., 1993). The relationship between depression and bullying may be related to this phenomenon. Future research with larger groups will help unearth these patterns in order to guide the development of effective intervention programs.

Considering the numerous needs of bullies and victims, it is imperative to develop appropriate interventions for this population. However, with few exceptions (Olweus & Limber, 1999; Pepler, Craig, Ziegler, & Charach, 1994; Ross, 1996; Smith & Sharp, 1994), the majority of interventions are not empirically validated and are not based on psychometrically sound approaches. Moreover, few interventions address the mental health needs of the bully or bully-victim in addition to victims. Finally, it seems imperative that interventions address the inherent differences among the subtypes of bullying discussed previously. In an effort to develop appropriate interventions for the mental health needs of bullies and victims, a first and necessary step is to better understand the differences between the bullying subtypes and mental health. This study adds to the research on bullying and mental health by focusing on internalizing factors related to the bully/victim continuum.

Schools are often called upon to adopt violence (e.g., bullying) prevention and intervention programs. Over 300 violence intervention programs are available (Howard, Flora, & Friffin, 1999). However, many of the programs are not empirically-validated and there is little guidance to help schools choose the program that will have the greatest impact. Results from this study suggest that a successful program for preventing and intervening with bullying will incorporate modules for coping with depressive and anxious symptoms. Hopefully, a comprehensive bullying prevention and intervention program that addresses internalizing symptoms will assist school personnel and mental health professionals in fostering an educational environment that is conducive to learning and free from all forms of violence.

NOTES

1. Inverse pairing causes F-tests to be liberal. Rejecting more often then should be done due to the violation of homogeneity of variance.
2. Games-Howell post hoc procedure for unequal variance conditions indicated statistically significant differences between these groups.
3. Games-Howell post hoc procedure for unequal variance conditions indicated statistically significant differences between these groups.

REFERENCES

Anderson, J. C., Williams, S., McGee, R., & Silva, P. A. (1987). DSM-III disorders in preadolescent children. *Archives of General Psychiatry, 44*, 69-76.

Angold, A. (1988). Childhood and adolescent depression I: Epidemiological and etiological aspects. *British Journal of Psychiatry, 152*, 601-617.

Austin, S. & Joseph, S. (1996). Assessment of bully/victim problems in 8 to 11 year-olds. *British Journal of Educational Psychology, 66*, 447-456.

Bailey, S. (1994). Health in young persons' establishments: Treating the damaged and preventing harm. *Criminal Behavior and Mental Health, 3*(4), 349-367.

Barrett, P. M., Rapee, R. M., Dadds, M. M., & Ryan, S. M. (1996). Family enhancement of cognitive style in anxious and aggressive children. *Journal of Abnormal Child Psychology, 24*(2), 187-203.

Batsche, G.M. (1997). Bullying. In G.G. Bear, K.M. Minke, & A. Thomas (Eds.), *Children's Needs II: Development, Problems, and Alternatives* (pp. 171-179). Bethesda, MD: National Association of School Psychologists.

Bernstein, J. Y., & Watson, M. W. (1997). Children who are targets of bullying: A victim pattern. *Journal of Interpersonal Violence, 12*(4), 483-498.

Biggam, F. H. & Power, K. G. (1999). Social problem-solving skills and psychological distress among incarcerated young offenders: The issue of bullying and victimization. *Cognitive Therapy and Research, 23*, 307-326.

Bosworth, K., Espelage, D. L., & Simon, T. R. (1999). Factors associated with bullying behavior in middle school students. *Journal of Early Adolescence, 19*(3), 341-362.

Boulton, M. J., & Underwood, K. (1992). Bully/victim problems among middle school children: Stability, self-perceived competence, peer perceptions and peer acceptance. *British Journal of Educational Psychology, 62*, 73-87.

Brady, E. U., & Kendall, P. C. (1992). Comorbidity of anxiety and depression in children and adolescents. *Psychological Bulletin, 111*, 244-255.

Callaghan, S. & Joseph, S. (1995). Self-concept and peer victimization among schoolchildren. *Personality and Individual Differences, 18*, 161-163.

Campbell, M. & Rapee, R. (1994). The nature of feared outcome representations in children. *Journal of Abnormal Child Psychology, 22*, 99-112.

Costello, E. J., Costello, A. J., Edelbrock, C., Burns, B. J., Dulcan, M. K., Brent, D., Janiszewski, S. (1988). Psychiatric disorders in pediatric primary care: Prevalence and risk factors. *Archives of General Psychiatry, 45*(12), 1107-1116.

Craig, W. M. (1998). The relationship among bullying, victimization, depression, anxiety, and aggression in elementary school children. *Personality and Individual Differences, 24* (1), 123-130.

Duncan, R.D. (1999a). Maltreatment by parents and peers: The relationship between child abuse, bully victimization, and psychological distress. *Child Maltreatment, 4*, 45-55.

Duncan, R. D. (1999b). Peer and sibling aggression: An investigation of intra-and extra-familial bullying. *Journal of Interpersonal Violence, 14*(8), 871-886.

Egan, S. K., & Perry, D. G. (1998). Does low self-regard invite victimization? *Developmental Psychology, 34*, 299-309.

Forero, R., McLellan, L., Rissel, C., & Bauman, A. (1999). Bullying behaviour and psychological health among school students in New South Wales, Australia: Cross sectional survey. *British Medical Journal, 319*, 344-348.

Furgusson, D. M., Horwood, L. J., & Lynskey, M. T. (1993). Prevalence and comorbidity of DSM-III-R diagnoses in birth cohort of 15 year olds. *Journal of the American Academy of Child and Adolescent Psychiatry, 32*, 1127-1134.

Graham, S., & Juvonen, J. (1998). Self-blame and peer victimization in middle school: An attributional analysis. *Developmental Psychology, 34*(3), 587-599.

Gray, J. A. (1987). *The psychology of fear and stress* (2nd ed.)., Cambridge: Cambridge University Press.

Hair, J. F., Anderson, R. E., Tatham, R. L., & Black, W. C. (1992). *Multivariate data analysis with readings* (3rd ed.). New York: Macmillan Publishing Co.

Harrington, R., Fudge, H., Rutter, M., Pickles, A., & Hill, J. (1991). Adult outcomes of childhood and adolescent depression: II. Links with antisocial disorders. *Journal of the American Academy of Child and Adolescent Psychiatry, 30*, 434-439.

Harter, S. (1993). Causes and consequences of low self-esteem in children and adolescents. In R. F. Baumeister (Ed.). *Self-esteem: The puzzle of low self-regard*. (87-116). New York: Plenum.

Hodges, E., & Perry, D. (1996). Victims of peer abuse: An overview. *Journal of Emotional and Behavioral Problems, 5*, 23-28.

Hoover, J. H., Oliver, R., & Hazler, R. J. (1992). Bullying: Perceptions of adolescent victims in the Midwestern U.S.A. *School Psychology International, 13*, 5-16.

Howard, K. A., Flora, J., & Griffin, M. (1999). Violence-prevention programs in schools: State of the science and implications for future research. *Applied & Preventive Psychology, 8*, 197-215.

Ialongo, N., Edelsohn, G., Werthamer-Larsson, L., Crockett, L., & Kellam (1996). The course of aggression in first-grade children with and without comorbid anxious symptoms. *Journal of Abnormal Child Psychology, 24*(4), 445-456.

Johnston, L. D., O'Malley, P. M., & Bachman, J. G. (1993). *Monitoring the future study for goal 6 of the national education goals: A special report for the National*

Education Goals Panel. Ann Arbor, MI: University of Michigan's Institute for Social Research.

Juvonen, J., Nishina, A., & Graham, S. (2000). Peer harassment, psychological adjustment, and school functioning in early adolescence. *Journal of Educational Psychology, 92*(2), 349-359.

Kaltiala-Heino, R., Rimpela, M., Marttunen, M., Rimpela, A., Rantanen, P. (1999). Bullying, depression, and suicidal ideation in Finnish adolescents: School survey. *British Medical Journal, 319*, 348-351.

Kann, L. Kinchen, S. A., Williams, B.I., Ross, J.G., Lowry, R., Hill, C.V., Grunbaum, J. A., Blumson, P.S., Collins, J.L., Kolbe, L.J. (1998). *Youth Risk Behavior Surveillance, 1997.* Atlanta, GA: Centers for Disease Control and Prevention. CDC Surveillance Summaries, August 14, 1998. MMWR; 47, (No. SS-3).

Kashani, J. H., Beck, N. C., Hoeper, E. W., Fallahi, C., Corcoran, C. M., McAllister, J. A., Rosenberg, T. K., & Reid, J. C. (1987). Psychatric disorders in a community sample of adolescents. *American Journal of Psychiatry, 144*, 584-589.

Kashani, J. H., Deuser, W., & Reid, J. C. (1991). Aggression and anxiety: A new look at an old notion. *Journal of the American Academy of Child and Adolescent Psychiatry, 30*(2), 218-223.

Kessler, R. C., McGonagle, K. A., Zhao, S., Nelson, C. B., Hughes, M., Eshleman, S., Wittchen, H. U., Kendler, K. S. (1994). Lifetime and 12-month prevalence of DSM-III-R psychiatric disorders in the United States: Results from the National Comorbidity study. *Archives of General Psychiatry, 51*, 8-19.

Kovacs, M. (1985). The Children's Depression Inventory. *Psychopharmacology Bulletin, 21*(4), 995-998.

Kovacs, M. (1992). *Children's Depression Inventory.* North Tonawanda, NY: Multi-Health Systems, Inc.

Kovacs, M. & Devlin, B. (1998). Internalizing disorders in childhood. *Journal of Child Psychology and Psychiatry, 39*(1), 47-63.

Kovacs, M., Paulauskas, S., Gatsonis, C., & Richards, C. (1988). Depressive disorders in childhood: III. A longitudinal study of comorbidity with and risk for conduct disorders. *Journal of Affective Disorders, 15*, 205-217.

Kumpulainen, K., Rasanen, E., Henttonen, I., Almqvist, F., Kresanov, K., Linna, S., Moilanen, I., Piha, J., Puura, K., & Tamminen, T. (1998). Bullying and psychiatric symptoms among elementary school-age children. *Child Abuse & Neglect, 22*, 705-717.

Lewinsohn, P. M., Roberts, R. E., Seeley, J. R., Rohde, P., Gotlib, I. H., & Hops, H. (1994). Adolescent psychopathology II. Psychosocial risk factors for depression. *Journal of Abnormal Psychology, 103*, 302-315.

Limber, S. P. & Small, M. A. (2000, August). *Self-reports of bully/victimization among primary school students.* Paper presented at the annual meeting of the American Psychological Association, Washington, D.C.

March, J. S. (1997). *Multidimensional Anxiety Scale for Children.* North Tonawanda, NY: Multi-Health Systems, Inc.

March, J. S., Parker, J. D., Sullivan, K., Stallings, P., & Conners, K. (1997). The Multidimensional Anxiety Scale for Children (MASC): Factor structure, reliability, and validity. *Journal of the American Academy of Child and Adolescent Psychiatry, 36*(4), 554-565.

Neary, A. & Joseph, S. (1994). Peer victimization and its relationship to self-concept and depression among schoolgirls. *Personality and Individual Differences, 16*(1), 183-186.

Olweus, D. (1978). *Aggression in the schools: Bullies and whipping boys.* Washington, DC: Hemisphere (Wiley).

Olweus, D. (1993). *Bullying at school.* Cambridge: Blackwell.

Olweus, D. (1994). Annotation: Bullying at school: Basic facts and effects of a school-based intervention program. *Journal of Child Psychology and Psychiatry, 35*, 1171-1190.

Olweus, D. (1995). Bullying or peer abuse at school: Facts and intervention. *Current Directions in Psychological Science, 4*, 196-200.

Olweus, D., & Alsaker, F. D. (1991). Assessing change in a cohort-longitudinal study with hierarchical data. In D. Magnusson, L. R. Bergman, G. Rudinger, & B. Rorestad (Eds.), *Problems and Methods in Longitudinal Research: Stability and Change.* Cambridge: Cambridge University Press.

Olweus, D. & Limber, S. (1999). Bullying Prevention Program. In D. S. Elliott (Ed.), *Blueprints for violence prevention.* Boulder, CO: Institute of Behavioral Science, Regents of the University of Colorado.

Paulk, D.L., Swearer, S.M., Song, S.Y., & Cary, P.T. (1999). *Teacher-, peer-, and self-nominations of bullies and victims of bullying.* Poster presented at the American Psychological Association National Conference; Boston, Massachusetts.

Pellegrini, A. D., Bartini, M., & Brooks, F. (1999). School bullies, victims, and aggressive victims: Factors relating to group affiliation and victimization in early adolescence. *Journal of Educational Psychology, 91*(2), 216-224.

Peppler, D.J., Craig, W.M., Ziegler, S., & Charach, A. (1994). An evaluation of an anti-bullying intervention in Toronto schools. *Canadian Journal of Community Mental Health, 13*, 95-110.

Perry, D., Kusel, S., & Perry, L. (1988). Victims of peer aggression. *Developmental Psychology, 24*, 807-814.

Perry, D. G., Williard, J. C., & Perry, L. C. (1990). Peers' perceptions of the consequences that victimized children provide aggressors. *Child Development, 61*, 1310-1325.

Petersen, A. C., Compas, B. E., Brooks-Gunn, J., Stemmler, M., Ey, S., & Grant, K. E. (1993). Depression in adolescence. *American Psychologist, 48*, 155-168.

Rey, J. M. (1994). Comorbidity between disruptive disorders and depression in referred adolescents. *Australian and New Zealand Journal of Psychiatry, 28*, 106-113.

Rigby, K. (1996). *Bullying in schools—and what to do about it.* Melbourne, Australia: The Australian Council for Educational Research.

Rigby, K. (1998). The relationship between reported health and involvement in bully/victim problems among male and female secondary schoolchildren. *Journal of Health Psychology, 3,* 465-476.

Rigby, K. (1999). Peer victimisation at school and the health of secondary school students. *British Journal of Educational Psychology, 69,* 95-104.

Ross, D. M. (1996). *Childhood bullying and teasing.* Alexandria: American Counseling Association.

Salmivalli, C., Karhunen, J., & Lagerspetz, K. M. J. (1996). How do the victims respond to bullying? *Aggressive Behavior, 22,* 99-109.

Slee, P. T. (1995). Peer victimization and its relationship to depression among Australian primary school students. *Personality and Individual Differences, 18*(1), 57-62.

Slee, P. T. (1994). Situational and interpersonal correlates of anxiety associated with peer victimization. *Child Psychiatry and Human Development, 25*(2), 97-107.

Smith, P. K. (1991). The silent nightmare: Bullying and victimization in school peer groups. *The Psychologist: Bulletin of the British Psychological Society, 4,* 243-248.

Smith, P. K. & Sharp, S. (Eds.) (1994). *School bullying: Insights and perspectives.* London: Routledge.

Stephenson, P. & Smith, D. (1989). Bullying in the junior school. In D. P. Tattum & D. A. Lane (Eds.), *Bullying in schools* (pp. 45-57). Stoke on Trent, England: Trendham Books Limited.

Stevens, J. (1996). *Applied multivariate statistics for the social sciences.* New Jersey: Lawrence Erlbaum Associates.

Strauss, C., Frame, C. L., & Forehand, R. (1987). Psychosocial impairment associated with anxiety in children. *Journal of Clinical Child Psychology, 16*(3), 433-443.

Strauss, C. C., Lahey, B. B., Frick, P., Frame, C. L., & Hynd, G. W. (1988). Peer social status of children with anxiety disorders. *Journal of Consulting and Clinical Psychology, 56*(1) 137-141.

Strauss, C. C., Last, C. G., Hersen, M., & Kazdin, A. E. (1988). Association between anxiety and depression in children and adolescents with anxiety disorders. *Journal of Abnormal Child Psychology, 16,* 57-68.

Swearer, S. M. & Paulk, D. L. (1998). *The Bully Survey.* Unpublished manuscript. University of Nebraska–Lincoln.

Tabachnick, B. G. & Fidell, L. S. (1989). *Using Multivariate Statistics: 2nd Edition.* New York: Harper Collins.

Walker, J. L., Lahey, B. B., Russo, M. F., Frick, P. J., Christ, M. A. G., McBurnett, K., Loeber, R., Stouthamer-Loeber, M., & Green, S. (1991). Anxiety, inhibition, and conduct disorder in children: I. Relations to social impairment. *Journal of the American Academy of Child and Adolescent Psychiatry, 30*(2), 187-191.

Whitney, I. & Smith, P. K. (1993). A survey of the nature and extent of bullying in junior/middle and secondary schools. *Educational Research, 35*(1), 3-25.

Zoccolillo, M. (1992). Co-occurrence of conduct disorder and its adult outcomes with depressive and anxiety disorders: A review. *Journal of the American Academy of Child and Adolescent Psychiatry, 31.* 547-556.

Bullying and Victimization During Early Adolescence: Peer Influences and Psychosocial Correlates

Dorothy L. Espelage
Melissa K. Holt

SUMMARY. This study examined the association between peer dynamics and bullying behavior among early adolescents. Participants ($N = 422$) included middle school students in grades 6 through 8 from a small midwestern town. Students completed a 40-minute survey that included demographic questions, self-report and peer-report measures of bullying and victimization as well as measures of other psychosocial variables. Male adolescents self-reported more bullying and were nominated as bullies more often than female adolescents, and older students self-reported more bullying behavior than younger students. Approximately 14.5% of the sample met the criteria for bullying frequently. Cluster analysis yielded five distinct groups of bully/victim subtypes. Bullies had the same number of friends as students who did not bully their peers,

Dorothy L. Espelage, PhD, is Assistant Professor of Counseling Psychology, and Melissa K. Holt, MA, is a doctoral candidate in the Counseling Psychology PhD program. Both authors are affiliated with the University of Illinois, Urbana-Champaign.

Address correspondence to: Dorothy L. Espelage, Department of Educational Psychology, University of Illinois, Urbana-Champaign, College of Education, 226 Education Building, 1310 South Sixth Street, Champaign, IL 61820-6990 (E-mail espelage@uiuc.edu).

This research was supported in part by an University of Illinois Research Board Grant.

[Haworth co-indexing entry note]: "Bullying and Victimization During Early Adolescence: Peer Influences and Psychosocial Correlates." Espelage, Dorothy L., and Melissa K. Holt. Co-published simultaneously in *Journal of Emotional Abuse* (The Haworth Maltreatment & Trauma Press, an imprint of The Haworth Press, Inc.) Vol. 2, No. 2/3, 2001, pp. 123-142; and: *Bullying Behavior: Current Issues, Research, and Interventions* (ed: Robert A. Geffner, Marti Loring, and Corinna Young) The Haworth Maltreatment & Trauma Press, an imprint of The Haworth Press, Inc., 2001, pp. 123-142. Single or multiple copies of this article are available for a fee from The Haworth Document Delivery Service [1-800-HAWORTH, 9:00 a.m. - 5:00 p.m. (EST). E-mail address: getinfo@haworthpressinc.com].

123

and the relation between popularity and bullying behavior was the strongest for 6th grade male adolescents. With respect to peer affiliation and bullying, 75% of bullies nominated fellow bullies as friends, suggesting that bullies hang out with other bullies. Twenty-percent of victims scored within the clinical range on a standard depression and anxiety measure. This study provides initial support for the notion that bullying or teasing might be a strategy for obtaining power and status within the middle school. *[Article copies available for a fee from The Haworth Document Delivery Service: 1-800-HAWORTH. E-mail address: <getinfo@haworthpressinc.com> Website: <http://www.HaworthPress.com> © 2001 by The Haworth Press, Inc. All rights reserved.]*

KEYWORDS. Bullying, peers, adolescence, middle school, victimization

INTRODUCTION

Aggression and violence during childhood and adolescence have been the focus of much research over the past several decades (Loeber & Hay, 1997; Loeber & Stouthamer-Loeber, 1998; Olweus, 1979; Patterson, Reid, & Dishion, 1992; Zumkley, 1994). These researchers have consistently demonstrated that serious forms of aggression remain relatively stable from childhood through adulthood; however, Loeber and Hay (1997) also argue that minor forms of aggression might have their onset during early or late adolescence. Despite their contention, very little research has been conducted on minor forms of aggression, such as bullying or teasing during the middle school years.

Although many studies on bullying have been conducted outside the United States, several recent reports provide some insight into the nature of this behavior within this country. Available data from cross-sectional studies in midwestern and southeastern U.S. schools suggest that bullying behavior is quite common. In a study of 200 junior and high school students from midwestern towns, 88% reported having observed bullying and 77% had been a victim of bullying during their school years (Hoover, Oliver, & Hazler, 1992). Similarly, 25% of students in grades 4 through 6 admitted to bullying another student with some regularity in the previous 3 months (Limber et al., 1997). Given that bullying is often a predecessor to more serious forms of aggression (Loeber & Hay, 1997), it behooves researchers to learn more about how bullying and victimization might emerge or continue during early adolescence.

One notable gap in the evolving literature on bullying and victimization during early adolescence is the role that peers play in promoting bullying and victimization by either reinforcing the aggressor, failing to intervene to stop the victimization, or affiliating with students who bully. During early adolescence the function and importance of the peer group changes dramatically (Crockett et al., 1984; Dornbusch, 1989). Adolescents, seeking autonomy from their parents, turn to their peers to discuss problems, feelings, fears, and doubts, thereby increasing the salience of time spent with friends (Sebald, 1992; Youniss & Smollar, 1985). However, this reliance on peers for social support is coupled with increasing pressures to attain social status (Corsaro & Eder; 1990, Eder, 1985). It is during adolescence that peer groups become stratified and issues of acceptance and popularity grow increasingly important. Research indicates, for example, that toughness and aggressiveness are important status considerations for boys, while appearance is a central determinant of social status among girls (Eder, 1995). Therefore, it is likely that this pressure to obtain peer acceptance and status might be associated with an increase in teasing and bullying to demonstrate superiority over other students for boys and girls either through name-calling or ridiculing.

International research with elementary school children supports the role of peer group members in reinforcing and maintaining bullying (Craig & Pepler, 1997; Salmivalli, Lagerspetz, Bjorkqvist, Osterman, & Kaukiainen, 1996). These authors contend that bullying can best be understood from a social-interactional perspective in which these bullying behaviors are considered a result of a complex interaction between individual characteristics (e.g., impulsivity) and the social context, including the peer group and school social system. Participation of peers in the bullying process was clearly evident when Pepler and her colleagues videotaped aggressive and socially competent Canadian children in grades 1 through 6 on the playground; peers were involved in bullying in an astounding 85% of bully episodes. This involvement, among other things, consisted of active participation in the episode (30%), observing the interaction (23%), and intervening (12%). Furthermore, peers were coded as being respectful to the bully in 74% of the episodes, but respectful to the victim in only 23% of the episodes. Similarly, in a survey study of 6th graders in Finland, the majority of students participated in the bullying process, in some capacity, and their various participant roles were significantly related to social status within their respective classrooms (Salmivalli et al., 1996). Clearly, peers play an instrumental role in bullying and victimization on elementary school playgrounds and within classrooms.

Less understood are the peer dynamics associated with bullying in the transition from elementary school to middle school. This transition can cause stress that might promote bullying behavior as students attempt to define their place in the new social structure. For example, changing from one school to another school often leads to an increase in other risk-taking behaviors, and bullying might be another way that young people deal with the stress of a new environment. In a short-term longitudinal investigation of over 500 middle school students (grades 6–8), we found an increase in bullying behavior among 6th graders over a 4-month period (Espelage, Bosworth, & Simon, under review). We speculated that the 6th graders were assimilating into the culture of this middle school, which had a certain rate of bullying behavior as seen in the initial scores for 7th and 8th graders. This is supported by the contention that bullying is a learned behavior and that the 6th graders as they enter middle school have not yet learned how to interact in the social milieu of the school. Many 6th graders who wish to "fit in" might adopt the behaviors–including teasing–of those students that have been in this school longer and have more of the power to dictate the social norm.

Two recent studies further examined the hypothesis that middle school students opt to bully their peers to "fit in" (Pellegrini, Bartini, & Brooks, 1999; Rodkin, Farmer, Pearl, & VanArcher, 2000). Pellegrini and colleagues found that bullying actually served to enhance within-group status and popularity among 5th graders (Pellegrini et al., 1999). Similarly, Rodkin and colleagues found aggressive 6th grade boys to be rated by their peers as some of the most popular students (Rodkin et al., 2000).

While these recent studies, and those conducted outside of the United States, indicate that peer interaction is intricately linked to bullying, methodological limitations warrant further research in the area of peer influences on bullying. First, although the observational methodology utilized by Debra Pepler has provided a wealth of information about the social-interactional components of bullying in school children and has enabled researchers to more closely examine the role of peers in bullying episodes, it is difficult to videotape middle school students. In fact, Pepler and Craig (1995) argue that by 11 to 12 years of age, children seem reticent when wearing microphones which is often a required component of this methodology. Therefore, this methodology has not been established as suitable for use with this age group. Because videotaping poises ethical and methodological challenges, U.S. researchers have developed methods of assessing peer influences, including self-report and peer-nomination tasks which have proven useful with this age group. Second, the previous literature has exclusively focused on elementary school children and no study has examined peer influences in middle school students. Therefore, the mechanisms through which peer interaction and the peer network structures influence bullying behaviors during early adolescence remains unclear. Further, it is unclear whether, and how, the influence of the peer group on bullying behaviors differs across sex, grade, or level of peer group status.

Examination of bullying in this study differs in several ways from previous investigations of aggression during early adolescence. First, given the results of ethnographic analysis of the middle school culture, in which teasing is more frequent than overt aggression (Eder, 1995), this paper deviates from the mainstream aggression literature by focusing exclusively on verbal teasing and threatening behaviors and eschews any attempt to measure overt, physical aggression. Therefore, bullying was defined as a subset of aggressive behavior that has potential to cause physical or psychological harm to the recipient. Second, unlike previous studies on bullying behavior where students were first presented with a definition of "bullying" (e.g., Salmivalli et al., 1996), socially desirable responding was minimized by asking students the frequency of behaviors without requiring students to evaluate the impact of their behavior (e.g., teasing, making fun of others). This is particularly important because students who tease others often do not define these behaviors as bullying or even hurtful, despite the findings that their victims report significant distress from low-level verbal aggression, such as teasing (Espelage & Asidao, in press). Third, given that bullying is often considered a subtype of aggression, cluster analysis was used to identify groups of students who differ or those who are similar in their self-reported bullying, fighting, and victimization experiences.

The primary objectives of this study were: (1) to examine the amount of bullying and victimization across sex and grade-level; (2) to explore the relation between popularity and bullying behavior across sex and grade level; (3) to determine the extent to which students who bully affiliate with one another; and (4) to identify groups of students who bully others and/or experience victimization in similar ways and determine the extent to which these groups differ on psychosocial measures. Based on previous research, we hypothesized that boys would report more bullying than girls, and older students (i.e., 8th graders) would report more bullying than younger students (i.e., 7th graders). Given the increasing importance of social status and popularity in the transition to adolescence and the centrality of dominance to determinations of these qualities for adolescents, we hypothesized that more "popular" and socially visible male and female peers would have higher mean levels of bullying behavior and lower victimization scores than less popular students. Conversely, victims of bullies were hypothesized to have a hard time fitting in, and would therefore be less popular. In order to identify groups of students with similar levels of bullying and victimization experiences, we hypothesized that several distinct clusters would emerge in the cluster analysis, including a large group of students that report few experiences of bullying others or being victimized. Furthermore, a group of victims would emerge along with a group of students who bully their peers but do not report being physically aggressive. Finally, two additional groups seen in the literature were expected to emerge–those students who bully others but are also physically aggressive and a group of students who are victimized and report bullying others as well.

METHOD

Students from a middle school in a small midwestern town were participants in this study during the fall 1999 and spring 2000 semesters. The middle school is located in a predominantly Caucasian and rural community, with a significant number of low SES households.

Participants

In early fall 1999, parent permission forms were sent to all 475 students registered at this school. Parents were asked to sign and return the consent form only if they did not want their child to participate in the study. Of the 475 students, 422 (93%) were granted permission from their parents to participate and 5 students returned permission forms from their parents denying permission. Of the 422 students in the study, 51% were girls ($n = 214$) and 49% were boys ($n = 208$), with 30% 6th graders ($n = 128$), 33% 7th graders ($n = 138$), and 37% 8th graders ($n = 156$). Approximately 93% were Caucasian, 1% were African American, 2% were biracial, and 4% were of other racial backgrounds.

Procedure

Participants completed the study survey during a free period on one day. Surveys were administered to groups of students ranging in size from seven to fifteen students. Students were situated such that they were not close to other students. Once students were arranged the project was introduced to them. Students were informed that we would be asking them questions about aggression, their feelings, and about their friends. They were told that they would receive a pencil and a highlighter for their participation and would be eligible for a drawing for a $10.00 gift certificate to a local music/bookstore. A drawing was conducted at the end of the survey administration in each classroom. Students were asked to give their written consent by signing their name on the front colored coversheet. Names were collected to allow for matching students' fall and spring data. Students were informed that their name would be converted to a number once we have collected their spring data and assured them of confidentiality and anonymity.

Once the project was explained to the class, students completed the survey which is discussed later in this section. In each classroom, one of two trained examiners read each item and response option aloud while a second team member monitored students' progress. The reader's speed varied based on the grade-level of the classroom. Students were allowed to ask questions if they had difficulty understanding any words.

Measures

The survey consisted of three sections: (1) demographic questions, (2) bullying/aggression, victimization, and other psychosocial likert-scale measures, and (3) peer nomination tasks and a sociometric item.

Demographic variables. Self-reports of gender, grade, and race were included as demographic characteristics.

Self-reported bullying, fighting, and victimization. Based on a comprehensive review of the research literature and existing bullying and victimization measures (Bosworth et al., 1999; Crick, 1996), 21 items assessing bullying, fighting, and victimization were included on the survey. The items were submitted to principal axis factoring (PAF) analysis to examine the factor structure of these data. Factors were extracted based on eigen values, percentage of variance explained, and examination of scree plots. Items that had factor loadings above .50 and those items that did not have cross-loadings above .30 on any other factor were retained. Three distinct factors emerged accounting for 49% of the variance, including a Bullying Scale with 9 items, a Fighting Scale with 5 items, and a Victimization Scale with 4 items. One item (i.e., "I took my anger out on an innocent person") was deleted because the factor loading on any factor was less than .50. Two additional items (i.e., "I made other students scared"; "I pushed, shoved, and slapped other students") were removed because they had equivalent cross-loadings on the Bullying and Fighting Scales (see Table 1).

Self-reported bullying behaviors. Bullying behavior was assessed with a scale that consists of 9 items including those related to teasing and name-calling, social exclusion, and rumor spreading. Students were asked to indicate the extent to which they did each behavior (e.g., "I teased other students") in the last 30 days. Factor loadings for these items ranged from .52 to .75 and this factor accounted for 31% of the variance in the factor analysis. Response options ranged from Never through 7 or more times. A Cronbach alpha coefficient of .87 was found for this sample and the Bullying Scale correlated .65 with the Youth Self-Report Aggression Scale (Achenbach, 1991) and was not significantly correlated with the Victimization Scale ($r = .12$).

Self-reported fighting. Fighting was measured with 5 items, and students were asked to indicate how many times in the last 30 days they engaged in each behavior (e.g., "I got in a physical fight"). Factor loadings ranged from .50 to

TABLE 1. Factor Loadings from Principal-Axis Factoring of Bullying, Fighting, and Victimization Items

Item	Factor Loadings			Communality
	Bully	Fight	Victim	
I teased other students.	.75	.26	.07	.64
In a group I teased other students.	.72	.02	−.05	.51
I upset other students for the fun of it.	.70	.28	.04	.57
I excluded others.	.64	.17	.02	.44
I encouraged people to fight.	.62	.25	.03	.51
I spread rumors about others.	.56	.16	.11	.35
I was mean to someone when angry.	.56	.17	.13	.35
I helped harass other students.	.54	.29	−.07	.40
I started arguments or conflicts.	.52	.26	−.20	.36
I got in a physical fight.	.18	.82	.07	.71
I got into a physical fight when angry.	.11	.82	.07	.68
I threatened to hit or hurt another student.	.30	.60	.11	.59
I hit back when someone hit me first.	.26	.55	.22	.49
I fought students I could easily beat.	.26	.50	−.02	.31
Other students made fun of me.	.03	.04	.92	.85
Other students picked on me.	-.03	.04	.90	.81
Other students called me names.	.11	.02	.85	.73
I got hit and pushed by other students.	.07	.18	.55	.34

Note. Boldface indicates highest factor loadings.

.82 for these items, and this factor accounted for 12% of the variance. Response options ranged from Never through 7 or more times, and a Cronbach alpha coefficient of .83 was found for this scale. This Fighting Scale was moderately correlated with the Bullying Scale ($r = .58$) and had a low correlation with the Victimization Scale ($r = .21$).

Self-reported victimization. Victimization from peers was measured with 4 items that asked about the frequency of being picked on, made fun of, called names, and hit or pushed. Factor loadings ranged from .55 through .92 for these items, which accounted for 6% of the variance in the factor analysis. Students were asked how often each behavior happened to him/her in the last 30 days. Again, response options ranged from Never through 7 or more times and higher scores indicated more self-reported victimization ($\alpha = .88$).

Peer-Nomination Tasks

Peer-nominations of bullying. Students were asked to list names of students for each of the following descriptors: students who are often teased by their peers and students who often tease other students. These names were converted to participant numbers and the number of nominations in each of the two categories (e.g., often teased by peers) was tallied to reflect the number of classmates that nominated each participant.

Friendship network data. Based on previous studies of adolescent friendship networks (Ennett & Bauman, 1994, 1996), students were asked questions about their friends at their school. Specifically, they were asked to identify and list up to eight friends similar in age (but not their siblings) with whom they hang out with most often. Students were allowed to nominate as few or as many students. Research team members emphasized that students differ in the number of friends they have.

Sociometric item. In addition, students were asked to list the most popular girls and boys in their grade.

Psychosocial Measures

With the exception of the Youth Self-Report (Achenbach, 1991), the psychosocial measures used in this study were drawn from a large violence prevention evaluation project (Bosworth, Espelage, & Simon, 1999; Bosworth, Espelage, Daytner, DuBay, & Karageorge, 2000). These measures were developed after a comprehensive review of the literature, focus groups with students that reviewed all of the items, and exploratory and confirmatory factor analysis with a predominantly Caucasian–with a small percentage of ethnic minority students–middle school sample ($n = 558$). A detailed explanation of this instrument development process can be found in Bosworth et al. 1999.

Perceived belonging at school was assessed with 4 of the 20 items from the Psychological Sense of School Membership scale (Goodenow, 1993). Students were asked how much they agreed with these four statements such as "I feel proud of belonging to my school" and "I am treated with as much respect as other students." Response choices included 0 = Strongly Disagree, 1 = Disagree, 2 = Neither Agree nor Disagree, 3 = Agree, and 4 = Strongly Agree (α = .67). Higher scores indicate a greater sense of belonging at school.

To assess students' *attitudes toward violence,* the 5-item Beliefs Supportive of Violence scale (Bosworth et al., 1999) was presented and participants were asked how much they agree or disagree with each statement, such as "If I walked away from a fight, I'd be a coward." Response choices ranged from 0 = Strongly Disagree through 4 = Strongly Agree (α = .71) and higher scores indicated more beliefs supportive of violence. *Positive adult messages about violence* was assessed with a four item scale (Bosworth et al., 1999) that asked students to report what adults tell them about fighting. Respondents were asked to think about the adults they spend the most time with, and indicate how many of them tell them things like "Fighting is not good there are other ways to solve problems." Response choices ranged from 0 = None through 3 = All (α = .75). Higher scores indicated more positive messages about violence from adults.

Selected scales from the Youth Self-Report (YSR; Achenbach, 1991) were completed by the students and the teachers. Internal consistency coefficients for each of the YSR scales were: *Aggressive Behaviors* (α = .88), *Delinquent Behaviors* (α = .75), *Anxiety/Depression* (α = .88), and *Withdrawn Behaviors* (α = .70).

Analytic Strategy

Our data analysis plan included several distinct stages. Preliminary analyses were conducted to evaluate the psychometric properties of study measures within and across sex and grade. Second, analyses were conducted to assess differences in bullying and victimization across sex and grade. Third, correlational analyses addressed the hypothesis of the association between popularity and bullying across sex and grade. Next, peer nomination data were evaluated to determine the extent to which bullies affiliated with other bullies. Finally, an investigation of the subtypes of bullies and victims was explored with k-means cluster analysis, and once groups were identified, differences between groups on psychosocial measures (e.g., belonging at school, peer and adult influences, depression, anxiety) shed some light on how these groups differ from one another.

RESULTS

Prevalence of Bullying, Fighting, and Victimization

Three two-way ANOVAs were calculated to examine sex and grade differences on the Bullying, Fighting, and Victimization Scales. Significant grade differences were followed up with Tukey post-hoc comparisons.

Self-reported bullying. Consistent with previous research, boys reported bullying their peers significantly more than girls ($p < .001$), and 7th and 8th graders indicated significantly more bullying than 6th graders ($p < .001$; see Table 2). To compare our results to previous studies, students who scored 1 standard deviation above the mean on the Bullying Scale were categorized as bullies and those scoring 1 standard deviation below the mean on the Bullying Scale were considered non-bullies. Based on this categorization, 61 students (14.5%) of the sample were in the bully group. A significant sex difference was found between the bully and non-bully group with 22% ($n = 47$) of the males and 7% ($n = 14$) females being placed in the bully group ($\chi^2 = 20.97, p < .001$). Although grade differences did not reach significance, there was a trend of an increase in the percentage of students classified as bullies across grade. Approximately 10% ($n = 13$) of 6th graders, 14% ($n = 19$) of 7th graders, and 18% ($n = 28$) of 8th graders were categorized as bullies ($\chi^2 = 3.58, p > .05$).

Self-reported fighting. As expected, a significant difference between males and females was found on the Fighting Scale, with males self-reporting more fighting in the last 30 days than females ($p < .001$). Grade differences also emerged with 6th graders indicating significantly less fighting than 7th and 8th graders ($p < .01$) (see Table 2).

Self-reported victimization. Sex differences emerged on the Victimization Scale, with males reporting more victimization than females ($p < .01$); however, there was no significant difference among the three grades (see Table 2).

Peer-Nominated Bullying and Victimization

Participants were asked to provide names of students who often teased other students. A frequency score was computed for each participant to reflect how many times he/she was nominated. Two two-way ANOVAs with sex and grade as independent variables evaluated mean differences in the number of bully and victim nominations. Consistent with self-report data, males were nominated more than females ($p < .001$), but no grade differences emerged. In addition, no sex or grade differences were found for the frequency of victim nominations (see Table 2).

Association Between Self-Reported and Peer-Nominated Bullying

To assess the association between self-reported and peer-nominated bullying, differences on peer-nominations between self-reported bullies (scored above 1 standard deviation on Bully Scale) and non-bullies were evaluated. A significant difference between bullies and non-bullies was found. On average, participants in the self-reported bully group received 3.50 bully nominations, whereas participants in the self-reported non-bully group received an average of .98 nominations ($t = -5.27, p < .001$).

Peer Influences on Bullying Behavior

Popularity and bullying. Relations between popularity and bullying behavior was evaluated with correlations between self-reported Bullying Scale scores and two measures of popularity. The first popularity index was com-

TABLE 2. Sex and Grade Differences on Bullying, Fighting, and Victimization Self-Report Scales and Bully and Victim Nominations

Variable	Male Students			Female Students			ANOVA F		
	6th	7th	8th	6th	7th	8th	Sex	Grade	Sex by Grade
Bullying Scale	1.67 (.71)	1.98 (.93)	1.95 (.78)	1.39 (.34)	1.50 (.45)	1.66 (.53)	29.47[b]	6.58[a]	1.00
Fighting Scale	1.51 (.88)	1.71 (.81)	1.54 (.66)	1.08 (.15)	1.26 (.37)	1.31 (.46)	39.52[b]	3.22[c]	1.38
Victim. Scale	2.22 (1.2)	2.42 (1.3)	2.00 (.98)	2.03 (1.1)	1.83 (1.1)	1.84 (.84)	9.14[a]	1.74	1.77
Bully Nomin.	1.94 (3.3)	2.33 (5.8)	2.18 (4.1)	.31 (.69)	.34 (1.1)	.83 (2.7)	23.67[b]	.42	.31
Victim Nomin.	1.42 (3.9)	2.83 (10)	2.37 (9.7)	.75 (2.1)	1.07 (5.8)	1.41 (4.7)	2.80	.66	.23

[a]$p < .01$, [b]$p < .001$.

puted as the number of times each participant was nominated as popular by his/her classmates. The second popularity index was the number of times each participant was nominated as a friend of his/her classmates. Because both sex and grade differences on the Bullying Scale scores emerged in the preliminary analyses, these correlation analyses were conducted separately for sex and grade (see Table 3). Significant correlations between self-reported bullying and popularity emerged for only the 6th grade females. In this case, greater self-reported bullying was associated with more friend nominations ($r = .31$, $p < .01$). It appears that self-reported bullying and popularity was not associated for the other participants.

Similarly, when differences on popularity were calculated between self-reported bullies and non-bullies-as determined by using a cutoff score of 1 standard deviation above the bully scale score mean–no significant findings emerged. Students in the bully group were on average nominated as a friend 4.92 times and students in the non-bully group were nominated approximately 4.73 times ($t = -.41, p > .05$), and those students in the bully group received an average of 3.65 popularity nominations compared to the 4.17 nominations among the non-bully group ($t = .31, p > .05$). These findings suggest that bullies and non-bullies have similar social standing within this school.

Next, the association between popularity and peer-nominated bullying was examined in another series of correlations. In this analysis, frequency scores on number of friends and popularity nominations were correlated with the number of times each participant was nominated as a bully by his/her peers. For 6th grade males, there were significant correlations between the number of

TABLE 3. Correlations Between Self-Reported Bullying and Peer-Nominated Bullying; Correlations Between Peer Nominated Bullying and Peer Nomination Popularity Indices by Sex and Grade

	Males			Females		
	6th	7th	8th	6th	7th	8th
Self-Reported Bully & No. of Friends (Nominations)	−.07	.17	−.04	.31*	.02	.04
Self-Reported Bully & Popularity (Nominations)	−.11	.02	−.03	.24*	−.09	.01
Peer-Nominated Bullying & No. of Friends (Nominations)	.47**	.26*	.10	.09	−.05	.15
Peer-Nominated Bullying & Popularity (Nominations)	.53**	.22	.05	.13	−.07	.22

*p < .05, ** p < .001.

friends and peer-nominated bullying ($r = .47$, p < .001) and the number of popularity nominations and peer-nominated bullying ($r = .53$, p < .001; see Table 3). These findings suggest that many of the students who bully their peers have friends and are rated as popular by students in this school. These associations remained significant for 7th grade males; however, the association was less significant ($rs = .26, 22; p < .05$), and these associations were no longer significant for 8th grade males. No significant associations between peer-nominated popularity and peer-nominated bullying were found for females.

Peer affiliation and bullying. Friendship nomination data was then evaluated to determine the extent to which students who bully their peers affiliate with other students who engage in the same amount of bullying. Of the 61 students who scored 1 standard deviation above the mean on the Bullying Scale (Bullies), 75% of them had a reciprocated friendship (i.e., both students indicated a friendship) tie with at least one student who self-reported bullying others at a similar rate.

Cluster analysis of bullying, fighting, and victimization scales. Cluster analysis was used to identify the types of bully/victim groups in the study sample. Mean scores on the Bullying, Fighting, and Victimization Scales were subjected to a k-means cluster analysis using SYSTAT. The k-means cluster analysis with five clusters provided the most meaningful solution and was consistent with the study hypotheses, which were based on groups that have emerged in the previous literature. Mean profiles from the five-cluster solution iterative partitioning cluster analysis for the participants are presented in Figure 1. The first group ($n = 253$) consisted of those students with scores on the scales below the scale means, indicating low mean levels of bullying, fighting, or victimization in the last 30 days (No Status). The second group ($n = 73$) had the highest value on the Victimization Scale with no elevations on the Bullying or Fighting Scale (Victims). A third group ($n = 64$) had the highest value–above the scale mean-on the Bullying Scale with small mean scores on the Fighting and Victimization Scales (Bullies). The

FIGURE 1. Bullying, Fighting, and Victimization Mean Scale Scores for Five Bully/Victim Subtype Groups

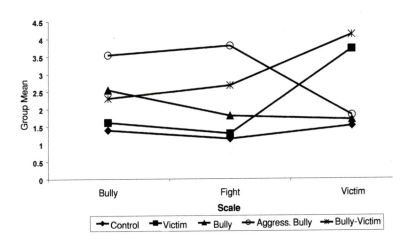

last two groups consisted of few students but were retained as these groups are often cited in the literature as important subtypes of bullying, including Aggressive Bullies ($n = 11$) and Bully Victims ($n = 21$). Sex and grade differences among these groups were evaluated using two Chi-square analyses. Consistent with other findings in this study, sex and grade differences emerged. Seventy-one percent of the females (71%) clustered in the No Status group, 17% in the Victim group, and 11% in the Bully group; whereas, 50% of males were in the No Status group, 17% in the Victim group, and 20% in the Bully group. No females were classified in the Aggressive Bully group and only 1% were Bully Victims. With respect to grade differences, there were significantly more 6th graders represented in the Victim group than 7th and 8th graders, whereas there were significantly more 8th graders in the Bully group than 6th graders (see Table 4).

Finally, differences on the number of friend nominations and psychosocial variables between these groups were examined. Given the small sample size in the Aggressive Bully and Bully Victim groups, these participants were not included in these analyses. Therefore, the sample size for these analyses was 386. To determine how the three groups (No Status, Victim, Bully) differed on the number of friend nominations, and how these differences varied across sex and grade, a two-way ANOVA with sex and grade as independent variables was performed with number of friendship nominations as the dependent vari-

TABLE 4. Demographic Characteristics of Bully-Victim Subtypes Generated from Cluster Analysis

	Bully-Victim Group					
	No Status (n = 253)	Victim (n = 73)	Bully (n = 64)	Aggress. Bully (n = 11)	Bully Victim (n = 21)	χ^2
Sex						34.55[a]
Males	106 (50%)	37 (17%)	42 (20%)	11 (5%)	18 (8%)	
Females	147 (71%)	36 (17%)	22 (11%)	0	3 (1%)	
Grade						25.89[a]
6th	87 (68%)	27 (21%)	5 (4%)	3 (2%)	6 (5%)	
7th	79 (57%)	24 (18%)	21 (15%)	4 (3%)	10 (7%)	
8th	87 (56%)	22 (14%)	38 (24%)	4 (3%)	5 (3%)	

[a] $p < .01$.

able. This analysis was not conducted with popularity nominations because there was too much missing data. Results yielded a significant main effect for group, with the Victims receiving fewer friend nominations (3.84) than No Status (5.15) and Bullies (4.97). No significant difference was found between No Status and Bullies. This main effect was qualified by a significant sex by group interaction with female victims receiving more nominations (4.69) than male victims (3.00). In addition, male bullies received more friendship nominations (5.32) than the female bullies (4.32).

With respect to psychosocial study measures, a series of ANOVAs were calculated to assess differences between the three groups. Significant differences emerged on school sense of belonging, beliefs supportive of violence, positive adult role models, and negative peer influence. Students in the Bully group reported less belonging at school, more beliefs supportive of violence, fewer positive adult role models, and more negative peer influences than students in the No Status experience group (see Table 5). On the Youth Self-Report scales, participants in the Bully group reported more YSR Aggression and Delinquency Scales than both students in the No Status and Victim groups. Victims, however, reported significantly more depression and anxiety than students in the other groups; 5% of the victims scored in the borderline clinical range with an additional 16% that scored in the clinical range. In contrast, only 2% of students in the No Status group and 5% in the Bully group scored in the clinical range. Finally, students in the Victim and Bully groups had significantly higher scores on the YSR Withdrawn scale than No Status students (see Table 5).

TABLE 5. Means (Standard Deviations) Among Bully/Victim Cluster Groups on Friendship Nominations and Psychosocial Measures

Variable	Bully/Victim Group			ANOVA F for Group
	No Status (n = 253)	Victim (n = 73	Bully (n = 64)	
No. of Friend Nominations	5.15 (3.42)	3.84 (3.19)	4.97 (3.35)	4.33[a]
No. of Victim Nominations	.60 (2.2)	4.47 (12.33)	.73 (1.72)	13.52[a]
No. of Bully Nominations	.86 (2.32)	.40 (.91)	3.50 (6.45)	19.32[b,c]
School Belonging	3.96 (.64)	3.80 (.75)	3.38 (.77)	18.01[b]
Beliefs Supportive of Violence	2.22 (.62)	2.48 (.66)	3.02 (.75)	38.00[a,b,c]
Positive Adult Models	3.41 (.67)	3.42 (.72)	2.80 (.63)	22.51[b,c]
Negative Peer Influences	1.38 (.36)	1.49 (.36)	1.97 (.57)	54.64[a,b,c]
YSR Aggression	.32 (.24)	.47 (.33)	.75 (.32)	67.28[a,b,c]
YSR Delinquency	.19 (.19)	.29 (.25)	.59 (.34)	72.94[a,b,c]
YSR Anxiety/Depression	.26 (.25)	.53 (.43)	.39 (.30)	24.97[a,b,c]
YSR Withdrawn	.39 (.33)	.58 (.42)	.46 (.33)	8.67[a]

[a] No Status differ from Victims
[b] No Status differ from Bullies
[c] Victims differ from Bullies

DISCUSSION

Only recently have researchers begun to investigate peer dynamics associated with bullying behaviors and the social standing of students who bully their peers during early adolescence (Pellegrini et al., 1999; Rodkin et al., 2000). Although these studies provided preliminary evidence that bullying and aggression might enhance students' status within their peer group, they did not explore these relations in children beyond 6th grade. However, the analyses in the present study of 6th through 8th grade students quite clearly indicate that students who bully their peers on a regular basis share the same amount of popularity or peer acceptance (i.e., number of friends) as those students who do not bully their peers. This finding suggests that students who bully others are not necessarily socially rejected but do have friends.

Even if bullies do have the same number of friends as other students, this does not necessarily mean that bullying also relates to popularity. Thus, this study further examined the association between popularity and bullying behavior. Students were asked to nominate the most popular students in their grade and to nominate students who often teased other students. Despite the finding that bullies as a group enjoy a strong friendship network, we found bullying and popularity to be differentially associated across males and females, as well as across the three grades. The most striking finding was the strong correlation ($r = .53$) between bullying and popularity among 6th grade males, which dropped considerably for 7th grade males and was not associated for 8th grade males. Without a longitudinal investigation of these behaviors, we can only speculate that bullying becomes less popular over the middle school years for many students. Nevertheless, it appears that the majority of the taunting and teasing within younger boys is seen as an effective and attractive means of interpersonal interaction. Perhaps, boys use these bullying tactics to obtain status within the social structure and over time other characteristics (e.g., athleticism) are more predictive of popularity in boys.

In addition to highlighting how bullying impacts students' social standing, this study also addressed the question of peer affiliation and bullying. For many years, researchers have found that adolescents tend to affiliate with students most like them and are strongly influenced by the behavior of their peers. More specifically, adolescents' health-related behavior (e.g., smoking, drug use, sexuality) has been the subject of much research, and strong support for peer influence on decision-making has consistently emerged (Bauman & Ennett, 1996; Eder, 1995). In line with extant research is our finding that bullies affiliate with students who are like them; that is, bullies hang out with other bullies. An overwhelming majority of students who self-reported bullying their peers at high levels had friends who reported similar levels of bullying. These findings suggest that our prevention and intervention programs should consider peer influences on bullying behavior for young adolescents, especially young males who are transitioning into middle school.

In addition to these findings related to peer influences, other results were consistent with previous literature, including our finding that males were more likely to bully their peers than females, even when bullying was constrained to verbal aggression. Grade differences also emerged with greater levels of self-reported bullying among 8th graders than younger students. Approximately, 14.5% (20% of the males; 7% of the females) of the study sample reported bullying their peers at a high rate (one standard deviation above the scale mean), which is consistent with previous research (Bosworth et al., 1999; Hoover et al., 1992).

Our final study objective and hypothesis related to the subtypes of bullies and victims. Using cluster analysis, we identified five groups of students, including those typically found in the literature (i.e., No Status, Bullies, Victims). While we found support for two additional groups–Aggressive Bullies and Bully-Victims–these groups consisted of a small number of students; therefore, we were not able to learn much about these subtypes. We did, however, find that about 1/5th ($n = 15$) of Victims reported clinical levels of de-

.pression and anxiety. Victims within elementary schools have perpetually been described as having psychological adjustment difficulties (Craig, 1998; Olweus, 1994), but few studies have included students in their middle school years. Our finding adds to this literature by finding that students who are victimized by their peers on a regular basis are at-risk for serious psychological adjustment problems which needs to be addressed by school administrators and personnel.

In summary, results from this investigation suggest that bullies share a similar number of friends as those students who do not bully. Furthermore, bullying among 6th grade males was associated with popularity; that is, students who often bullied their peers were among the most popular students. This relationship was not as strong in 7th or 8th graders, which suggests that teasing and bullying among 6th graders might represent a strategy for negotiating the new environment as well as a tactic to gain power and prestige within one's primary peer group. Results also confirmed the previously untested hypothesis that students who tease other students are affiliated with students who report similar levels of bullying. Together, these findings suggest that–like other health-related behaviors (e.g., sex, smoking, drug use)–peers do impact whether a student bullies another student and in some cases bullying or teasing might serve to enhance the status of students within their primary peer group.

We can no longer assume that bullying among young adolescents is a simple interaction between a bully and a victim, rather there are groups of students that are supporting their peers and sometimes participating in teasing and harassing other students. Prevention and intervention programs will be effective only if we learn more about how bullying occurs within a middle school environment where students are vying for power and status within peer groups. Only then can we begin to design programs to educate students about the harmful effects of teasing and harassment and give them the skills to manage, and potentially change, the pressure to hurt their classmates in order to "fit in."

Although our findings provide initial support for the importance of examining the influence of peers on understanding bullying, the study is limited in several respects. First, the data were obtained from self-report and peer-report. Second, bullying was measured in terms of behavior in the past thirty days. Thus, the systematic or chronic nature of bullying behaviors was not assessed. These students did participate in a similar survey later in the school-year, which will allow us to evaluate the stability of bullying and victimization as well as the predictors of these behaviors over the course of a year. Third, the research was conducted with a sample that consisted primarily of White students, with relatively few minorities, and the age range of participants was narrow. However, a particular strength of this study is the high participation rate. These study design problems limit our ability to generalize the results of this research to a more ethnically diverse population from a different age group.

REFERENCES

Achenbach, T.M. (1991). *Manual for the Youth Self-Report and 1991 Profile.* Burlington, VT: University of Vermont Department of Psychiatry.

Bauman, K.E., & Ennett, S.T. (1996). On the importance of peer influence for adolescent drug use: Commonly neglected considerations. *Addiction, 91,* 185-198

Bosworth, K., Espelage, D., & Simon, T. (1999). Factors associated with bullying behavior among early adolescents. *Journal of Early Adolescence, 19,* 341-362.

Bosworth, K., Espelage, D., DuBay, T., Dahlberg, L., & Daytner, G. (1996). Using multimedia to teach conflict resolution skills to young adolescents. *American Journal of Preventive Medicine, Suppl. 12,* 229-255.

Bosworth, K., Espelage, D.L., Daytner, G., DuBay, T., & Karageorge, K. (2000). The effectiveness of a multimedia violence prevention program for early adolescents. *American Journal of Health Behavior, 24,* 268-280.

Corsaro, W.A., & Eder, D. (1990). Children's peer cultures. *Annual Review of Sociology, 16,* 197-220.

Craig, W.M. (1998). The relationship among bullying, victimization, depression, anxiety, and aggression in elementary school children. *Personality and Individual Differences, 24,* 123-130.

Craig, W.M., & Pepler, D.J. (1997). Observations of bullying and victimization in the school yard. *Canadian Journal of School Psychology, 13,* 41-59.

Crick, N.R. (1996). The role of relational aggression, overt aggression, and prosocial behavior in the prediction of children's future social adjustment. *Child Development, 67,* 2317-2327.

Crockett, L.J., Losoff, M., & Petersen, A.C. (1984). Perceptions of the peer group and friendship in early adolescence. *Journal of Early Adolescence, 4,* 155-181.

Dornbusch, S.M. (1989). The sociology of adolescence. *Annual Review of Sociology, 15,* 233-259.

Eder, D. (1985). The cycle of popularity: Interpersonal relations among female adolescents. *Sociology of Education, 58,* 154-165.

Eder, D. (1995). *School Talk: Gender and Adolescent Culture.* New Brunswick, New Jersey: Rutgers University Press.

Ennett, S.T. & Baumann, K.E. (1994). The contribution of influence and selection to adolescent peer group homogeneity: The case of adolescent cigarette smoking. *Journal of Personality and Social Psychology, 67,* 653-663.

Ennett, S.T. & Baumann, K.E. (1996). Adolescent social networks: School, demographic, and longitudinal considerations. *Journal of Adolescent Research, 11,* 194-215.

Espelage, D., & Asidao, C. (in press). Interviews with middle school students: Bullying, victimization, and contextual factors. Journal of Emotional Abuse.

Espelage, D.L., Bosworth, K., & Simon, T.S. (under review). Short-term stability and prospective correlates of bullying in middle School students: An examination of potential demographic, psychosocial, and environmental correlates. Manuscript being considered for publication at *Violence and Victims*.

Goodenow, C. (1993). The psychological sense of school membership among adolescents: Scale development and educational correlates. *Psychology in the Schools, 30*, 79-90.

Hoover, J.H., Oliver, R., & Hazler, R.J. (1992). Bullying: Perceptions of adolescent victims in the midwestern USA. *School Psychology International, 13*, 5-16.

Limber, S.P., Cummingham, P., Florx, V., Ivey, J., Nation, M., Chai, S., & Melton, G. (1997, June/July). *Bullying among school children: Preliminary findings from a school-based intervention program.* Paper presented at the Fifth International Family Violence Research Conference, Durham, NH.

Loeber, R., & Hay, D. (1997). Key issues in the development of aggression and violence from childhood to early adulthood. *Annual Review of Psychology, 48*, 371-410.

Loeber, R., & Stouthamer-Loeber, M. (1998). Development of juvenile aggression and violence: Some common misconceptions and controversies. *American Psychologist, 53*, 242-259.

Moffitt, T.E., Caspi, A., Dickson, N., Silva, P. & Stanton, W. (1996). Childhood-onset versus adolescent-onset antisocial conduct problems in males: Natural history from ages 3 to 18 years. *Development and Psychopathology, 8*, 399-424.

Olweus, D. (1979). Stability of aggressive reaction patterns in males: A review. *Psychological Bulletin, 86*, 852-875.

Olweus, D. (1994). Bullying at school: Long-term outcomes for the victims and an effective school-based intervention program. In L.R. Huesmann, *Aggressive behavior: Current perspectives* (pp. 97-130). New York: Plenum.

Patterson, G.R., Reid, J.B., & Dishion, T.J. (1992). *A social interactional approach: IV. Antisocial boys.* Eugene, OR: Castalia.

Pellegrini, A.D., Bartini, M., & Brooks, F. (1999). School bullies, victims, and aggressive victims: Factors relating to group affiliation and victimization in early adolescence. *Journal of Educational Psychology, 91*, 216-224.

Pepler, D.J., & Craig, W.M. (1995). A peek behind the fence: Naturalistic observations of aggressive children with remote audiovisual recording. *Developmental Psychology, 31*, 548-553.

Rodkin, P.C., Farmer, T.W., Pearl, R., & Van Acker, R. (2000). Heterogeneity of popular boys: Antisocial and prosocial configurations. *Developmental Psychology, 36*, 14-24.

Salmivalli, C., Lagerspetz, K., Bjorkqvist, K., Osterman, K., & Kaukiainen, A. (1996). Bullying as a group process: Participant roles and their relations to social status within the group. *Aggressive Behavior, 22*, 1-15.

Sebald, H. (1992). *Adolescence.* New Jersey: Prentice Hall, Inc.

Youniss, J., & Smollar, J. (1985) *Adolescent Relations with Mothers, Fathers, and Friends.* Chicago: University of Chicago Press.

Zumkley, H. (1994). The stability of aggressive behavior: A meta-analysis. *German Journal of Psychology, 18*, 273-281.

Middle School Bullying as a Context for the Development of Passive Observers to the Victimization of Others

Linda R. Jeffrey
Demond Miller
Margaret Linn

SUMMARY. School bullies create a climate of fear and intimidation that may affect not only those students who are the direct targets of the bullying but also the secondary victims (i.e., those students who witness

Linda R. Jeffrey, PhD, is Professor of Psychology, Rowan University, and Director, Rowan Center for Addiction Studies, and is a licensed New Jersey psychologist. Demond Miller, PhD, is Assistant Professor of Sociology, Rowan University and Director, Rowan Liberal Arts and Science Institute. Margaret Linn is a graduate of the Rowan University Master of Arts in the Applied Psychology program and is pursuing licensure as a professional counselor.

Address correspondence to: Linda R. Jeffrey, PhD, Psychology Department, Rowan University, 201 Mullica Hill Road, Glassboro, NJ 08028 (E-mail: LindaJ2@attglobal.net).

An earlier form of this paper was presented at the Victimization of Children & Youth Conference: An International Research Conference sponsored by the Family Research Laboratory & Crimes Against Children Research Center, June 27, 2000.

[Haworth co-indexing entry note]: "Middle School Bullying as a Context for the Development of Passive Observers to the Victimization of Others." Jeffrey, Linda R., Demond Miller, and Margaret Linn. Co-published simultaneously in *Journal of Emotional Abuse* (The Haworth Maltreatment & Trauma Press, an imprint of The Haworth Press, Inc.) Vol. 2, No. 2/3, 2001, pp. 143-156; and: *Bullying Behavior: Current Issues, Research, and Interventions* (ed: Robert A. Geffner, Marti Loring, and Corinna Young) The Haworth Maltreatment & Trauma Press, an imprint of The Haworth Press, Inc., 2001, pp. 143-156. Single or multiple copies of this article are available for a fee from The Haworth Document Delivery Service [1-800-HAWORTH, 9:00 a.m. - 5:00 p.m. (EST). E-mail address: getinfo@haworthpressinc.com].

the victimization of peers). Results from a survey of New Jersey middle school students indicate that eighth graders were significantly more indifferent to bullying and less sympathetic to victims than fifth graders. Older students were also more likely to identify themselves as outsiders and bully's assistants in bullying situations. In the absence of bullying prevention programs, witnesses to peer aggression become less willing to intervene on behalf of victims and more indifferent to the distress of the victim. The implications of these findings for the prevention of bullying and the achievement of civic responsibility are discussed. *[Article copies available for a fee from The Haworth Document Delivery Service: 1-800-HAWORTH. E-mail address: <getinfo@haworthpressinc.com> Website: <http://www.HaworthPress.com> © 2001 by The Haworth Press, Inc. All rights reserved.]*

KEYWORDS. Bullying, witnesses to victimization, social context effects, middle school socialization, aggression

Bullying has traditionally been viewed as a normative social experience of childhood endured by many but damaging only to a small proportion of individuals. Being bullied has been seen as an unpleasant but inescapable, and for the most part, ultimately benign part of schooling. In an influential educational psychology text from the 1930s, Wheeler and Perkins offered advice about bullying:

> Ordinary teasing, especially on the part of boys, is a common expression of aggressiveness. When it is a source of difficulty in school situations, the victims of the teasing can usually be taught to laugh their way to freedom, or effectively to ignore the teaser. It should be explained to them that teasing is done for its effect and lacking the effect, it will cease. (1932, p. 433)

Teachers and school administrators generally greeted the problem with fatalistic resignation, minimized its possible consequences, and placed responsibility for its solution on the bully's victim.

Contemporary research findings (Olweus & Limber, 1999; Boulton & Hawker, 1997) indicate that the victims of bullying can rarely be taught to "laugh their way to freedom" from bullying. The emotional and social problems associated with a history of being bullied are now well documented (Olweus, 1993a; Egan & Perry, 1998; Duncan, 1999). Students who are chronic victims of even mild bullying are likely to view school as an unsafe and unhappy place.

Bullying is not only a problem for the direct victims of bullying but also fosters an environment where a hierarchy of domination is maintained through perceived force. A key feature of bullying is its essential public nature: bullying routinely occurs in the presence of other students (Greene, in press; Craig, 1998). Bullies create a climate of fear and intimidation that may also affect secondary victims of bullying (i.e., those students who are not directly the victims of bullying but witness the victimization of peers) (Ross, 1996). While there has been considerable progress in the last decade in the understanding of the effects on children of witnessing domestic violence, (Holden, Geffner, & Jouriles, 1998), the effects of witnessing peer aggression have yet to be fully mapped.

Batsche and Knoff (1994) observe that students are poorly equipped to respond to bullies. The use of power and intimidation by bullies and the lack of effective intervention by school personnel can create an environment where few students wish to spend their day. Sadker and Sadker (1994) suggest that bullying is part of the "hidden" or "evaded" curriculum that must be uncovered in order to create a climate of respect and learning in the whole-school community.

For bullies, victims and bystanders, bullying is a formative social experience with long-term developmental implications. Previous research has investigated the negative consequences of bullying for the victims (Duncan, 1999; Salmivalli et al., 1996; Olweus, 1993b; Sharp, 1995), and for the bullies (Kumpulainen et al., 1998; Stephenson & Smith, 1989; Whitney & Smith, 1993). Research has also addressed children who both bully others and are bullied themselves (Boulton & Smith, 1994). More recently, attention has been focused on the role of bystanders in the maintenance of bully behavior. Sutton and Smith (1999) note that bullying research has shifted from a dyadic focus on the characteristics of the bully and victim to the recognition of bullying as a whole group of processes in which a number of children play a role.

Attention to the psychology of bystanders to bullying is important for two reasons. First, bystander psychology is important because witnesses to bullying learn to be passive observers of the victimization of others, and this behavior is not in keeping with the democratic principles underlying public education. Bystanders who are helpless in the presence of another student's victimization learn passive acceptance of injustice. Second, bystander psychology is important because peer reactions may sustain bullying. Mobilizing peer reaction is a promising avenue to preventing bullying.

BYSTANDERS TO BULLYING AND SOCIAL JUSTICE

School-based peer aggression is a context that teaches bystanders as well as bullies and victims important social knowledge. Most school mission statements include goals such as the achievement of student efficacy and empowerment as well as civic responsibility and civility. When bullying is allowed to take place in a school, students learn different lessons than those promised by the mission statements. Bullying undermines the central mission of schools in that it robs children of the safe environment needed to learn. Moreover, bystander students who are helpless in the presence of another student's victimization learn to be dominated and powerless in the face of force and intimidation and have important experiences in failing to defend the human rights of others. Hazler (1994, p. 40) observed that the way school authorities deal with bullying teaches all the "children about gaining, using, and abusing power; listening versus telling; negotiating versus demanding; considering the needs, behaviors, and feelings of other people; and the real values of cooperation."

Atlas and Pepler (1998) found that peers were present in 85% of bullying episodes, but intervened in only 10% of bullying episodes to stop the bullying. Smith (1991) referred to bullying as the "silent nightmare" because there is a code of secrecy (i.e., bully victims and witnesses are unlikely to report the act). Reasons suggested for the failure of bystanders to report or intervene include their fear that they will be the next victim (Olweus, 1978, 1993b); their uncertainty about how to help, their focus on the classroom activity, or their lack of confidence in obtaining teacher support to stop the bullying (Atlas & Pepler, 1998); and their embarrassment and fear of retaliation (Clarke & Kiselica, 1997). Pepler et al. (1994) found that 33% of the students did nothing to stop the bullying but thought they should do something. In essence, because there is no reliable way to ensure a bystander's personal safety, many bystanders remain paralyzed by fear, discomfort and anxiety.

A range of bystander attitudes toward bullying has been identified. Some peer witnesses experience discomfort and anxiety (Atlas & Pepler, 1998). Ziegler and Pepler (1993) found that 61% of Toronto students sampled reported that witnessing bullying is unpleasant, but approximately 33% of peers reported that they could join in and bully another student. One-fifth of the students in a study by Whitney and Smith (1993) indicated that they might join in if they saw someone being bullied. In a study by Boulton and Underwood (1992), 29% of the students stated they would not intervene even though they thought that they should help. Boulton and Flemington (1996) reported that nearly one quarter of the children viewing a video of bullying incidents found them "amusing." Rigby and Slee (1991) indicated that there is a developmental trend whereby sympathy for the victims decreased with age. Greene (in press) observes that peers may not act to prevent or interrupt bullying out of a sense of relief that they themselves are not being bullied or from distain for the bully victims.

Randall (1995) measured the child attitudes toward the victims bullying in high-bullying areas. He found that the majority of children were opposed to bullying, perceived bullying as undesirable, and believed that it should be stopped. He concluded that high rate bullying in an area is not associated with weaker provictim responses.

PEERS AND THE PREVENTION OF BULLYING

Peers provide the audience for bullying, but most do not intervene. Peers are both part of the problem and may be part of the solution to school bullying (Atlas & Pepler, 1998). Greene (in press) suggests that bullies are typically supported in their bullying through the attitudes, norms and behavioral responses of their peers.

Olweus (1993b) identified four processes that may influence peers' behavior in bullying episodes: modeling and reinforcement, social contagion, diffusion of responsibility, and social reputation of bullies and victims. Olweus (1991, p. 445) identified three class rules against bullying defining appropriate witness behavior: "We shall not bully other students, we shall try to help students who are being bullied, and we shall make a point to include students who become easily left out."

Atlas and Pepler (1998) suggest that intervention with peers to combat bullying requires defining bullying for students, providing strategies, and developing a language or script for intervening. Pepler et al. (1993) suggests that students may need assistance in becoming aware of how they may inadvertently support bullying. Sharp (1996) emphasizes the importance of rehearsal and role-play to develop verbal defense strategies. Sharp and Cowie (1994) have advocated the training of peer helpers to intervene in bullying episodes.

Olweus and Limber (1999) identified seven roles for peer bystanders to bullying: those who (1) initiate the bullying behavior; (2) actively support the bully; (3) less actively support the bully; (4) passively support the bully; (5) are disengaged onlookers; (6) show distain for the bully; and (7) defend the victim. Sutton and Smith (1995) identified four bystander roles: (1) reinforcer; (2) assistant or follower; (3) defender of victim; and (4) outsider (doing nothing or staying away).

The purpose of this study was to obtain information about the attitudes and feelings of middle schoolers about bullying, bullies and victims, and the roles that they identified with in the bullying interaction. This information allows the social mapping of bullying to be more fully defined for age and gender. Based upon previous research findings (Salmivalli et al., 1996; Randall, 1995), it was hypothesized that female students would be more sympathetic to victims than male students, and that the male students would more often identify with roles supportive of bullying. It was also hypothesized that younger children (i.e., fifth graders) would be more sympathetic toward victims than older children (Rigby & Slee, 1991).

METHOD

The student body of a public middle school in an ethnically diverse, southern New Jersey suburban school district was surveyed with a modified English version of the questionnaire used by Olweus in Norway (Olweus, 1995). The sample included five classes of fifth grade (n = 123), five classes of sixth grade (n = 124), five classes of seventh grade (n = 113), and five classes of eighth grade (n = 110). The total number of subjects surveyed was 470, 236 boys and 234 girls. Parental consent was obtained for participation in the study. The questionnaires were administered within a one-week period in classroom settings during the regular school day. Thirty-five questions were asked with respect to age, gender, number of friends, and bullying behavior of self and others. Five additional questions concerning students' feelings and attitudes about the bully, victim, and bullying were also asked.

RESULTS

Frequency of Victimization

The numbers of students indicating that they have been bullied are reported by grade in Table 1 and by gender in Table 2. By sixth grade the majority of students had been bullied. Seventh grade had the highest bullying rate. Seventh graders also reported the highest rate of race-related name-calling. Fifth and eighth graders reported the highest weekly experience of bullying. Having been bullied was a normative experience for the eighth graders. According to chi-square analysis, significantly more fifth graders describe themselves as never having bullied another child [X^2 = 42.446, p < .000] when compared to eighth graders. Over 60% of eighth graders indicated that they had bullied other children at least once. Only 20% of fifth graders reported that they had bullied others.

Gender and Bullying

The majority of both male and female students reported being bullied. About 30% of both male and female students reported being bullied within five days of completing the survey. Female students reported more occasional bullying, but almost twice as many males than females reported weekly bully-

TABLE 1. Number of Students Bullied in Middle School (by Grade of Victim)

Frequency of being bullied	5th grade	6th grade	7th grade	8th grade
Never	52.8%	46.3%	38.7%	42.7%
Once or twice	25.2%	37.4%	33.3%	35.5%
Once a month	10.6%	11.4%	20.7%	10%
Once a week Several times a week	5.7%	2.4%	5.4%	3.6%

TABLE 2. Number of Students Bullied (by Gender of Victim)

Frequency of being bullied	Male Students	Female Students
Never	49.6%	41.2%
Once or twice	29.5%	36.1%
Once a month	10.3%	15.9%
Once a week or more	10.7%	6.8%

ing experiences. Male students were more frequently hit, kicked or hurt in other physical ways. Females were more frequently the recipients of indirect bullying, such as exclusion from a group. Most students reported being bullied by a student in the same grade. Although both males and females report being bullied by males, it was found to be more common for females to be bullied by males [$X^2 = 55.6, p < .000$].

Student Attitudes and Feelings About Bullying

More males than females reported that they think it is fun to make trouble for other students [$X^2 = 30.9, p < .000$]. The rate of reports of indifference about other children being bullied varied four-fold from 9% of the fifth graders to 36% of the eighth graders. While almost 30% of fifth graders indicated that bullying upset them a lot, only 12% of the eighth graders felt upset about bullying.

The feelings that eighth graders associated with witnessing bullying were indifference (36%), helplessness (23%), excitement (17%), fear (15%), and relief (9%). In contrast, fifth graders felt fear (49%), helplessness (28%), indifference (9%), excitement (8%) and relief (6%). Chi-square analysis indicates a statistically significant difference in the responses of the fifth and eighth graders [$X^2 = 44.35, p < .000$]. Fifth graders appear to be more helpless and fearful because they may have no power to control a given situation whereas the eighth graders tend to be more indifferent. For both the younger and older middle schoolers, relief at not being the target of the bullying was less frequently reported than other reactions.

Gender differences in emotional reactions to bullying were evident. Male students felt fear (29%), excitement (23%), indifference (19%), helplessness (19%) and relief (10%). Female students felt fear (34%), helplessness (31%), indifference (22%), relief (8%), and excitement (6%). Overall, more female students reported feelings of helplessness while male students reported excitement when watching someone being bullied [$X^2 = 28.94, p < .000$]. (See Table 3.)

Student Attitudes and Feelings About Bullies

By far, fifth graders were statistically less likely than eighth graders to report that they feel indifferent about the bully [$X^2 = 41.67, p < .000$]. The fifth graders were more likely than eighth graders to indicate that they are angry when they saw another student bullied [$X^2 = 14.41, p < .000$]. Few students reported admiration for the bully at any grade level, especially eighth grade. However, more male students (15%) expressed admiration for bullies than did female students (4%). (See Table 4.)

Student Attitudes and Feelings About Victims

The indifference of eighth graders toward bullying was also evident in their reported attitudes towards the victim. Eighth graders reported indifference toward the victim of bullying significantly more frequently than fifth graders [$X^2 = 4.14, p < .05$]. The majority of fifth graders (64%) felt unhappiness for the victim. Almost 60% of female students expressed unhappiness about the victim. Males more often than female students felt satisfied that the victim was receiving what he/she deserved [$X^2 = 10.10, p < .001$].

Student Identification with Bullying Roles

Students were asked what role they played in bullying: bully, victim, bully's assistant, victim's defender, or outsider. Eighth graders were more likely to as-

TABLE 3. When You See Someone Being Bullied, How Do You Feel? (by Gender of Respondent)

	Percentage of Student Response by Gender	
	Male	Female
Excited, because I like a good fight.	23.4%	6.2%
Fearful, because I am not sure what will happen next.	29.3%	33.5%
Indifferent, because I do not really care.	18.9%	21.6%
Relieved, because it is not happening to me.	9.5%	7.5%
Helpless, because I do not believe that I can stop it.	18.9%	31.3%

TABLE 4. When You See Someone Bullying Another Student, How Do You Feel About the Bully? (by Grade of Respondent)

	Percentage of Students by Grade			
	5th	6th	7th	8th
I admire him/her	9.6%	10.6%	9.2%	6.4%
I feel angry toward him/her.	66.1%	47.2%	43.1%	37.6%
Indifferent I do not care one way or another.	7%	23.6%	29.4%	43.1%
Helpless, because I do not believe I can stop him/her.	13%	17.9%	15.6%	11.9%

sist the bully while fifth graders were more likely to defend the victim [X^2 = 9.58, $p < .002$]. While over half (52%) of the eighth graders view themselves as outsiders, only 38% of the fifth graders view themselves as outsiders.

Males were just as likely as females to assist bullies or defend victims. Both male and female students most frequently reported being outsiders.

When asked to select a role, that of bully or victim, fifth graders were more likely to select victim and less likely than eighth graders to select bully [X^2 = 60.862, $p < .000$]. (See Table 5.)

CONCLUSION

Students bullying others and being bullied is common in the southern New Jersey suburban middle school surveyed in this study. In the absence of a

TABLE 5. When a Bullying Incident Occurs, Rate Yourself in One of the Following Categories (by Gender of Respondent)

	Male	Female
Bully	12.7%	6.7%
Victim	14.5%	6.7%
Assistant to bully	9.1%	6.2%
Defender of victim	23.2%	32%
Outsider (doesn't take sides, stays away)	40.5%	48.4%

whole-school prevention program, by fifth grade close to half of the students have been bullied, and by eighth grade the majority of students, both male and female, have been bullied. Moreover, over one-tenth of both fifth and eighth graders reported being bullied weekly. Almost one-third of both male and female students reported being bullied at least once in the last five days.

The specific bullying experiences reported by the students were emotionally and physically abusive, and included racially-based name-calling. Students reported being hit, kicked or hurt in other ways, in the context of bullying. More male students were directly physically bullied while more female students reported indirect bullying.

Both gender and grade effects were evident in student attitudes and feelings about bullying. Many male students reported that they think it is fun to make trouble for other students. Male students reported feeling excitement and fear while witnessing bullying while female students reported feeling fear and helplessness. Twice as many male as female students reported the belief that victims get what they deserve.

Eighth graders were significantly more indifferent to bullying and to the victim than fifth graders. Moreover, while the majority of fifth graders reported feeling anger toward the bully, the most frequent response to bullies by eighth graders was indifference.

In this study, the students were asked to identify the role that they play in a school bullying situation, i.e., bully, victim, bully's assistant, victim's defender, or outsider. The outsider is a student who pretends not to notice what is happening, does not do anything to stop the bullying or take sides, and tries to stay away. More students in the higher grades identified themselves as outsiders than did the fifth graders. Eighth graders were more likely to report assisting the bully while fifth graders were more likely to defend the victim. When asked to select a role, bully or victim, eighth graders were more likely than fifth graders to select bully.

If bullying is the middle school context for learning the hidden curriculum of peer aggression, power and control, what are the lessons students learn in this public school district? In the absence of a whole-school bullying prevention program, the anger and distress expressed by the fifth graders may become the indifference reported by the eighth graders. Students may lose their sense of righteous indignation at the victimization of others. If adults do not provide information and instruction to combat bullying nonviolently, students fall back on the resources available to them. One way students feel safer is to develop the avoidance skills of the outsider role and to become emotionally indifferent to bullying and the distress of the victim. This indifference to bullying then further contributes to the school culture that makes bullying possible.

Another way available to students to help themselves feel safer is to become the bully's assistant and to identify more with bullies than victims. The results of this study indicate that the eighth graders in this school district are using these strategies to deal with the threat of bullying. Because they seek safety from bullying, students who enter middle school viewing themselves as victim's defenders may leave middle school acting as the bully's assistant.

Taking the role of the outsider, i.e., seeking safety by removing oneself from the fray, has its own negative consequences. The middle school student learns self-protective distancing from aggression that carries with it the price of loss of sympathy and identification with the victim. A valuable opportunity for learning personal efficacy and social empowerment is lost. Students are taught to act cowardly in the face of bullying. Instead of a just community based on the democratic principles of individual rights and social responsibility, a group of isolated outsiders emerges.

In this study eighth graders expressed little admiration for bullies but selected the role of bully over that of victim. It is possible that their role selection was based on a perception of the discomfort associated with being a victim more than a desire to be a bully. The results of this study present a developmental anomaly: the younger children reported a more mature concern for victims and their distress than did the older children. Longitudinal research · tracking the social cognition of middle schoolers as they progress from fifth through eighth grade may shed further light on these differences.

The gender effects reported in this study also suggest the importance of systematic incorporation of nonviolent concepts of masculinity and femininity into bullying prevention programs. Given the traditional central importance of aggression in the definition of masculinity for many in our society, there is a need to address and understand gender role differences in bullying and incorporate this knowledge in prevention programs. The range of responses, as noted by this study, for male students in their attitudes toward bullying may provide an opportunity for intervention program design. Efforts to combat sexual harassment, racial discrimination and bullying can be linked in the prevention of victimization.

The results of this study suggest that a window of opportunity for building a community of peer justice exists with fifth graders. One-third of fifth graders reported their identification with defending those who are being victimized. This suggests an openness to education that would provide the skills and language necessary to be supportive of their classmates. The anger of the fifth graders toward bullying could be mobilized in the service of building a just school community. Fifth graders have not yet become desensitized to the victimization of their classmates. Further research about the reduction of bullying through community building and enhanced belongingness is needed.

A disturbing finding in this study is the deficit in the older students' sense of personal responsibility to intervene to stop victimization. Middle schools may unfortunately serve as laboratories for the development of individuals who feel indifferent to the victimization of others.

REFERENCES

Atlas, R., & Pepler, D. (1998). Observations of bullying in the classroom. *Journal of Educational Research, 92,* 1-86.

Batsche, G., & Knoff, H. (1994). Bullies and their victims: Understanding a pervasive problem in the schools. *School Psychology Review, 23,* 165-174.

Boulton, M., & Flemington, I. (1996). Social roles and aspirations of bullies and victims. *Aggressive Behavior, 15,* 80-115.

Boulton, M., & Hawker, D. (1997). Verbal bullying–the myth of 'sticks and stones' In D. Tattus & G. Gerbert (Eds.). *Bullying: Home, School and Community* (pp. 53-63). London, UK: David Fulton Publishers.

Boulton, M., & Smith, P. (1994. Bully/victim problems in middle-school children. Stability, self-perceived competence, peer perceptions and peer acceptance. *British Journal of Developmental Psychology, 12,* 315-329.

Boulton, M., & Underwood, K. (1992). Bully/victim problems among middle school children. *British Journal of Educational Psychology, 62,* 73-87.

Clarke, E., & Kiselica, M. (1997). A systemic counseling approach to the problem of bullying. *Elementary School Guidance & Counseling, 31,* 310-326.

Craig, W. (1998). The relationship among bullying, victimization, depression, anxiety, and aggression in elementary school children. *Personality and Individual Differences, 24,* 123-130.

Duncan, R. (1999). Maltreatment by parents and peers: The relationship between child abuse, bully victimization, and psychological distress. *Child Maltreatment, 4,* 45-56.

Egan, S., & Perry, D. (1998). Does low self-regard invite victimization? *Developmental Psychology, 34,* 299-309.

Greene, M. (In press). Bullying and harassment in schools. In R. S. Moser & C.E. Frantz (Eds.). *Shocking violence: Youth perpetrators and victims. A multidisciplinary perspective.* Springfield, IL: Charles C. Thomas.

Hazler, R. (1994). Bullying breeds violence: You can stop it. *Learning, 22,* 38-41.

Holden, G., Geffner, R., & Jouriles, E. (Eds.). (1998). *Children Exposed to Marital Violence. Theory, Research, and Applied Issues.* Washington, DC: American Psychological Association.

Kumpulainen, K., Rasanen, E., Henttonen, I., Almqvist, F., Kresanov, K., Molanen, B., Piha, F., & Tamminen, T. (1998). Bullying and psychiatric symptoms among elementary school age children. *Child Abuse and Neglect, 22,* 703-717.

Olewus, D. (1978). *Aggression in the schools: Bullies and whipping boys.* New York: Wiley.

Olewus, D. (1991). Bully/victim problems among school children, In D. Pepler & K. Rubin (Eds.) *The development and treatment of childhood aggression.* Hillsdale, NJ: Erlbaum.

Olweus, D. (1993a). Victimization by peers: Antecedents and long-term consequences. In K.H. Rubin & J.B. Asendorph (Eds,), *Social withdrawal, inhibition, and shyness in childhood* (315-341), Hillsdale, NJ: Lawrence Erlbaum.

Olweus, D. (1993b). *Bullying at school: What we know and what we can do.* Oxford, UK: Blackwell Publishers.

Olweus, D., & Limber, S. (1999). *Bullying prevention program.* Boulder, CO: Center for the Study and Prevention of Violence.

Olweus, D., & Smith, P. (1995). *The bully/victim questionnaire* (English version). Oxford, UK: Blackwells.

Pepler, D., Craig, W., Ziegler, S., & Charach, A. (1993). A school-based anti-bullying intervention: Preliminary evaluation. In D. Tattum (Ed.), *Understanding and managing bullying* (pp. 76-91). Oxford, UK: Heinenmann.

Randall, P. (1995). A factor study on the attitudes of children to bullying. *Educational Psychology in Practice, ll,* 22-26.

Rigby, K., & Slee, P. (1992). Bullying among Australian school children: Reported behavior and attitudes toward victims. *Journal of Social Psychology, 131,* 615-627.

Sadker, M., & Sadker, D. (1994). *Failing at fairness: How America's schools cheat girls.* New York: Charles Scribner's Sons.

Salmivalli, C., Karhunen, J., & Lagerspetz, K. (1996). How do the victims respond to bullying? *Aggressive Behavior, 22,* 99-109.

Sharp, S. (1995). How much does bullying hurt? The effects of bullying on the personal wellbeing and educational progress of secondary aged students. *Educational and Child Psychology, 12,* 81-88.

Sharp. S. (1996). The role of peers in tackling bullying in schools. *Educational Psychology in Practice, 11,* 17-22.

Sharp, S. (1996). Self-esteem, response style and victimization: Possible ways of preventing victimization through parenting and school based training programmes. *School Psychology International, 17,* 347-357.

Sharp, S., & Cowie, H. (1994). Empowering pupils to take positive actions against bullying. In P.K. Smith & S. Sharp (Eds.). *School bullying: Insights and perspectives* (pp. 108-131). London, UK: Roultedge.

Slee, P. (1995). Peer victimization and its relationship to depression among Australian primary school students. *Personality & Individual Differences, 18,* 57-62.

Smith, P. (1991). The silent nightmare. Bullying and victimization in school peer groups. *The Psychologist, 4,* 243-248.

Stephenson, P., & Smith, D. (1989). Bullying in the junior high. In D. Tattum & D. Lane (Eds.), *Bullying in schools* (pp. 45-48). Stoke-on-Trent: Trentham Books.

Sutton, J., & Smith, P. (1999). Bullying as a group process: An adaptation of the participant role approach. *Aggressive Behavior, 25,* 97-111.

Wheeler, R. & Perkins, F. (1932). *Principles of mental development.* New York: Thomas Y. Crowell Company.

Whitney, I.,& Smith, P. (1993). A survey of the nature and extent of bullying in junior, middle, and secondary schools. *Educational Research, 35,* 3-25.

Ziegler, S., & Pepler, D. (1993). Bullying at school: Pervasive persistent. *Orbit, 24,* 29-31.

Preventing Bullying and Sexual Harassment in Elementary Schools: The Expect Respect Model

Ellen Sanchez
Trina Reed Robertson
Carol Marie Lewis
Barri Rosenbluth
Tom Bohman
David M. Casey

SUMMARY. The Expect Respect Elementary School Project, funded by the U. S. Centers for Disease Control and Prevention, established a

Ellen Sanchez, MEd, AASECT, is Project Coordinator; Trina Reed Robertson, MA, is Project Evaluator, Expect Respect: Elementary School Project. Carol Marie Lewis, PhD, is Associate Director, Center for Social Work Research, University of Texas-Austin. Barri Rosenbluth, LMSW-ACP, is Director of School Based Services, SafePlace: Domestic Violence and Sexual Assault Survival Center. Tom Bohman, PhD, is Manager, Research Consulting, Academic Computing and Instructional Technology Services, University of Texas-Austin. David M.Casey, PhD, is Human Development and Family Sciences, University of Texas-Austin.

Address correspondence to: Ellen Sanchez, SafePlace, P. O. Box 19454, Austin, TX 78760 (E-mail:esanchez@austin-safeplace.org).

This report was prepared on contract with the Family and Intimate Partner Violence Prevention Team of the National Centers for Disease Control and Prevention. The views expressed are those of the authors and do not necessarily represent the views of the Centers for Disease Control and Prevention.

[Haworth co-indexing entry note]: "Preventing Bullying and Sexual Harassment in Elementary Schools: The Expect Respect Model." Sanchez, Ellen et al. Co-published simultaneously in *Journal of Emotional Abuse* (The Haworth Maltreatment & Trauma Press, an imprint of The Haworth Press, Inc.) Vol. 2, No. 2/3, 2001, pp. 157-180; and: *Bullying Behavior: Current Issues, Research, and Interventions* (ed: Robert A. Geffner, Marti Loring, and Corinna Young) The Haworth Maltreatment & Trauma Press, an imprint of The Haworth Press, Inc., 2001, pp. 157-180. Single or multiple copies of this article are available for a fee from The Haworth Document Delivery Service [1-800-HAWORTH, 9:00 a.m. - 5:00 p.m. (EST). E-mail address: getinfo@haworthpressinc.com].

model for the primary prevention of dating violence by addressing bullying and sexual harassment on public school campuses. This three-year project was based on the belief that when bullying and sexual harassment go unchecked in elementary schools, these behaviors condition students to accept mistreatment in their peer relationships, laying the foundation for abuse in future dating relationships. The Expect Respect Project assisted six public elementary schools in Austin, TX in taking a whole school approach to stopping bullying, sexual harassment and gender violence by providing staff training, classroom education, parent education, assistance with policy development, and support services. Data from the first year of implementation showed students in the intervention schools had a significant increase in their: (1) ability to identify sexual harassment; (2) awareness of school policy to protect them from sexual harassment by other students; and, (3) willingness to intervene on behalf of another student. This article represents the project's findings from the first year of implementation. *[Article copies available for a fee from The Haworth Document Delivery Service: 1-800-HAWORTH. E-mail address: <getinfo@haworth pressinc.com> Website: <http://www.HaworthPress.com> © 2001 by The Haworth Press, Inc. All rights reserved.]*

KEYWORDS. Bullying, sexual harassment, school violence, gender violence, school-based prevention, elementary school, victimization

The school shootings of the past two years and the recent incident in Central Park force us to face issues that up until now we've allowed to remain somewhere far from the forefront of our minds. We no longer have the luxury of ignoring what has been an ugly part of our common culture and a painful part of growing up for most American children. Bullying, sexual harassment and gender-based violence create a range of social and academic problems for many of our young people, beginning in elementary school and continuing through high school. They always have. The recent tragedies move us as a nation to confront these abusive behaviors and search for ways to stop them.

HISTORY OF THE PROJECT

SafePlace: Domestic Violence and Sexual Assault Survival Center is the Austin/Travis County community's primary provider of comprehensive sexual and domestic violence prevention, intervention, education and advocacy services. Since the inception of SafePlace's parent agencies in the mid-1970s SafePlace has developed and provided domestic violence and sexual assault and abuse services in response to the needs of the community. In the late 1980s, when counselors from local schools began requesting counseling for girls in violent dating relationships, domestic violence counselors began providing support to students at school, beginning a nationally-recognized dating and sexual violence prevention and intervention program for boys and girls now known as *Expect Respect*. After more than a decade, SafePlace has continually provided school-based sexual harassment and dating violence prevention and intervention to Austin-area youth.

Sexual harassment and dating violence as well as the bullying behaviors that precede such gender-based violence are rampant in schools and among school-age youth. However, a majority of school personnel and teachers are not properly addressing these behaviors with the seriousness they demand. Often teachers and school personnel are not confident in their ability to intervene on behalf of the victim. Some school personnel discount these behaviors as inconsequential or consider them to be flirting or teasing, leaving the victims feeling powerless and giving the perpetrators carte blanche to abuse again. Students, after seeing a lack of action by school personnel, do not help victims of harassment, knowing they will not have the support of adults in charge.

Numerous studies and surveys have found that sexual harassment is a significant problem in schools, particularly middle and high schools. A survey of students in grades 8-11 found that 81% of the respondents reported some experience of sexual harassment in school. Of these, 66% said they had been harassed at least once in the halls, 55% in the classroom, 43% on other school grounds, 39% in the gym or other athletic area, 34% in the cafeteria, and 23% in the parking lot. (AAUW, 1993) Such high rates of harassment indicate a lack of action by school personnel. As one 14-year-old female student stated, "I've been harassed in front of teachers and hall monitors, maybe even a janitor or two, and certainly other students, none of whom took any action. They probably dismissed it as flirting, or maybe they were just ignorant or didn't care"(Stein, Marshall and Tropp, 1993, p. 3,5).

The AAUW survey also gauged the educational and behavioral impacts of sexual harassment on the targets. From one-fifth to one-third of harassed girls reported experiencing the following educational consequences: not wanting to go to school; not wanting to talk as much in class; finding it hard to pay attention in class; staying home from school or cutting a class; and/or making a lower grade on a test or in a class. Behavioral consequences of sexual harassment included avoiding the person, staying away from a particular place, changing seats in class, and withdrawing from a particular activity or sport.

State and local data also demonstrate that students experience violent and controlling behavior at alarming rates in their dating relationships. A study of 8th and 9th grade male and female students in North Carolina indicated that 25% had been victims of non-sexual dating violence and 8% had been victims of sexual dating violence. A 1997 Massachusetts Youth Risk Behavior Survey, using a statewide and scientific sample of high school students, reported that 14% of students experienced dating violence (7% males and 20% females), 11% had been physically hurt, and 7% had been hurt sexually by someone they were dating. Of 7,000 Austin Independent School District students who participated in educational presentations on dating and sexual violence during the 1998-1999 school year, 11% reported past abuse by a dating partner, 3% reported having abused a dating partner, 29% had a friend that had been abused by a dating partner, 22% had a friend that had abused a dating partner, and 65% knew someone who had been raped or sexually assaulted (SafePlace, Final Evaluation, 1999).

Sexual harassment, dating violence and sexual assault and abuse among school-age youth are not phenomena that occur without warning. In fact, aggressive and harassing behaviors begin much earlier among students in the primary grades. "The antecedents of peer-to-peer sexual harassment in schools may be found in 'bullying,' behaviors children learn, practice, or experience beginning at a very young age . . . Left unchecked and unchallenged, bullying may in fact serve as fertile practice ground for sexual harassment." (Stein, 1999, p. 50; Stein, 1993, Stein, 1995) The National Educational Association estimates that 160,000 students miss school every day or 28 million days per year, due to fear of attack or intimidation by a bully (Fried & Fried, 1996).

MODEL: EXPECT RESPECT ELEMENTARY SCHOOL PROJECT

In 1997, SafePlace received one of ten grants awarded by the Centers for Disease Control and Prevention to develop, implement and evaluate an intimate partner violence prevention program in twelve Austin Independent School District (AISD) elementary schools. The project was rooted in the belief that social acceptance of violence in personal relationships is a major cause and perpetuating factor in the occurrence of dating and domestic violence, and that children exposed to a culture which accepts bullying and sexual harassment in school or domestic violence at home are at increased risk for using and accepting violence in their own relationships. The project was designed to assist schools in addressing bullying and sexual harassment on their campuses, which, left unchecked, condition students to accept mistreatment in their peer relationships and lay the foundation for dating and domestic violence later in their lives.

For the Expect Respect Elementary School Project, SafePlace conducted a survey of 1,500 fifth graders in 12 AISD elementary schools. As expected, many of the students had been bullied during school hours on school grounds. The survey revealed that 45% of respondents experienced bullying at school or on the bus in the preceding three months. Incidents of bullying occurred in the classroom, in the cafeteria, on the playground, and in the bathrooms.

The Expect Respect Elementary School Project utilized a whole school approach to improve the climate on six intervention campuses. The following five components are described below: (1) classroom education; (2) staff training; (3) policy and procedure development; (4) parent education; and (5) support services

Classroom Education

All fifth grade students in the intervention schools received 12 weekly sessions adapted from *Bullyproof: A Teachers Guide on Teasing and Bullying for Use with Fourth and Fifth Grade Students* (Stein, 1996) facilitated by the project's educators and the classroom teacher or school counselor. The *Bullyproof* lessons helped the students distinguish between playful teasing/joking around and hurtful teasing/bullying. They enhanced students' knowledge about bullying and sexual harassment and developed their skills for responding to bullying and sexual harassment as targets and as bystanders by focusing on courage and taking action. The lessons included writing assignments, role plays and class discussions and were correlated with the state's curriculum requirements by project staff.

Staff Training

All adults working on campus received training to raise their awareness of bullying and sexual harassment and prepare them to respond effectively when they witness incidents among students or have incidents reported to them. Training included discussion of the research on bullying and sexual harassment; strategies for building a consistent response at the individual, classroom and school-wide levels; strategies for classroom management that enhance mutual respect among students; practice using lessons from the prevention curricula; and methods for integrating the lessons into many areas of the curriculum, i.e., social studies, language arts, health. Campus administrators were urged to include all staff in training, and schools were reimbursed for the cost of substitute teachers when required. Special training was delivered to school bus drivers and their supervisors, as much of bullying and sexual harassment occur on the ride to and from school. Intervention schools had a six-hour start-up training by Nan Stein and an additional three hours of training each academic year by project staff.

Policy and Procedure Development

Campus policy and procedures were developed and adopted to facilitate a consistent response by all staff members to incidents they witness or about which they are told. These documents include a statement of philosophy, working definitions of bullying and sexual harassment, expectations for action in response to incidents and reports, and a statement of commitment to maintaining confidentiality of targets, witnesses who report incidents, and students accused of bullying or harassing. These documents were developed with input from staff at all levels and approved for adoption by the school principal and the campus advisory council (made up of staff and parent representatives). The principal at each campus provided training for all staff on the policy and procedures and the documents were distributed to all staff.

Parent Education

Information about bullying and sexual harassment was offered to parents to facilitate their support of the program and to provide them with a common language with which to respond to incidents or discussions with their children in a manner consistent with the project objectives. Parent education seminars were offered and newsletters were sent home with children. Seminars provided information about bullying and sexual harassment, the vocabulary being used with students, ways to respond to and prevent sibling bullying at home, and community resources for help with bullying, sexual harassment, gender violence and domestic violence.

Support Services for Individual Students

Individual and group counseling was made available to students through the school counselor. Special attention was paid to students who were routinely bullied or who were bullying others repeatedly. The Expect Respect Project provided school counselors with a manual of community resources and information about sexual harassment, bullying, and dating and domestic violence. Counselors from SafePlace provided individual counseling to students struggling with any or all of these issues.

Partnerships

SafePlace was the lead agency of the project. As such, SafePlace was financially and programmatically responsible for the all aspects of the project, from development of the design through implementation and evaluation. SafePlace had two partners in addition to the CDC, which provided the funding and technical assistance. The University of Texas at Austin was responsible for the evaluation component of the project. Staff from the Center for Social Work Research of the School of Social Work, the School of Nursing, and the College of Education served as technical advisors and conducted the data analysis. The Austin Independent School District (AISD) had twelve schools represented in the project–six intervention schools and six comparison schools. In addition, Nan Stein, Senior Researcher at the Wellesley College Center for Research on Women served as a consultant to the project. Stein contributed her expertise to all aspects of the project's design and provided initial training on her *Bullyproof* curriculum to SafePlace and AISD staff.

STUDY DESIGN

This study involved a pretest posttest design with four groups, two groups (fall and spring cohorts) of intervention schools and two groups of comparison schools. Each group included three schools. During the 1998-99 and 1999-2000 school years, services were delivered and data was collected for the two groups of intervention schools. Data was also collected from the two groups of comparison schools, although the comparison schools did not receive any of the program services. All project participants were nested within schools (Cook & Campbell, 1979).

During the two years of the project implementation, student and staff surveys conducted at the comparison and intervention schools were collected for analysis of the effectiveness of the services at meeting the project objectives. Staff at both intervention and comparison schools received the staff survey at the beginning of the year and as a follow-up at the end of the school year. Fifth grade students at the intervention and comparison schools received the student survey at the beginning of the year, at mid school year, and at the end of the school year. The fifth grade teachers also received the mid school year survey along with their classes so that analysis could be done measuring the relationship between the survey responses of the teachers and the survey responses of students in their individual classes.

Sample Selection and Size

Elementary schools were selected for this project due to the significant amount of bullying and student-to-student sexual harassment occurring at the elementary school level. Fifth grade students were selected for the classroom education component for three reasons. First, as the oldest students at the elementary schools they serve as role models for younger children. They are also preparing to go to middle school where they may be at risk for more serious forms of bullying and student-to-student sexual harassment. And finally, many fifth graders have already begun to experiment with new roles of boyfriend and girlfriend. It is, therefore, a time when they would benefit from lessons that address safety and respect in personal relationships.

Six pairs of schools that represent a cross-section of the Austin Independent School District were selected. The school pairs were matched on variables including ethnicity, limited-English proficiency, and the socio-economic status of students, the schools' passing rates on the statewide academic skills test (TAAS), total school population, and fifth grade population. Schools in each pair were randomly assigned to either an intervention or a comparison group.

DATA ANALYSIS METHODS–QUANTITATIVE

The study included 1243 fifth-graders from 12 elementary schools within the Austin Independent School District (Austin, Texas). Six schools received the *Bullyproof* curriculum (intervention group), three in the fall of 1998 and three in the spring of 1999. In an attempt to have an equal demographic representation in each of the subgroups (e.g., gender and ethnicity), each of the six intervention schools (intervention group) was matched with one of the six comparison schools (comparison group) that was similar on the proportion of these variables in the school population. The intervention school was randomly selected in each matched pair of schools. The 1243 fifth grade students completed a survey at three time points: pretest at the beginning of the school year (Time 1), late fall (Time 2), and spring (Time 3). A total of 496 students were eliminated from the current analysis for the following reasons: Students were not included in the analysis if they did not take the survey at all three time points; if they had completed the Spanish version of the survey (n = 20)[1]; and if they had changed schools during the school year. Consequently, 747 students from 12 schools were included in the current analysis[2]. Of the students included in the analysis, 362 (48%) were students at the intervention schools.

Due to a small sample size, American Indian (n = 3) and Asian (n = 33) were grouped together with White. Consequently, for analysis purposes there were only three categories for ethnicity: African American, Hispanic, and White/Other. Data on socioeconomic status (SES) was based on whether or not the student and/or their sibling(s) were receiving free or reduced-price lunches. For analysis purposes, students receiving free or reduced-price lunches (low SES group) were compared with the students who did not receive free or reduced-price lunches (non-low SES).

The intervention group consisted of 48% males and 52% females. Of those, 16% were African American, 26% Hispanic, and 58% White/American Indian/Asian. Sixty-seven per cent of students were non-low SES and 33% were low SES (see Figures 1, 2 and 3).

DATA ANALYSIS STRATEGY–QUANTITATIVE

Analyses are based on student answers to a 27-question survey that consisted of multiple-choice and yes-no questions. The two primary methods of analysis of the student survey consisted of multilevel or hierarchical linear models and chi-square analysis. The chi-square analyses were used to analyze changes in student responses to the multiple-choice items on the survey. A six-cell matrix was used to compare the number of students who changed their answers from Time 1 to Time 3 in a desirable or an undesirable direction to students whose answers were consistent for both survey administrations. The responses of students at intervention schools were matched to students at the comparison schools to determine the effect of the project.

Multilevel or hierarchical linear models were fit using the SAS MIXED procedure (SAS Institute, 1996) in order to properly account for variation in bullying and sexual harassment knowledge due to school membership in determining the project effect on bullying and sexual harassment knowledge. One of the dependent variables used in the multilevel analysis was the composite score for bullying (see Appendix). The reliability (Cronbach Alpha) of the composite score was adequate at each of the time points (.67, .69, & .62). The other dependent variable used in the multilevel analysis was the composite score for sexual harassment (see Appendix). The reliability (Cronbach Alpha) of the composite score was adequate at each of the time points (.66, .64, & .62).

Quantitative Results

Knowledge of Bullying and Sexual Harassment

Students in both the intervention and comparison groups showed slight improvement in their knowledge of bullying. However, the hierarchical linear

FIGURE 1. Gender of Students Included in Analysis

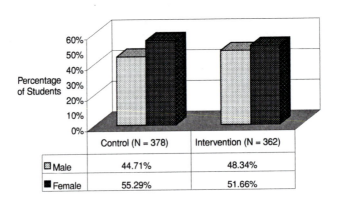

	Control (N = 378)	Intervention (N = 362)
Male	44.71%	48.34%
Female	55.29%	51.66%

FIGURE 2. Ethnicity of Students Included in Analysis

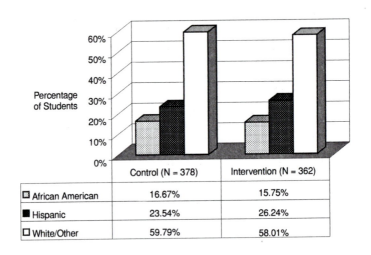

	Control (N = 378)	Intervention (N = 362)
African American	16.67%	15.75%
Hispanic	23.54%	26.24%
White/Other	59.79%	58.01%

modeling (HLM) did not indicate that the classroom education had a significant effect on bullying knowledge for students at the intervention schools. As part of the hierarchical linear model analyses, four separate models were fitted for the bullying dependent variable. Each model tests the effect of the interaction of different groupings of the variables: time, group, cohort and ethnicity and SES. While there were increases over time, none of these models indicated

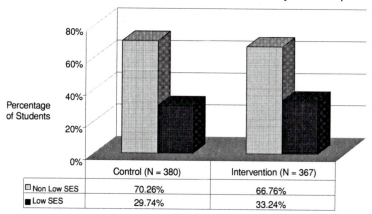

FIGURE 3. SES of Students' Families for Analyzed Group

	Control (N = 380)	Intervention (N = 367)
☐ Non Low SES	70.26%	66.76%
■ Low SES	29.74%	33.24%

statistically significant differences between the intervention and comparison groups resulting from exposure to the classroom education.

In contrast, the hierarchical linear modeling (HLM) indicated that the classroom education did have a significant effect on sexual harassment knowledge for students at the intervention schools. Four separate models were also fitted for the sexual harassment dependent variable. Descriptions of the models are included in Table 1 as well as a table of the F-ratios, degrees of freedom, and significance levels. The Cohort by Time interaction was determined to be significant for sexual harassment knowledge. Therefore the change in sexual harassment knowledge over time can be partially explained by which cohort students were in, i.e., students in the fall cohort showed greater increases in knowledge between Time 1 and Time 2 than the spring cohort, who had not yet received the classroom education. There was a statistically significant effect of measurement time $F(2, 2204) = 113.46, p < .001$. Sexual harassment awareness increased from Time 1 ($M = 7.05, SE = .102$) to Time 2 ($M = 7.65, SE = .098$) to Time 3 ($M = 7.96, SE = .097$). This main effect was qualified by an intervention Group by Time interaction, $F(2, 2204) = 3.59, p < .05$. Figure 4 illustrates the interaction and shows that the intervention group had a larger increase over time relative to the comparison group.

The Group by Time interaction remained statistically significant across the four models. Gender and SES by Time also remained significant in both the models that introduced them as variables.

Figure 5 shows the interaction by plotting the means for each cell in the interaction. The non-low SES intervention group appears to have started higher than other groups and showed consistent increases from Time 1 to Time 3. The

TABLE 1. F-Ratios and Significance Levels for Fitted Effects Models with the Sexual Harassment Dependent Variable

Sexual Harassment Predictors	Numerator DF	Model 1 DDF = 2204	Model 2 DDF = 2200	Model 3 DDF = 2198	Model 4 DDF = 2178
Group	1	2.51	3.39	5.31*	4.26*
Time (Ntime)	2	113.46***	107.18***	108.51***	85.61***
Group X Time	2	3.59*	3.45*	3.59*	3.48*
Cohort (Time)	1	-	0.00	0.06	.05
Group X Cohort	1	-	3.22		-
Time X Cohort	2	-	6.01**	6.07**	6.23**
Time X Group X Cohort	2	-	0.36	-	-
Gender	1	-	-	32.31***	32.60***
Ethnicity	2	-	-	0.34	0.32
SES	1	-	-	7.27**	6.83**
Gender X Group	1	-	-	-	0.89
Ethnicity X Group	2	-	-	-	0.44
SES X Group	1	-	-	-	1.29
Gender X Time	2	-	-	-	0.20
Ethnicity X Time	4	-	-	-	0.60
SES X Time	2	-	-	-	0.09
Gender X Group X Time	2	-	-	-	3.69*
Ethnicity X Group X Time	4	-	-	-	1.08
SES X Group X Time	2	-	-	-	3.89*

Note: DDF = Denominator Degrees of Freedom.   Note * = $p < .05$; ** = $p < .01$; *** = $p < .001$

Model 1 consisted of the intervention group, time of measurement, and the interaction of these two predictors.
Model 2 contained the same predictors as Model 1 with the addition of the cohort (Fall versus Spring) effect.
Model 3 contained the same predictors as Model 1 with the addition of respondent's gender (male versus female), ethnicity (African-American, Hispanic, White/Asian/American Indian), and socioeconomic status (low SES versus non-low SES) as main effect predictors.
Model 4 contained the same predictors as Model 3 with the addition of the interactions of gender, ethnicity, and socioeconomic status (SES) with intervention group, time of measurement, and the intervention group by time interaction.

low SES intervention group showed an increased change from Time 1 to Time 2 but then leveled off from Time 2 to Time 3. The non-low SES comparison group shows a fairly similar increase from Time 1 to Time 2 compared to the low SES intervention group. The low SES intervention group shows a consistent increase over time.

FIGURE 4. Interaction Between Measurement Time and Group for Sexual Harassment Score

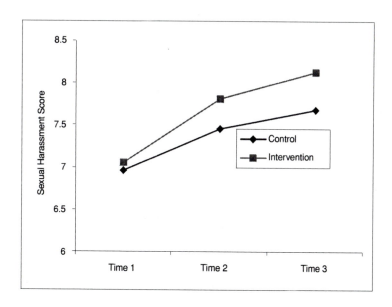

FIGURE 5. Interaction Between Time, Group (Intervention versus Comparison) and Social Economic Status (Free Lunch versus No-Free Lunch)

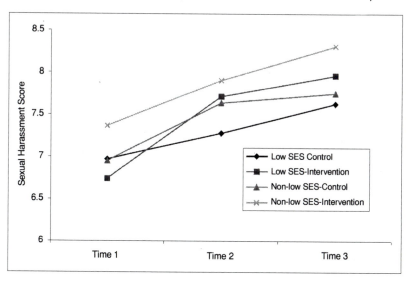

There was also an interaction of Group by Time by Gender, $F(2, 2178) =$ 3.89, $p < .05$. Figure 6 shows the interaction that indicates that males in the intervention group showed a greater gain than males in the comparison group from Time 2 to Time 3. Females in the intervention group showed a greater increase than females in the comparison group from Time 1 to Time 3.

Awareness of Bullying at School

Students were asked, "How often in the past week have you seen any bullying at school or on the bus?" Response options were "not at all," "once or twice," or "almost everyday." The difference in the change scores between the comparison and intervention schools was statistically significant, $X^2(2, N = 723) = 7.00$, $p < .05$. More students at the intervention schools reported seeing bullying more often at Time 3 than they did at Time 1 (see Figure 7). At Time 3, 59% of all students reported that they that they had seen bullying "once or twice" or "almost everyday" in the past week (45% and 14% respectively).

Although change scores were not significant in Year 1, it is also interesting to note that 20% of students reported at Time 3, after the intervention, that they had bullied another student in the past week. Also, at Time 3, 37% of students surveyed reported that they had been bullied in the past three months.

FIGURE 6. Interaction Between Time, Group (Intervention versus Comparison) and Gender (Females versus Males)

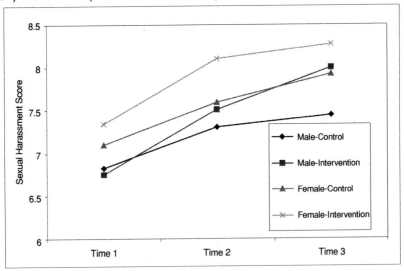

FIGURE 7. "How Often in the Past Week Have You Seen Any Bullying at School or on the Bus?" Change Scores for Response Options: "Not At All," "Once or Twice," or "Almost Everyday"

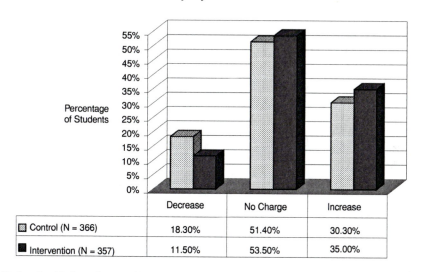

	Decrease	No Charge	Increase
Control (N = 366)	18.30%	51.40%	30.30%
Intervention (N = 357)	11.50%	53.50%	35.00%

Behavior Related to Bullying at School

The project had the effect of increasing the students' expectations of themselves, rather than that of the school staff. Students in the intervention group indicated that following the project they were more likely to take personal action on behalf of a target. Their responses also indicated that after the project they were less likely to tell an adult about a name-calling incident. There was statistically significant change for the intervention group on the question, "What would you do if you heard students calling another student mean names?" Fewer students at intervention schools indicated at Time 3 that they would "tell an adult at school" about a name calling incident when compared to the percentage for the same response item at Time 1, $X^2(2, N = 747) = 4.275$, $p < 0.05$ (see Figure 8).

There was also a statistically significant difference between the intervention and comparison groups on this question. At Time 3, 56% of the comparison group compared to 47% of the intervention group reported that they would tell an adult (see Figure 9). This change was statistically significant at conventional level $p < 0.05$, $X^2(2, N = 747) = 5.94$.

There was also a significant difference at Time 3 for the change in reports between the intervention and comparison groups for the response group "take personal action," $X^2(2, N = 747) = 4.12$, $p < 0.05$. That is, a greater percentage

FIGURE 8. "What Would You Do if You Heard Students Calling Another Student Mean Names?" Intervention Group: Change From Time 1 to Time 3

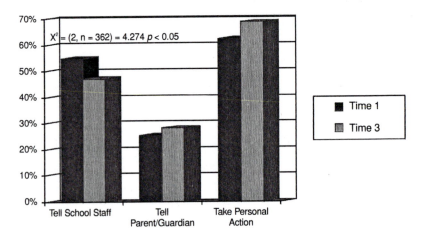

FIGURE 9. "What Would You Do If You Heard Students Calling Another Student Mean Names?" Intervention Group vs. Comparison Group at Time 3

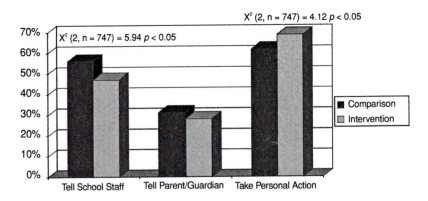

of the intervention group compared to the comparison group indicated that they would "tell the students to stop calling another student mean names," "help the student get away from the bully" or "hit, kick or shove the bully" (see Figure 9).

When students were asked, "What would you do if you saw one student beating up another student at school?" personal action again included the response options 'tell the bully to stop," "help the student get away from the bully" and "hit, kick or shove the bully." There was a significant difference for the change in reports from Time 1 to Time 3 for the intervention groups on the response options indicating that they would take personal action, X^2 (2, n = 362) = 16.927 $p < 0.001$ (see Figure 10). The change intervention students indicated in their intention to tell an adult at school or a parent about this kind of bullying did not meet the conventional definition of statistical significance.

At Time 3, there was also a significant difference between the intervention and comparison groups, $X^2(2, N = 747) = 4.80, p < 0.05$. Specifically, 61% of the intervention group compared to 49% of the comparison group indicated they would "tell the bully to stop beating up another student."

DATA ANALYSIS METHODS–QUALITATIVE

Focus group interviews were conducted at each of the six intervention schools. The focus groups sessions were divided into three distinct participant groups: girls, boys and 5th grade teachers.[3] All teachers were invited to participate in the focus group discussions and only one teacher chose not to participate. Students were selected at random based on previous parental permission to participate in the evaluation of the Expect Respect Project. Students were

FIGURE 10. "What Would You Do if You Saw One Student Beating Up Another Student at School?"

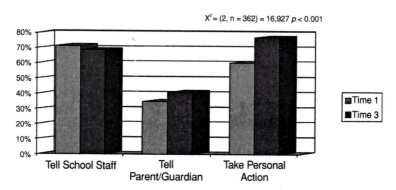

Intervention Group Change Over Time

$$X^2 = (2, n = 362) = 16,927 \, p < 0.001$$

At Time 3, there was also a significant difference between the intervention.

also given an opportunity to choose not to participate. No student exercised that option.

The focus group sessions were audio-taped and lasted one hour (plus or minus 15 minutes). The project evaluator facilitated all focus groups. A research assistant was present to take notes. Teacher sessions were held after school, with the exception of one school where arrangements were made to conduct the focus group session during school hours. Student sessions were all held during school hours.

Tapes were transcribed then reviewed and coded for themes. The themes and transcripts were then reviewed again to ensure that coding was consistent with the identified themes. A report was presented to the project evaluator by staff at the Center for Social Work Research. The report was then compared to the theme analysis by the project evaluator.

QUALITATIVE RESULTS

In examining the transcripts from student and teacher focus groups, two specific themes were identified related to the project's impact on students. The themes were: (1) students' conceptual awareness of bullying and sexual harassment; and (2) students' behavior. The data supports the finding of greater student awareness of bullying and sexually harassing behavior, their own and that of their peers. Although staff and students reported that students were more likely to intervene when someone was being bullied, neither reported that bullying had stopped.

Awareness of Bullying at School

Both students and teachers reported that the project increased student awareness of the behavior that constitutes bullying and sexual harassment, the potential impact on targeted students, and strategies for handling it. The students said:

> I learned . . . that just because of their gender and their body parts doesn't mean that you have to make fun of them, because it is like a part of nature.

> We learned how to respect each other.

> If someone is bothering you, you could be like tell the teacher, or just walk away and ignore them, or tell an adult.

Some teachers expressed surprise at the students' expression of empathy and internal questioning. Teachers described the project's effect on student awareness with the following statements:

It helped establish clear boundaries between acceptable and unacceptable behavior.

And I basically feel that the program really helped establish an awareness of the bullying concepts and sexual attitudes, and sexist attitudes that we are dealing with in society, so I think it was very informative for the children. I could really see them soul-searching, okay, who did I hurt and how is that going to be perceived.

I guess maybe the surprise that might have hit me the most maybe how, was how some of the students were kind of empathetic towards one student who acts out a lot in my classroom. And so, I mean, because he acts out that he's setting himself up to be an easy target. But yet, there was instead of . . . I don't know attacking him or, you know, bullying him in a sense, they, there was some empathy there.

They were made aware of each other, being able to identify other children's behavior. Their behavior did not necessarily improve, but I think the awareness gave them a little more strength in not accepting bullying . . . The bully has not got the power that maybe they had before.

Teachers also reported that the project improved the students' vocabulary for describing bullying situations. Before the project, bullying reports were often labeled as "tattling" and dismissed. Following the project, students and teachers had a common language with which to define incidents, behavior, and expectations more precisely. Many teachers reported a noticeable increase in reports of bullying.

The students' ability to describe bullying and sexual harassment with specific vocabulary seemed to make them more conscious about the issues of bullying and sexual harassment, and what they say to each other.

I think it's been more positive in my class. It's given us a point of reference to deal with situations. Hasn't necessarily gotten any better, but we've dealt with it more effectively.

For me, I don't think there were more instances, probably [*sic*] people were finally telling us about it. They felt much more comfortable reporting.

Like she said, it wasn't tattling anymore, it was a real problem. It's something that could be dealt with. They finally came up to us and then we would acknowledge it instead of, "go settle it on your own."

Behavior Related to Bullying at School

While some students and teachers reported that bystander behavior did not change, others gave specific examples of students intervening on behalf of another student who was being bullied. The students indicated in the surveys that they were more likely to intervene on behalf of a target and, on the whole, the focus group data supports these findings. Students said:

> Before Expect Respect I wasn't standing up for my friends and stuff [*sic*] and they would get somebody to jump me or something. With Expect Respect Mr. Johnson told us not to be scared and to show our feelings. Then when they were picking on my friend, I said now leave her alone because I got tired of them picking on her everyday . . .

> Some people they taking up for people. Before Expect Respect . . . they take up for people now . . . well sometimes.

> This boy has learning problems and he has a really nice sister, a lot of people tease and bully him. And now I stand up for him, now I know who his sister is and she's really nice. Sometimes I feel bad because if there wasn't Expect Respect I probably wouldn't stick up for him.

Many of the teachers expected that students would stop bullying each other as a result of the *Bullyproof* lessons in their classrooms. The project staff did not share this expectation due to the limited time that students would be discussing the issues during the Expect Respect sessions. Focus group data is inconclusive on this point. Some students and teachers reported positive change, while others reported negative change or no change at all. In some of the focus group sessions there were individuals who gave conflicting opinions about behavior change. For example, one student said:

> Some people they still fighting and fussing at each other. A whole bunch of people, they're not fighting and fussing at each other, but sometimes they are. We don't have a lot of fights in our class no more . . .

While teachers at different schools said:

> It was disturbing to me at the first when I saw more bullying, it really was.

> I think awareness is probably the biggest thing, and probably the biggest disappointment is behavior did not really change.

Teachers across the six schools also indicated that some students were using mild cases of bullying to get attention. Many of the teachers acknowledged this testing of new limits as typical behavior for this age group.

I think about 2 or 3 weeks into the project they started trying out the scenes on us, and seeing how far we would let it go if we knew it was happening. Like they really wanted to make us aware we're doing this, what are you going to do about it now?

But as we mentioned, I think the other thing is that it also gave them, some . . . not ideas, but it made them think, "Well, if we do this, then we'll get this kind of attention." It's almost like they are working at trying to get some of the attention now. It seems almost like deliberate choices are being made.

Teachers at one school specifically noted that the severity of bullying that students were involved in was less than in years before the project began.

Well, actually I meant, you know, going back, for me, I've been thinking about it, getting back from it though, and going back over the last couple of years, especially the last couple years, previous to this year. I think that [*sic*] our 5th graders are a lot less prone to be very hurtful.

DISCUSSION OF RESULTS

The Expect Respect Project evaluation examined the project's effect on students' knowledge, awareness and behavior related to bullying and sexual harassment at school. The multilevel analysis indicated that the project had an impact on sexual harassment knowledge. Students in both groups, intervention and comparison, had improvements in their scores for sexual harassment knowledge, but students at the intervention schools demonstrated greater increases in scores for these questions than students at the comparison schools. Knowledge about bullying, however, was not significantly affected by the project according to the multilevel analysis. This can be partially explained by the fact that students had relatively high initial scores on the bullying knowledge questions. It is also worth mentioning that the response pattern for students at the comparison schools suggest that repeated exposure to the project survey may have had some teaching effect for the comparison school students.

Both the chi-square and focus group data analyses indicate that the students developed greater awareness of concepts and recognition of bullying in their environment. In particular, teachers said that the students' increased vocabulary made it much easier to deal with bullying incidents when they occurred.

·When approaching the teachers about bullying situations the students were better able to articulate the specific problems.

The chi-square analyses indicate that students at the intervention schools were significantly more likely to identify bullying more often and in more places at their school after the intervention. The students at the intervention schools were also more likely to take personal action on behalf of a target of bullying when compared to the students at the comparison schools. Students and teachers indicated in focus groups that they saw some increased intervention by fifth grade students in bullying situations.

Important project effects are indicated in three areas of student growth and development: sexual harassment knowledge; awareness of bullying and its' effects; and willingness to intervene on behalf of someone being bullied. One unintended effect of the project as reported by some teachers was an increase in mild bullying by some students. However, teachers indicated much of this increase seemed to be either attention-seeking behavior or normal testing of new limits typically demonstrated by students at this age.

Successes

The Expect Respect Elementary School Project successfully increased student's knowledge of sexual harassment, their awareness of bullying on campus, and the likelihood of them intervening on behalf of a target. The project also increased public awareness through local workshops, media exposure, and through presentations at state and national conferences. As the nation has recognized the relationship between bullying and school violence, requests for help have also increased. In Austin, ten schools that did not participate in the research project requested and received student and staff training from project staff. The school intends to support K-12 prevention education district wide, and SafePlace continues working with the district to develop and implement student-to-student sexual harassment policy and training.

Challenges

A primary challenge to the success of the project was it's applicability to Latino students and their families. Austin's school population is 41% Latino. There are many recent immigrants among this group, and many monolingual Spanish-speaking students. There is no term in Spanish that is equivalent to *bully or bullying* in English. Neither the term nor the concept translates accurately. Difficulty also lies in cultural differences. Gender role expectations vary from culture to culture and with them so do definitions of healthy relationships. This project did not have the resources to adequately address these differences.

The other substantial challenge was getting sufficient time allotted for teachers to be adequately trained on the use of the curriculum and on effective responses to incidents. The emphasis in Texas on standardized test scores has intensified the pressure on teachers and administrators to use all available time for test preparation. As a result, getting a commitment of time for training was extremely difficult.

RECOMMENDATIONS

Addressing bullying and sexual harassment on school campuses requires full support of the campus staff. As mentioned earlier, two factors that are critical to changing the school climate from one that allows mistreatment to one that promotes respect among students are: (1) the adults intervene immediately and in a consistent manner when they witness bullying or sexual harassment, and (2) students are prepared and motivated to take personal action on behalf of a target. The key element in creating this change is the support and investment of the school's principal. S/he establishes expectations for staff behavior and sets priorities for their time and the focus of their attention. A school-wide commitment to the project's goals, as established by the principal, also determines the continuation of activities after the project ends. For a community-based agency to work effectively in schools, time and resources must be allocated to gaining the commitment and full investment of school principals. The project director must be knowledgeable of, and sensitive to school culture and the logistical and political pressures on the administrators and teachers. In the case of the Expect Respect Elementary School Project, a strong relationship between SafePlace and the AISD laid the foundation for a successful partnership.

NOTES

1. The difficulty in administration of Spanish language surveys made the validity of their results highly questionable.

2. There were significant differences between the 496 excluded and the 747 included students, in terms of student's gender, $X^2(1, N = 1186) = 5.27, p < .05$; ethnicity,

$X^2(2, N = 1186) = 18.4, p < .001$; and SES, $X^2(2, N = 1233) = 17.63, p < .001$. There were fewer males, more females, fewer African Americans and Hispanics and more Whites, and more non-low SES students in the included group than the excluded sample.

3. Originally the sessions were divided into only two groups, students and 5th grade teachers. The decision to separate the girl and boys was made after the first student focus group session.

APPENDIX
Questions on Bullying and Sexual Harassment Knowledge

Students were asked to answer the following two questions to assess their bullying and sexual harassment knowledge. Students received composite scores for each question. The composite scores were then used in the multilevel analyses to determine the project effect on each knowledge base.

Which of these would you call bullying?

Check as many as you call bullying

❑ Name calling
❑ Pushing someone
❑ Telling someone to leave you alone
❑ Crowding or cornering someone
❑ Making fun of a person's body
❑ Telling on someone who did something wrong
❑ Hitting someone
❑ Telling mean jokes about someone
❑ Taking things from someone without asking
❑ Not sharing your lunch or snack
❑ Shooting the finger at someone
❑ Not telling someone about your birthday party
❑ None of the above
❑ Other (please write it in)

Which of these would you call sexual harassment?

Check as many as you call sexual harassment

❑ Touching someone in ways that are not OK with him or her
❑ Making fun of someone's private body parts
❑ Having a dream about someone you like
❑ Passing a note that says sexual things about someone's body
❑ Continuing to tell dirty jokes around someone after he or she has asked you to stop
❑ Letting someone know that you like her or him
❑ Asking for someone's phone number
❑ Asking the counselor for information about sex
❑ Pressuring someone for sex
❑ None of the above
❑ Other (please write it in)

Self-Efficacy in a New Training Model for the Prevention of Bullying in Schools

Natasha M. Howard
Arthur M. Horne
David Jolliff

SUMMARY. The present study examined the effectiveness of an intervention program designed to increase teachers' knowledge and use of effective intervention skills for decreasing bullying in middle schools. The project is a replication of a program created at the University of Georgia and piloted in Athens. The *Bullybusting: A Psychoeducational Program for Helping Bullies and Their Victims* program was evaluated to determine its impact on the rate of reported aggressive behavior as well as teachers' perceived efficacy in intervening in bullying situations. Research participants ($N = 11$) were sixth grade teachers employed at a public middle school in Fort Wayne, Indiana; the program was included as a component of the staff development training. The effectiveness of the psychoeducational program was assessed by comparing pre- and

---

Natasha M. Howard, MA, is affiliated with the University of Georgia. Arthur M. Horne, PhD, is affiliated with the University of Georgia. David Jolliff, PhD, is affiliated with Phoenix Associates, Fort Wayne, Indiana.

This study was supported by Project A.C.T. Early, funded by field-initiated grants (R306F60158, R305T990330) from the Institute for At-Risk Children of the Office of Educational Research and Improvement, United States Department of Education and the Centers for Disease Control Multi-Site Violence Prevention Project for Middle Schools.

[Haworth co-indexing entry note]: "Self-Efficacy in a New Training Model for the Prevention of Bullying in Schools." Howard, Natasha M., Arthur M. Horne, and David Jolliff. Co-published simultaneously in *Journal of Emotional Abuse* (The Haworth Maltreatment & Trauma Press, an imprint of The Haworth Press, Inc.) Vol. 2, No. 2/3, 2001, pp. 181-191; and: *Bullying Behavior: Current Issues, Research, and Interventions* (ed: Robert A. Geffner, Marti Loring, and Corinna Young) The Haworth Maltreatment & Trauma Press, an imprint of The Haworth Press, Inc., 2001, pp. 181-191. Single or multiple copies of this article are available for a fee from The Haworth Document Delivery Service [1-800-HAWORTH, 9:00 a.m. - 5:00 p.m. (EST). E-mail address: getinfo@haworthpressinc.com].

181

post-test scores on the Teacher Efficacy and Attribution Measure (TEAM) and the Teacher Inventory of Skills and Knowledge (TISK). Repeated measures and chi-square analyses were employed to test four research hypotheses. Results indicate that the intervention program is effective in increasing teachers' knowledge of bullying intervention skills, teachers' use of bullying intervention skills, and teachers' general sense of self-efficacy in working with students, and reducing the rate of bullying incidents. *[Article copies available for a fee from The Haworth Document Delivery Service: 1-800-HAWORTH. E-mail address: <getinfo@haworthpressinc.com> Website: <http://www.HaworthPress.com> © 2001 by The Haworth Press, Inc. All rights reserved.]*

KEYWORDS. Teacher training, teacher efficacy, bullying

Schools cannot be effective institutions of learning if they are not first and foremost safe. Olweus (1993) estimates that one in seven students is involved, either as victim or perpetrator, in bullying behavior. Because 160,000 children miss school each day due to fear (Lee, 1993), we must take a closer look at one of the major causes of that fear: bullying and related violence. Bullying occurs three criteria are met: (1) there is an imbalance of power in a relationship, (2) the more powerful individual intentionally inflicts, or attempts to inflict, an injury or discomfort onto another individual, and (3) these acts of aggression are repeated over time (Newman, Horne, & Bartolomucci, 2000; Olweus, 1994). Bullying can be either physical or psychological and committed by individuals or groups (Byrne, 1994; Hoover, Oliver, & Hazler, 1992; Olweus, 1993; Stephenson & Smith, 1988). Physical bullying can include kicking, pushing, or beating the victim, while the most common means of psychological bullying are teasing and exclusion. Regardless of its form, bullying disrupts both the educational process and the educational community as a whole (Oliver, Hoover, & Hazler, 1994).

Often considered a rite of childhood and adolescence, bullying engenders a number of negative social, psychosexual, and academic consequences for both the victims and the perpetrators of the aggression (Anderson, 1982; Gilmartin, 1987; Olweus, 1978). Victims of bullying have been found to be anxious, insecure, lacking in self-esteem, and socially withdrawn (Byrne, 1994; Olweus, 1993). The overrepresentation of students as victims in special education classrooms and the poorer performances on intelligence tests by victims is also troubling (Hoover, Oliver, & Hazler, 1992; Roland, 1989b). Similarly, the bullies, or perpetrators of the bullying behavior, have an extended prognosis of problems both in school and out, for they become social isolates from average children or become involved in community problems resulting in police and/or court involvement.

Teachers are an obvious choice for intervening in attacks on students in schools; yet, few make active attempts to decrease bullying. Some teachers remain inactive because they feel ill-equipped to deal with the issue (Stephenson & Smith, 1989) while others believe any action by them would result in more vicious retaliatory attacks or would simply make the attacks more covert (Besag, 1989; Hoover, Oliver, & Hazler, 1992). These and other reservations lead students to believe that teachers are unaware of the bullying endured on a daily basis. Hazler, Hoover, and Oliver (1992, p. 20) noted that the students they surveyed "by and large indicted adults for failing to recognize the severity of the problem." Indeed, some teachers may not be fully aware of the magnitude of the problem as students tend not to turn to teachers or other school staff until there is a particularly troubling or serious issue (Byrne, 1994). Teachers' rate of intervention has been reported to be only 40 percent (Olweus, 1993). It is critical that this rate of intervention be increased, and a key component of facilitating further action is focusing on teachers' control and prevention power in the classrooms (Newman, 1999).

REVIEW OF RELATED LITERATURE

One of the early difficulties encountered by researchers in attempting to draw conclusions about the frequency and effects of bullying in schools was forming a complete definition of what constitutes bullying. Olweus (1973) first began describing aggressive behavior by groups of students toward a victim and naming the phenomenon "mobbing." The definition has since been expanded to include acts by an individual perpetrator (Byrne, 1994; Hoover, Oliver, & Hazler, 1992; Olweus, 1993; Stephenson & Smith, 1988). For the purposes of this research, Roland's (1989a) definition will be used:

> Bullying is long-standing violence, physical or psychological, conducted by an individual or a group, and directed against an individual who is not able to defend himself in the actual situation. (p. 143)

In recent years, bullying has lost much of its playground anonymity and has been studied along several dimensions. Craig (1998) investigated the relationship among bullying, victimization, depression, anxiety, and aggression, finding that male bullies and victims report higher levels of both physical and verbal aggression than do girls. Craig also concluded that anxious children are more likely to be victimized, thereby increasing already high levels of anxiety. The differences between groups of students identified as bullies or victims has been examined, and extensive work has concentrated on differing between direct and indirect bullying (Olweus, 1978, 1993; Pelligrini, 1998) and aggressive and passive bullies (Dodge & Coie, 1987). These works highlight the need for intervention programs to increase teachers' awareness of various types of bullying scenarios as well as improve recognition of different kinds of bullies.

Olweus' (1973) early studies penned the term "whipping boys" for victims of repeated acts of aggression or violence and stressed that these boys (and girls) are actively abused rather than being merely disliked or unpopular. Several researchers (Besag, 1989; Byrne, 1994; Olweus, 1978) have made attempts to classify victims into a number of subgroups, including passive/submissive or provocative. While physical bullying may be both more easily recognized by and more troubling to adults, students consistently indicate that psychological aggression is more difficult to tolerate (Hazler, Hoover, & Oliver, 1992).

THEORETICAL BACKGROUND

"Children learn what they live." "It takes a village to raise a child." We often dismiss these sayings as mere political sound bites, but the adages embody the tenets of social learning theory. Behavior is a direct result of observation (Bandura, 1973). Because children spend such a large proportion of their waking hours in school, it is logical to view the school environment as both the problem for victims of bullying, and as the possible solution to the bullying problem. Ineffective or absent discipline for aggressive acts reinforces children's belief that aggressive acts will achieve a desired goal without negative consequences. Lack of action on the part of teachers and other school personnel may be interpreted as tacit approval (Newman, 1999; Newman, Horne & Bartolomucci, in press).

Teachers will not intervene in bullying behaviors consistently until they feel adequately equipped to act. Action is based more on individual beliefs than on reality (Bandura, 1995). Beliefs in one's ability to organize and execute a course of action is referred to as self-efficacy (Bandura, 1995). The acquisition of cognitive, behavioral, and self-regulatory tools is necessary in building a strong sense of self-efficacy (Bandura, 1995). A successful intervention program, then must have as a central aim an increase in teachers' perception of self-efficacy, the development of appropriate skills, and an understanding of the importance of intervening when bullying occurs.

TEACHER EDUCATION AND INTERVENTION

Recently a new program has been developed to assist teachers and other school personnel in their efforts to become more effective in reducing aggression in the form of bullying behavior. The program, *Bullybusting: A Teacher's Manual for Helping Bullies, Victims, and Bystanders* (Newman, Horne, & Barolomucci, 2000), has been examined for effectiveness in four domains: (1) increasing teachers' knowledge of bullying intervention skills, (2) increasing teachers' use of bullying intervention skills, (3) increasing teachers' self-efficacy, and (4) decreasing the amount of bullying in the school environment (Newman, 1999; Newman, Horne, & Bartolomucci, in press). The authors found that the program was effective in each of the domains examined, resulting in significant increases in teacher knowledge, skills, and efficacy, and a significant decrease in reported bullying, both in the classroom and in discipline referrals to the office. Based upon their research, Newman, Horne, and Bartolomucci report the program to be successful.

The present project sought to replicate and extend the work of the original investigators. Although the results of the original evaluation project by Newman, Horne, and Bartolomucci are impressive, the program's effectiveness should be tested with facilitators other than the original program developers, and there is a need to evaluate the program in additional settings. The developers and investigators of the original study were involved in all facets of the program implementation and analyses. The positive results may reflect the effectiveness of the program, or it may be that the effectiveness found for the program was a result of the involvement of the program's original developers, training instructors, support team leaders, data collectors, and data analyzers. Additionally, not only does the program need to be implemented and evaluated by facilitators other than the program developers, it should also be implemented in a different school setting in order to eliminate the possibility that the program's effectiveness was a function of unique characteristics of the pilot school. The present study implemented the Bullybusters program by a facilitator not involved in the program development or original pilot testing, and in a different area of the country, thereby affording the opportunity to examine possible regional effects. The specific questions examined in the present study were:

1. Does the *Bullybusting: A Psychoeducational Program for Helping Bullies and Their Victims* (Newman, Horne, & Bartolomucci, 2000) program result in an increase of teachers' knowledge of bullying intervention techniques?

2. Does the *Bullybusting: A Psychoeducational Program for Helping Bullies and Their Victims* program result in an increase in teachers' use of bullying intervention techniques?
3. Does the *Bullybusting: A Psychoeducational Program for Helping Bullies and Their Victims* program result in an increase in teachers' self-efficacy?

METHOD

Participants

Research participants for the present study were eleven sixth grade teachers employed at Portage Middle School in Fort Wayne, Indiana. Participation in the psychoeducational intervention program was approved as a component of the school system's staff development activities. Participants received a stipend for participation in the research activities associated with this project.

Treatment Program

This project utilized the *Bullybusting: A Psychoeducational Program for Helping Bullies and Their and Victims* (Newman, Horne, & Bartolomucci, 2000) treatment program. Participants received training in the recognition of bullies and victims as well as specific techniques to address bullying with students. The program was implemented during two six-hour professional development workshops. During the workshops, participants received information dealing with a broad range of issues related to bullying in middle schools. The training proceeded in accordance to specific goals in each of seven modules presented in the *Bullybusting* manual: Awareness, Recognizing the Bully, Recognizing the Victim, Taking Charge: Interventions for Bullying Behavior, Assisting the Victims: Interventions and Recommendations, Bullyproofing Your Classroom: The Role of Prevention, and Bullyproofing Yourself: Relaxation and Coping Skills.

Instruments

Teacher Inventory of Skills and Knowledge (TISK). The TISK assesses teachers' knowledge and use of bullying intervention techniques and was specifically developed for use with the *Bullybusting: A Psychoeducational Program for Helping Bullies and Their Victims* (Newman, Horne, & Bartolomucci, 2000). The TISK is a 58-item self-report questionnaire containing two subscales, "Knowledge" and "Use" of bullying intervention techniques. Six dimensions are assessed on each of the two subscales: prevention, intervention (bully), intervention (victim), intervention (bully/victim), resource, and awareness. Participants identified each item on the Knowledge subscale as U (Unfamiliar), S (Somewhat familiar), or V (Very familiar). Relatedly, items on the Use subscale are responded to with N (Never), S (Sometimes), or A (Always). Newman's (1999) study included analysis of internal consistency reliability yielding Cronbach's alpha coefficients between .79 and .92 for the six dimensions of the Knowledge scale and a range of .71 to .88 for the six dimensions of the Use scale. Our own analysis yielded reliability coefficients ranging between .88 and .98 on the Knowledge scale and .68 to .92 on the Use scale.

Teacher Efficacy and Attribution Measure (TEAM). The TEAM asks participants to respond to a series of seven descriptions of children they may encounter in class. The vignettes were designed in accordance to the seven behavior typologies derived from the Behavioral Assessment Scale for Children (BASC) as applied in the ACT Early Program at the University of Georgia. Those identified behavior typologies are: (1) well-adapted, (2) average, (3) learning problems, (4) mildly disruptive, (5) physical complaints, (6) disruptive behavior problems, and (7) severe psychopathology (Kamphaus et al., 1999). Following each vignette, participants respond to questions relating to attributions for the child's behavior, their expectations for future outcomes, and their sense of efficacy in dealing with this type of behavioral presentation. The expectations and efficacy questions are answered on a five point Likert scale ranging from 1 (Highly confident) to 5 (Highly uncertain). Analysis of inter-item consistency for teacher efficacy items in the original study (Newman, 1999) produced Cronbach's alpha coefficients ranging from .84 to .95 for the seven typologies. In our study, the reliability analysis yielded alpha coefficients between .8 and .96.

Procedure

Upon consenting to participate in the program, participants completed the pre-test measures, the TISK and TEAM. Participants also completed a demographic questionnaire that included information about gender, race, educational background, and years of teaching experience. Following completion of these measures, group training workshops began. The workshops were conducted over the course of two days for a total of 12 hours. During these training workshops, participants received instruction on the recognition and intervention of bullying behaviors. Discussions centered on the practical application of knowledge in the classroom and school-wide setting. Following the training period, participants met every other week for six weeks of ongoing support team meetings. All workshops and support group meetings were facilitated by a doctoral-level licensed psychologist in conjunction with a school counselor. Upon completion of the support group meetings, participants again completed the TISK and the TEAM.

Research Design

A quasi-experimental pre-test/post-test design was utilized in this study. Participants served as their own controls and are compared to the control group of the original study.

RESULTS

Before testing our primary hypotheses, intercorrelations for pre-intervention and post-intervention study variables were computed and are displayed in Table 1.

Paired samples t-tests were employed to test each hypothesis. For our first two hypotheses, results showed that teachers' knowledge and use of bullying intervention skills significantly improved following the intervention program. Means, standard deviations, and paired samples t-tests results are displayed in Table 2.

Our third hypothesis, that teachers' self-efficacy in dealing effectively with students representing all seven of the BASC typologies (Kamphaus et al., 1999), was also supported empirically. Paired samples t-tests for each of the seven typologies were non-significant. However, a general pattern of improved efficacy emerged for all but one of the typologies. Thus, we combined all of the typologies to examine an overall efficacy difference between pre- and post-intervention tendencies. This finding was statistically significant and is also displayed in Table 2.

To test our final hypothesis, that the amount of bullying in the school environment would decrease as a result of the bullying intervention program, we employed a chi-square analysis. Since the first step of the training model involves awareness of bullying behavior, and because the delivery of the program began in March, we excluded the frequency of March bullying incidents from the analysis. This resulted in a more conservative test of the final hypothesis. The average number of bullying incidents for the last two pre-intervention months (January and February) was 13.50, while the average frequency for the two post-intervention months (April and May) was 5.50. The frequency of pre-intervention bullying incidents was significantly different from post-intervention incidents $c^2(1, N = 38) = 6.74, p < .01$.

TABLE 1. Correlation Matrix of Pre- and Post-Intervention Study Variables

Variable	1	2	3	4	5	6	7	8	9
1. BIS Knowledge	-	.19	.26	.46	−.10	−.14	−.15	−.49	.25
2. BIS Use	.93*	-	−.07	.22	.72*	.46	.45	.55	.73*
3. E–WA	−.17	−.26	-	.52	−.46	−.32	−.32	−.48	−.32
4. E–A	.05	−.11	.58	-	−.02	.16	.16	−.30	.45
5. E–DBD	.42	.30	−.43	.04	-	.88*	.82*	.87*	.61
6. E–LD	.37	.29	−.55	−.11	.82*	-	1.00**	.77*	.47
7. E–PCW	.61*	.59	−.34	.13	.70*	.84*	-	.77*	.48
8. E–SP	.26	.20	−.41	.25	.52	.78*	.71*	-	.27
9. E–MD	−.12	−.20	−.01	.28	.17	.37	.18	.74*	-

Note. BIS = Bullying Intervention Skills; E = Efficacy with Behavior Assessment System for Children Typologies; WA = Well-Adapted; A = Average; DBD = Disruptive Behavior Disorder; LD = Learning Disorder; PCW = Physical Complaints and Worry; SP = Severe Pathology; MD = Mildly Disruptive. Pre-intervention correlation coefficients are below and post-intervention correlation coefficients are above the diagonal.
*$p < .05$; **$p < .01$.

TABLE 2. Paired Samples T-Tests Assessing Differences Between Pre- and Post-Intervention Variables

	Pre-Intervention		Post-Intervention		
Variable	M	SD	M	SD	t
BIS Knowledge	1.82	.37	2.48	.42	−4.28*
BIS Use	1.76	.29	2.02	.19	−2.89*
E–WA	4.78	.30	4.90	.32	−1.02
E–A	4.67	.37	.480	.43	−.69
E–DBD	3.12	.89	3.47	.53	−1.39
E–LD	2.95	.75	3.23	1.02	−.85
E–PCW	2.93	.72	3.23	1.00	−.80
E–SP	2.80	.87	2.78	1.27	.04
E–MD	3.28	.95	3.75	.81	−1.60
Overall Efficacy	3.50	1.05	3.74	1.10	−2.12*

Note. BIS = Bullying Intervention Skills; E = Efficacy with Behavior Assessment System for Children typologies; WA = Well-Adapted; A = Average; DBD = Disruptive Behavior Disorder; LD = Learning Disorder; PCW = Physical Complaints and Worry; SP = Severe Pathology; MD = Mildly Disruptive.
*$p < .05$.

CONCLUSIONS

The results of the study indicate that the *Bullybusting: A Psychoeducational Program for Helping Bullies and Their Victims* (Newman, Horne, & Bartolomucci, 2000) is effective in increasing teachers' knowledge and use of bullying intervention skills, increasing teachers' sense of efficacy in working with students to prevent bullying and decreasing the frequency of bullying behaviors in the school. Correlational analyses also indicated that teachers' efficacy in utilizing bullying intervention skills are more strongly related to particular BASC typologies.

Results of the TEAM point to an increase in participants' efficacy in working with six of the BASC typologies: Well-Adapted, Average, Learning Disorder, Physical Complaints and Worry, Disruptive Behavior Disorder, and Mildly Disruptive. The only typology in which there was no evidence for an increase in teachers' efficacy was the Severe Psychopathology cluster. This may be due in part to the unpredictable behavior these students often display, making it difficult for teachers to anticipate appropriate intervention techniques.

Two limitations of the present study must be taken into account when evaluating the results and planning replications. First, the sample size was very small. A larger sample size is likely to yield stronger empirical results, as several of the specific typology efficacy scores were near the point of statistical significance. Secondly, a control group is strongly recommended to limit the possibility of variables outside the scope of the investigation affecting the results. Subsequent investigations of the effectiveness of this prevention program should involve potential changes in teachers' expectations for and attributions of student behaviors in addition to perceived efficacy.

REFERENCES

Anderson, C.S. (1982). The search for school climate: A review of the research. *Review of Educational Research, 52*, 368-420.

Bandura, A. (1973). *Aggression: A social learning analysis*. Englewood Cliffs, NJ: Prentice Hall.

Bandura, A. (1995). *Self-efficacy in changing societies*. New York: Cambridge University Press.

Besag, V. (1989). *Bullies and victims in schools*. Milton Keynes: Open University Press.

Byrne, B. (1994). *Coping with bullying in schools*. London: Cassell.

Craig, W.M. (1998). The relationship among bullying, victimization, depression, anxiety, and aggression in elementary school children. *Personality and Individual Differences, 24*(1), 123-130.

Dodge, K.A., & Coie, J.D. (1987). Social information processing factors in reactive and proactive aggression in children's peer groups. *Journal of Personality and Social Psychology, 53*, 1146-1158.

Gilmartin, B.G. (1987). Peer group antecedents of severe love shyness in males. *Journal of Personality, 55*, 467-489.

Hazler, R.J., Hoover, J.H., & Oliver, R. (1992). What kids say about bullying. *The Executive Educator, 14*, 20-22.

Hoover, J.H., Oliver, R., Hazler, R.J. (1992). Bullying: Perceptions of adolescent victims in the Midwestern USA. *School Psychology International, 13*, 5-16.

Kamphaus, R.W., Petoskey, M.D., Cody, A.H., Rowe, E.W., Huberty, C.J., & Reynolds, C.R. (1999). A typology of parent rated child behavior for a national U.S. sample. *Journal of Child Psychology and Psychiatry and Allied Disciplines, 40*(4), 607-616.

Lee, F. (1993, April 4). Disrepsect rules. *The New York Times Educational Supplement*, p.16.

Newman, D. (1999). The effectiveness of a psychoeducational intervention for classroom teachers aimed at reducing bullying behavior in middle school students (Doctoral dissertation, University of Georgia, 1999). *Dissertation Abstracts International, 60* (5-A).

Newman, D., Horne, A., & Bartolomucci, C. (2000). *Bullybusting: A psychoeducational program for helping bullies and their victims*. Champaign, IL: Research Press.

Newman, D., Horne, A, Bartolomucci, C. (in press). The effectiveness of a psychcoeducational intervention for classroom teachers aimed at reducing bullying behaviors in middle school students.

Oliver, R., Hoover, J., & Hazler, R. (1994). The perceived roles of bullying in small-town Midwestern schools. *Journal of Counseling and Development, 72*(4), 416-420.

Olweus, D. (1978). *Aggression in the schools: Bullies and whipping boys*. Washington, D.C.: Hemisphere.

Olweus, D. (1993). *Bullying at school: What we know and what we can do*. Oxford: Blackwell Publishers.

Pelligrini, A.D. (1998). Bullies and victims in schools: A review and call for research. *Journal of Applied Developmental Psychology, 19*, 165-176.

Roland, E. (1989a). A system oriented strategy against bullying. In E. Roland & E. Munthe (Eds.), *Bullying: An international perspective* (pp. 143-151). London: David Fulton.

Roland, E. (1989b). Bullying: The Scandinavian research tradition. In D.P. Tattum & D.A. Lane (Eds.), *Bullying in schools* (pp. 21-32). Stoke-on-Trent: Trentham Books.

Stephenson, P., & Smith, D. (1989). Bullying in the junior school. In D. Tattum & D. Lane (Eds.), *Bullying in schools* (pp. 45-57). Stoke-on-Trent: Trentham Books.

Index